Corporate Social Responsibility

For my parents, Ma and Babuji.
For my sister, Moni.

And for Goldie, my everything.

Corporate Social Responsibility

The Good, the Bad and the Ugly

Subhabrata Bobby Banerjee

Professor of Management and Associate Dean of Research, College of Business, University of Western Sydney, Australia

Edward Elgar
Cheltenham, UK • Northampton, MA, USA

Published by
Edward Elgar Publishing Limited
Glensanda House
Montpellier Parade
Cheltenham
Glos GL50 1UA
UK

Edward Elgar Publishing, Inc.
William Pratt House
9 Dewey Court
Northampton
Massachusetts 01060
USA

A catalogue record for this book
is available from the British Library

Library of Congress Cataloguing in Publication Data
Banerjee, Subhabrata Bobby.
    Corporate social responsibility : the good, the bad and the ugly /
Subhabrata Bobby Banerjee.
        p. cm.
    Includes bibliographical references and index.
    1. Social responsibility of business. 2. Business and politics. 3.
Corporations—Political aspects. 4. Corporate power. 5. Human rights. 6.
Sustainable development. I. Title.
    HD60.B335   2007
    658.4'08—dc22
                                                            2007029863

ISBN 978 1 84542 976 8

Typeset by Manton Typesetters, Louth, Lincolnshire, UK
Printed and bound in Great Britain by MPG Books Ltd, Bodmin, Cornwall

Contents

Tables

Abbreviations

ABB	Asea Brown Boveri
ANC	African National Congress
ANWR	Arctic National Wildlife Refuge
ASEAN	Association of South East Asian Nations
ATCA	Alien Tort Claims Act
CBD	Convention on Biodiversity
DFE	design for environment
FSC	Forest Stewardship Council
ICCPR	International Covenant on Civil and Political Rights
ICESCR	International Covenant on Economic, Social and Cultural Rights
IIFC	International Indigenous Forum on Climate Change
ILO	International Labour Organization
IMF	International Monetary Fund
INBio	Instituto Nacional de Biodiversidad
IPC	Intellectual Property Committee
IPR	intellectual property rights
LCA	life cycle assessment
NAFTA	North American Free Trade Agreement
NGO	non-governmental organization
OECD	Organisation for Economic Co-operation and Development
TNC	transnational corporation
TQEM	total quality environmental management
TQM	total quality management
TRIPS	trade-related intellectual property rights; Agreement on Trade-Related Aspects of Intellectual Property Rights
UDHR	Universal Declaration of Human Rights
WCED	World Commission for Economic Development
WSF	World Social Forum
WTO	World Trade Organization

It is not a sign of good health to be well adjusted to a sick society.

J. Krishnamurti

Introduction

In January 2001 Kofi Annan, then secretary general of the United Nations, delivered the keynote address to the United States Chamber of Commerce. The topic of his speech was the 'revolutionary role business can play in the fight against HIV/AIDS'. Announcing the creation of the Global AIDS and Health Fund to support national programs to fight the epidemic, Annan urged business leaders to join the global fight against HIV/AIDS. According to Annan it was important for business to do so not just for humanitarian reasons but

> because your business will see benefits on its bottom line. You will see direct benefits, such as protecting investment and reducing risk. And you will make less tangible, but no less important, gains in assets such as reputation and customer loyalty. In fact, there is a happy convergence between what your shareholders pay you for, and what is best for millions of people the world over.

In his address he also urged business leaders to join the Global Compact, which he had launched in January 1999. The Global Compact is a voluntary initiative between the United Nations and business, which encourages corporate responsibility in the areas of human rights, core labor standards and the environment.

My intention in writing this book is to critically analyse contemporary notions of corporate social responsibility (CSR). Corporate social responsibility has become a mini-industry these days both in academia and in the business world. A recent Google search with the keywords 'corporate social responsibility' yielded over 77 million hits. A search of books available at Amazon.com with 'corporate social responsibility' in the title resulted in 1035 books dating back to 1973. More than 70 percent of these books were published in the last ten years targeting a wide audience including business practitioners, policy makers, academics, students and social workers. If, as Kofi Annan claims, corporations are to become agents for positive social change, it becomes important to critically analyse theories and practices that enable corporations to address social issues. This book is an attempt to develop such a critique. I argue that 'enlightened self-interest', the fundamental philosophy driving CSR, can only go so far in terms of producing positive social outcomes. I want to problematize the notion that corporate initiatives designed to address social misery are perfectly compatible with the shareholder wealth-maximizing model. Ultimately the limits of corporate rationality determine the limits of corporate social responsibility. Thus, to quote Bakan (2004: 50), if 'a corporation can do good only to help itself do well, there is a profound limit on just how much good it can do'. Any meaningful and sustainable corporate involvement in addressing global social problems requires a radical rethinking of the purpose and legal personality of the corporation accompanied by structural changes in the larger political economy.

In this book I try to describe the good, the bad and the ugly faces of corporate social responsibility. The good focuses on what CSR discourses tell us: about what CSR is, why business firms should be accountable to the broader society and what corporations should do to become more responsible. The bad is what these ideas and discourses conceal: how the imperatives of profit accumulation and shareholder value maximization do not always create win–win situations but often result in dispossession, and how the current political economy results in an economic capture of the social that marginalizes millions of people in the world. And the ugly is about how relentless corporate and government public relations campaigns create an illusory perception of good when describing the bad.

The current debate about CEO compensation is a case in point. A recent study has shown increases in CEO compensation has little to do with increasing shareholder value: in fact the study found a *negative* relationship between CEO pay and stock performance: the CEOs of ten large US corporations that posted negative returns in terms of their 2003 stock performance received significant pay increases in terms of salaries, bonuses and stock options (Strauss, 2003). Total compensation of the top five American CEOs between 1993 and 2002 was $260 billion, increasing from 5.7 percent of gross corporate income to 10 percent (Madrick, 2004). Another study found that the biggest CEO raises were linked to the largest layoffs. While the median pay increase for CEOs was 6 percent in 2002, the figure for CEOs of 50 companies that announced the biggest layoffs in 2001 jumped to 44 percent (Kristof, 2003). Of course all of these 50 companies produce slick, glossy corporate social responsibility reports annually. And the oft-repeated mantra that layoffs, like inflated CEO salaries, are an inevitable part of any corporate strategy because ultimately they are good for the global economy begs the question: whose globe and whose economy?

The book is organized as follows: Chapter 1 provides a historical background of corporate social responsibility. Using archival data this chapter discusses how the modern corporation took shape in the United States. It critically analyses different theories of the firm and discusses how political, economic, social and legal forces produced the currently dominant view of the corporation as a shareholder value-maximizing entity. Chapter 2 provides a critical review of contemporary concepts and theories of CSR. More than 50 years of research on corporate social responsibility have produced a plethora of models, frameworks and taxonomies of CSR. This chapter discusses and critiques the fundamental assumptions of CSR. Chapter 3 discusses the emergence of the stakeholder view of the firm as an alternative to the dominant shareholder value maximization view. It discusses theoretical and practical approaches to identify a firm's primary and secondary stakeholders and describes several case studies of conflicts between corporations and their stakeholders as well as the power dynamics underlying relationships between governments, non-governmental organizations, international institutions, and corporations. Chapter 4 discusses the emergent literature on corporate citizenship and its relation to CSR. It discusses and critiques various models of citizenship that are found in the literature. Chapter 5 discusses the dilemmas and paradoxes of CSR and corporate citizenship. It discusses a variety of cases to show the problems faced by corporations and stakeholders in implementing CSR. Chapter 6 provides a critical review of current debates on sustainability. It discusses the three major themes of environmental, economic and social sustainability and the challenges of integrating social and environmental issues into corporate strategy. Chapter 7 provides a critical analysis of the role of human rights and its relationship to CSR. It describes various human rights initiatives like the United Nations Global Compact and industry and corporate human rights codes of conduct and discusses their limitations. It also describes the emergence of new social movements such as farmers' rights movements in developing countries protesting the patenting of seeds by TNCs, environmental movements, fair wage and anti-sweatshop movements and indigenous rights movements.

In Chapter 8 the focus shifts from the individual corporation to an analysis of networks of power in the political economy. By drawing on insights from political economy and sociology the chapter discusses how discursive formations of the economic produce particular forms of social arrangements of various actors, institutions and networks that constitute a particular image of the 'social' and the inclusions and exclusions that result. In the final chapter I discuss some alternate visions that may allow us to rescue the social from the economic. I discuss alternate formations of the corporation that could make them more effective agents of social change. I discuss possible reforms in the operations of international agencies and outline new approaches to corporate governance. The chapter concludes by discussing directions for the future and provides a critical research agenda for corporate social responsibility.

I do not take a moral approach to CSR in this book: many other writers have already done that. Rather I focus my arguments on the political aspects of CSR discourse: how power dynamics between actors and institutions in the political economy produce particular representations of CSR and the inclusions and exclusions that result. If, as Kofi Annan claims, there is indeed a convergence between maximizing shareholder value and 'what is best for millions of people the world over' a critical analysis of CSR will enable us to identify which millions in the world are served best and which millions marginalized by corporations.

1. Corporate social responsibility: a historical review

Since trade ignores national boundaries and the manufacturer insists on having the world as a market, the flag of his nation must follow him, and the doors of the nations which are closed against him must be battered down. Concessions obtained by financiers must be safeguarded by ministers of state, even if the sovereignty of unwilling nations be outraged in the process. Colonies must be obtained or planted, in order that no useful corner of the world may be overlooked ... The seed of war in the modern world is industrial and commercial rivalry. (Woodrow Wilson, 1907)

As a field of study in management, CSR probably emerged in the 1950s in the United States. Business practices in the 1900s that could be termed socially responsible took different forms: philanthropic donations to charity, service to the community, enhancing employee welfare and promoting religious conduct. Early proponents were CEOs and business leaders from the big oil and energy companies, telecommunication corporations and automobile manufacturers of the 1920s (Frederick, 2006). For instance, in 1951 Frank Abrams, Chairman of the Board of Standard Oil (now Exxon), in an article in the *Harvard Business Review* called for top management to become 'good citizens', aspire to a 'higher duty of professional management' and contribute to the 'solution of the many complex social problems of our times' because business firms were 'man-made instruments of society' (Abrams, 1951). Abrams was not alone in articulating the social role of corporations: a series of articles appeared in the *Harvard Business Review* in the 1950s written by a diverse range of authors including theologians, philosophers, economists, business leaders and historians all advocating a broader role for business. The titles of these papers reflected the ideas of the times: 'Management's responsibilities in a complex world', 'Management's mission in a new society', 'Can the businessman apply Christianity?', 'Can Christianity produce corporate good?', 'Business and religion' and 'Has business developed a conscience?' are some examples. A notable exception in this collection of authors was Theodore Levitt (1958), who described social responsibility as 'a happy new orthodoxy, a prevailing vogue, a new tyranny of fad and fancy' that could harm business interests. Milton Friedman was a powerful advocate of this line of thinking when he claimed some years later in his book *Capitalism and Freedom* (1962) that social responsibility was a 'fundamentally subversive doctrine in a free society', arguing that profit itself was a social good and that society was best served when corporations maximized shareholder value.

It is interesting to note that some writers who were strongly advocating a socially responsible corporation in the 1950s also warned that CSR could be used as window-dressing. For instance, in his article exploring the relationship between religion and business, Johnson (1958) discussed the 'dualistic nature of man' in Christian theology where 'man as angel' could use business to serve a social purpose whereas 'man as devil' could misuse corporate power and responsibility. Believing that their corporations served a larger social purpose could lead managers to 'assume exaggerated views of their abilities, judgments, and contributions to the enterprise of which they are a part' (Johnson, 1958: 72). He described two hypothetical scenarios:

> Company executives may stress that their 'socially responsible' philosophy works to the general benefit; yet basically such a philosophy may be a subtle device to maintain economic power in their own hands by extending their influence and decision-making power into so many nonbusiness areas that they become benevolent dictators.

> Corporations may give funds to charitable or educational institutions and may argue for them as great humanitarian deeds, when in fact they are simply trying to buy community good will.

Johnson thus anticipated the term 'greenwashing' which entered the popular lexicon nearly 50 years later. The *Oxford English Dictionary* defines 'greenwash' as 'disinformation disseminated by an organization so as to present an environmentally responsible public image'. The non-governmental organization CorpWatch has a less charitable definition of 'greenwash': 'the phenomenon of socially and environmentally destructive corporations attempting to preserve and expand their markets by posing as friends of the environment and leaders in the struggle to eradicate poverty'.

The ideology of CSR in the 1950s was primarily based on an assumption of the obligation of business to society. This obligation arose because some scholars and practitioners saw business as an instrument of society and managers as public trustees whose main job was to balance often competing demands of employees, customers, suppliers, communities and shareholders (the term 'stakeholder' to define these different groups was coined 30 years later). Most of the academic research over the next few decades took an instrumental approach to CSR by describing the ways and means by which corporations could meet their social obligations without losing sight of their main shareholder value-maximizing function (Jones, 1995). As we shall see in the next chapter there was a shift in CSR thinking in the 1990s from fulfilling societal obligations through philanthropy to a more strategic level that attempted to tie corporate social initiatives to corporate objectives.

One of the earliest books on CSR, *The Social Responsibilities of the Business-man*, was written by Howard Bowen in 1953. Bowen argued that since social institutions shaped economic outcomes it was to be expected that business firms as an economic outcome of societal interests should consider the social impact of business activity. It took less than 50 years for this argument to come full circle: as we shall see in a later chapter neoliberal political economy, which is dominant in most parts of the world, is based on an ideology that economic institutions should shape social outcomes. Enlightened self-interest was a key assumption of CSR where social responsibility was to be manifested through philanthropic activity, community service and employee welfare, all of which were supposed to serve the public interest. Frederick (2006) notes that Bowen took a more skeptical view of CSR in the 1970s when he stated, 'voluntary social responsibility cannot be relied upon as a significant form of control over business. The power of business overcomes the weak reed of voluntary social responsibility. The social responsibility concept is of minimal effectiveness.' However, the effectiveness or lack thereof of CSR appears to be irrelevant going by the hundreds of books and papers written on CSR since the 1970s. And this attention is not just generated by academics: every Fortune 500 company and thousands more across the world have some sort of corporate social responsibility statement in their annual reports; government leaders, CEOs, policy makers and academic bodies regularly host CSR conferences; and international bodies like the United Nations, World Bank, and International Monetary Fund all publicly affirm their commitment to social responsibility. However, if we do accept Bowen's general argument that because business is an instrument of society it must consider societal interests then we need to understand what social, economic and political forces created the modern corporation. If corporations and management scholars invented CSR then let us go back even further in time to see how the corporation itself was invented.

SOCIAL RESPONSIBILITY AND THE MODERN CORPORATION

In his excellent book *Organizing America*, Charles Perrow (2002) described how economic, political and social forces combined to create a legal revolution that created the modern corporation in the United States. The earliest form of the corporation, apart from artists' and professional guilds, was the chartered corporation created as a result of royal corporate charters granted by the British monarchy in the 1700s and 1800s. After independence American colonists in an effort to distance themselves from colonial rule developed a system that replaced royal charters by state charters giving state legislatures the power to grant charters to corporations. The terms and conditions of a chartered corporation specified what business the corporation was allowed to conduct, how long it could exist and its obligation to serve the public interest. States could legally revoke a corporation's charter in nineteenth-century America if corporations failed to operate by the terms of the charter. One legal ruling in 1815 declared that 'a private corporation created by the legislature may lose its franchise by a misuser or nonuser of them. This is the common law of the land, and is a tacit condition annexed to the creation of every such corporation' (*Terret v. Taylor*, 1815). Revocation of a corporation's charter was not just a legal artifact: several states routinely revoked corporate charters if corporations failed to act in the public interest. For instance, banks lost their charters in Mississippi, Ohio and Pennsylvania for 'committing serious violations that were likely to leave them in an insolvent or financially unsound condition'. In Massachusetts and New York, charters of turnpike corporations were revoked for 'not keeping their roads in repair' (Derber, 1998: 124).

However, by the end of the nineteenth century, restrictions around incorporation had all but disappeared. A series of legal rulings in the 1800s essentially freed corporations from restrictions imposed by state charters and rules of incorporation, creating the first privately owned corporations free from state control and possessing private property rights. The landmark decision of the US Supreme Court that removed corporations from state control was *Dartmouth College v. Woodward* in 1819. The case completely redefined the identity and role of a corporation. The state of New Hampshire had enacted legislation in order to convert Dartmouth College, originally founded in 1769 as a charter between King George and the college, from a private college to a public institution. Thomas Jefferson in his statement to the governor of New Hampshire supporting the legislation wrote:

> The idea that institutions established for the use of a nation cannot be touched or modified may perhaps be a salutary provision against the abuses of a monarch, but it is most absurd against the nation itself. To make a corporate charter sacrosanct would lead to the belief that the earth belongs to the dead, and not to the living.

In its effort to oppose a state charter the trustees of Dartmouth College argued in the courts that the 1769 charter represented a contract and thus was entitled to protection under Article 1 Section 10 of the US constitution that prohibited states from 'impairing the obligations of contracts'. While the New Hampshire court ruled in favor of the state, Dartmouth College appealed the verdict in the Supreme Court, arguing that the rights of private corporations and private rights in general must be 'protected from the rise and fall of popular parties and the fluctuations of political opinions' (Perrow, 2002: 41). The presiding judge agreed, ruling that 'a corporation is an artificial being, invisible, intangible. And existing only in contemplation of law' (Chief Justice John Marshall, *Dartmouth College v. Woodward*, 1819). And so the modern corporation was born, defined as a 'fictitious legal person, an artificial legal entity' distinct from its owners and officers (Hessen, 1979: xiv).

This court ruling had two immediate effects: first, it effectively put an end to the argument that the corporation was a creature of the state, thus limiting public representation. Second, by conferring private rights on corporations, rights normally held by individuals, the court automatically guaranteed a system that would protect those rights. Thus, an artificial legal entity like a corporation became entitled to protection under the 14th Amendment of the US Constitution which guarantees all persons 'due process' and 'equal protection under the law'. A series of subsequent court rulings across the country reinforced the view of a corporation as a person whose rights are protected under the 14th Amendment, the same law that was used to abolish slavery in the United States. It is indeed ironic that in the first 15 years of the adoption of the 14th Amendment less than 0.5 percent of the cases involved protection of the rights of African-American slaves while more than 50 percent of the cases involved corporations (Justice Hugo Black, *Connecticut General Life Insurance Company v. Johnson*, 1938). As we shall see these legislative requirements were designed to protect private interests, often at the expense of the public. The legal personality of the modern corporation was created by certain interests to deliver specific outcomes that needed a particular form of organization, and a strong state presence was inimical to these interests. It is interesting to note that, 170 years after corporations freed themselves of state charters, consumer and environmental activists of the 1960s and 1970s were campaigning for a system of federal charters to 'rein in the power of large corporations'. In a call for a congressional hearing on the issue, Ralph Nader declared, 'The corporation is, and must be, the creature of the State. Into its nostrils the State must breathe the breath of a fictitious life' (Nader et al., 1976: 15).

Thus, the current notion of a corporation as a nexus of private contracts designed to enhance shareholder value must be seen as a peculiar American invention that emerged from a specific historical context as an outcome of particular power relations. As Perrow (2002: 41) argues, the removal of legal restrictions on corporate activity was not 'a mistake, an inadvertence, a happenstance in history, but a well-designed plan devised by particular interests who needed a ruling that would allow for a particular form of organization'. God did not come down to earth to tell us that corporations should maximize shareholder value. And even if she did, she got a lot of help from powerful business and legal interests in eighteenth-century America. If the corporation was ruled to have the legal identity of a person what kind of personality does it have? A Canadian sociologist, Joel Bakan, analysed a range of corporate behaviors using a personality diagnostic test found in the World Health Organization's *Manual of Mental Disorders*. The corporation was diagnosed with a personality disorder – it had the personality of a 'psychopath' because it displayed the following traits: 'Callous unconcern for the feelings of others; incapacity to maintain enduring relationships; reckless disregard for the safety of others; deceitfulness: repeated lying and conning others for profit; incapacity to experience guilt; and failure to conform to social norms with respect to lawful behaviours' (Bakan, 2004).

The new identity of the corporation as an artificial legal entity meant that there was no official or legal requirement to serve the public interest, which was the case when state charters defined the corporation's identity and purpose. This process of redefinition was an exercise of political and economic power by a minority interest group promoting a particular ideology that 'redefined the character of the Republic in order to justify the new opportunities that the corporation offered for the accumulation of private wealth' (*Harvard Law Review*, 1989: 1886–7). As the legal personality of the modern corporation evolved in the 1800s, contestations in the public, political and legal spheres revolved around the conflict between public and private interests. The new system of property rights that were bestowed to the corporation also became a primary incentive to maximize economic returns for shareholders. Any reference to 'social good' was at best symbolic and derivative in that the economic function provided the social good. The corporation as an artificial person could now enter into contracts, sue and be sued, and enjoy property rights. Its social responsibility, once an integral part of its personality, now became a discretionary activity, a strategic choice influenced by market and competitive factors. The separation of the social from the economic also reflected the canons of economic theories of the time – the economic concept of externalities, for example, which shifted the burden of responsibility for managing the negative social and environmental effects of economic activity from economic entities to governments. There was little recognition, at least in legislative circles, that the way profit-seeking corporations were organized determined social costs borne by society as well as established the powers and freedoms enjoyed by corporations (Perrow, 2002: 143).

New laws in the 1800s further consolidated property rights of corporations allowing states to allocate property to private corporations. Perrow (2002) describes how powerful private interests in the railroad industry, the big business of the 1800s, with a combination of creative legal interpretations of property rights along with other activities of dubious legality, were able to obtain rights of way on public land at virtually no cost. In the political, economic and legal climate of the time public purpose was defined so broadly that protection of corporate rights allowed corporations to externalize costs in the name of prosperity and growth. Perrow (2002: 45) described an 1839 court decision on a petition by Louisville residents protesting the company's decision to lay rail lines across their neighborhood:

A railroad will be allowed to run its locomotives into the heart of Louisville despite the noise and pollution from its smokestacks (the externality), because so necessary are the agents of transportation in a populous and prospering country that private injury and personal damage must be expected. (1839 Kentucky court decision, cited in Perrow, 2002)

Other cases brought to court by individuals and groups of cattle farmers against railroad corporations were dismissed on similar grounds. It would be naïve of us to ignore the powerful political and economic interests that were responsible for influencing court rulings that allowed a new definition of a corporation. Large corporations in the 1800s wielded considerable economic and political power, and some nineteenth-century corporate political strategies would even make the crooks that ran Enron blush: judges and legislators were routinely bought, stock was diluted through dubious financial dealings, dividends were misused, public funds were obtained through deception, funds were misused and laws were broken. In fact, the level of corruption was such that Perrow (2002: 143) argues ease of corruption should be added to the usual factors of production such as land, labor, capital, technology and organizational form. He rightly points out that corruption involved considerable social costs in terms of wasting a society's resources, risking the lives and health of communities and workers owing to evasion of environmental health and safety laws, and increasing negative externalities. Corrupting the legislature and judiciary meant that corporations could shape their own powers and freedoms. As he argues:

Corruption meant that the profits were not returned to either the government that subsidized so much of the railroads, or even to many of the private investors, but to a small group of executives and financiers. This concentrated wealth and the power that comes with it. Corruption counts, but few historians and social scientists have done any counting. Instead, they tend to blame the victims, not the perpetrators – the large organizations. There are no accounts of railroads as corporations engaged in lobbying, joining with merchants and shippers in getting public funds, fighting regulation and accountability, and generally using the organizational tool to shape the commercial world to their liking. (Perrow, 2002: 144)

It is important to realize that the legal developments that created the modern corporation did not go uncontested. Anti-corporate protests were strong in the mid-1850s as they were on the streets of Seattle 150 years later. But, as Perrow (2002) points out, these protests were more a reflection of the anxiety about the growing powers of corporate capitalism as opposed to any resistance to capitalist ideals per se. Individual entrepreneurs, workers and artisans with restricted access to capital supported private property rights for individuals because it could provide freedom from wage dependence. However, they opposed property rights for corporations without a state charter because that would limit opportunities for self-employment. There were also public concerns about the effect of unbridled commerce on society. There was a fear that relaxing state control would dramatically expand the power of corporations, creating a new form of aristocracy 'depending for its wealth on government privileges and therefore with an interest in corrupting government by diverting it from the public good' (*Harvard Law Review*, 1989: 1891). Small entrepreneurs, artisans and farmers were also concerned their livelihoods would be destroyed because of the new privileges granted to corporations. A community of self-employed artisans and traders with shared interests was seen as a public good that was threatened by permanent wage dependence (Perrow, 2002). Intellectuals, workers, union officials, artisans and entrepreneurs voiced their concerns in several sections of the business press of the time. For example, a union publication declared in 1835: 'We entirely disapprove of the incorporation of Companies, for carrying on manual mechanical business, inasmuch as we believe their tendency is to eventuate in and produce monopolies, thereby crippling the energies of individual enterprise, and invading the rights of smaller capitalists' (cited in *Harvard Law Review*, 1989: 1989).

Debates about the role of corporations in their new entity centered around two assumptions: that the corporation was inherently guided by self-interest or that a corporation had an 'enduring capacity to operate on the basis of civic virtue' (Regan, 1998: 305). The first notion was also reflected in economic theories of the firm where the focus was on efficiencies required to maximize rent-seeking opportunities. The second notion refers to the legitimacy of a corporation and its role in society. Thus, to quote Dahl (1973: 11):

> Business corporations are created and survive only as a special privilege of the state. It is absurd to regard the corporation simply as an enterprise established for the sole purpose of allowing profit making. One has simply to ask: Why should citizens, through *their* government, grant special rights, powers, privileges, and protections to any firm except on the understanding that its activities are to fulfill *their* purposes? Corporations exist because we allow them to do so.

The problem with the efficiency–legitimacy dichotomy as with all dichotomies is that one category tends to define the other. For example, in economic policy it is often the case that legitimacy becomes subordinate to efficiency because notions and terms of legitimacy are discursively produced and defined by economic efficiency criteria. As Regan (1998) has argued, both assumptions are problematic for society. Assuming that the corporation is solely guided by narrow economic self-interest tends to reinforce structures that will lead to this outcome. A second outcome of the self-interest assumption is that it leads to a free rider scenario where corporations will not usually take the socially responsible course of action unless it meets their profitability criteria (Regan, 1998). This view is reflected in the 'corporate social responsibility is good for business' refrain heard from many CEOs, government officials, academics, NGOs and the like. If the sole obsession is with profits then governments and other agencies need to regulate business to produce socially beneficial outcomes, which is another shortcoming with this approach. Laws are usually created after the fact and cannot anticipate every instance of social evil. Monitoring compliance in a command and control system can be an expensive process involving high transaction costs. Moreover, it is naïve to think that laws governing the behavior of corporations are made in isolation and not without active involvement from industry. Political lobbying as a corporate strategy has been around for more than 200 years.

The implications of the second assumption, that a corporation is capable of operating on the basis of civic virtue, serves to limit legal constraints on a virtuous corporation with the corresponding risk that managers can operate with impunity and without accountability. In a relaxed legal environment, competitive pressures and market demand and supply become the only key drivers of corporate behavior, which could have negative social outcomes. The mechanisms of both the market and the law appear to preclude civic virtue. However, as Regan (1998: 305) points out, 'both expecting civic virtue from corporations and denying its possibility create risks that may exacerbate rather than resolve the tension'.

Disputes between social and corporate interests that entered the legal arena tended to muddy social responsibilities of the modern corporation and narrow the focus of the board of directors to generating shareholder wealth. In one celebrated case, the Ford Motor Company was taken to court by its shareholders, who contested the company's plan to forgo the payment of special dividends. Henry Ford, in the middle of implementing one of his social engineering plans, declared to the court that he chose to forgo the dividend payment because the company wanted 'to employ still more men; to spread the benefits of this individual system to the greatest possible number; to help them build up their lives and their homes' (Henry Ford, 1919, cited in Regan, 1998). The court disagreed, ruling that 'A business organization is organized and carried on primarily for the profit of the stockholders. Directors cannot shape and conduct the affairs of a corporation for the mere incidental benefit of shareholders and for the primary purpose of benefiting others' (*Dodge v. Ford Motor Company 1919*, cited in Regan, 1998).

Now a literal interpretation of this ruling could mean that it is illegal to be socially responsible. However, managers do have some discretion in determining the best way to enhance shareholder value. Had Henry Ford, not known for his modesty, chosen to be a little less grand about his plans for society and restated his argument concentrating on the long-term financial benefits of his 'social investment', the court may well have accepted his argument. Hertz (2001) mentions a similar case where the court ruled that a donation to a civil rights group by Kodak was not a 'financially responsible investment' and ordered the company to accede to shareholders' demand to pay the amount as dividends instead. However, some recent rulings have attempted to include some level of stakeholder recognition by emphasizing that directors do not 'have a duty to the shareholders but instead have a duty to the corporation' (Cunningham, 1999: 1294). Another ruling stated that directors in considering the best interests of the corporation consider 'the effects of any action upon any or all groups affected by such action, including shareholders, employees, suppliers' (Cunningham, 1999: 1294). However, this simply allows company directors to consider public interests; it is not legally binding in any way, thus limiting whatever attention corporate elites will give to social concerns. For instance, the American Bar Association states: 'While allowing directors to give consideration to the interests of others, the law compels them to find some reasonable relationship to the long-term interests of shareholders when so doing' (American Bar Association, 1990). Thus, as Regan (1998: 305) puts it, 'the operation of both law and the market therefore systematically tend to deprive corporations of the capacity to cultivate civic virtue'.

The philosophy driving CSR discourses from the 1950s onwards was an attempt to cultivate civic virtue in corporations. In the 1980s, the focus of CSR shifted from CSR as obligation ('doing good to do good') to CSR as strategy ('doing good to do well') (Vogel, 2005). Criticisms of CSR have focused around either its inability to overcome the profit-maximizing motive of corporations or the dangers posed by CSR activities in diverting resources from the economic mission of the firm to meet social goals. The 'new' CSR allegedly overcomes both these problems by linking corporate strategies with social goals. Let us now turn our attention to understanding the key theoretical and practical features of contemporary discourses of CSR.

2. Corporate social responsibility: theoretical perspectives

> Did you ever expect a corporation to have a conscience, when it has no soul to be damned and no body to be kicked? And by God, it ought to have both! (First Baron Thurlow (1731–1806), Lord Chancellor of England)

The above quote attributed to the first Baron Thurlow was made in the heyday of what was probably the world's first multinational corporation – I refer of course to the infamous East India Company. In an era of British colonial expansion, the company was engaged in conquering markets, eliminating competition, securing cheap sources of raw material supply and building strategic alliances – strategies consistent with securing competitive advantage according to current strategic management textbooks. Colonial expansionist practices of the British empire in the 1800s involved both capital appropriation and permanent destruction of manufacturing capacities in the colonies – the 'technological superiority' of the British textile industry, for example, was established as much by invention as by a systematic destruction of India's indigenous industry involving innovative competitive strategies such as the severing of the thumbs of master weavers in Bengal, forced cultivation of indigo by Bihar's peasants and the slave trade from Africa that supplied cotton plantations in the US with free labor (Dutt, 1970; Shiva, 2001: 34).

The end of direct colonialism shifted the powers of chartering corporations from the British monarchy to state legislatures. A series of court rulings in the mid-nineteenth century succeeded in freeing corporations from state control and created the legal fiction of a corporation as an artificial person. The corporate body was now defined as a 'nexus of contracts' between wealth-maximizing rational actors. The focus was on identifying institutions, markets and governance structures that could align incentives of managers with interests of shareholders (Yingyi and Weingast, 1997). The emergence of corporate social responsibility in the mid-twentieth century can be seen as an attempt to create a soul for the corporate body based on its obligation to society – doing good to do good. However, as we have discussed in the last chapter these efforts were by no means universally accepted. Some critics saw CSR as an 'ideological movement' intended to legitimize the power of multinational corporations (Mitchell, 1989). Others saw CSR activity as 'theft' from a firm's key stakeholder groups: shareholders, customers and employees (Friedman, 1962). The ambiguity around the concept of CSR also arises from some confusing terminology. The 'good' done by corporations goes by many names: corporate citizenship, corporate ethics, corporate social responsiveness, corporate philanthropy, societal marketing, social marketing and corporate community involvement are some examples. The emerging discourse on corporate citizenship warrants some attention because it appears to reflect new directions of CSR, and I will discuss some key concepts of corporate citizenship in Chapter 4. Given these divergent interpretations it will be useful if we examine some basic definitions and concepts of CSR before we examine its theoretical and practical implications. Some popular definitions of corporate social responsibility are:

> The firm's consideration of, and response to, issues beyond the narrow economic, technical and legal requirements of the firm to accomplish social benefits along with the traditional economic gains which the firm seeks. (Davis, 1973: 312)

> Encompassing the economic, legal, ethical and discretionary expectations that society has of organizations at a given point in time. (Carroll, 1979: 500)

> Actions that appear to further some social good beyond the interests of the firm and that which is required by law. (McWilliams and Siegel, 2001: 117)

> The ways in which an organization exceeds the minimum obligations to stakeholders specified through regulation and corporate governance. (Johnson and Scholes, 2002: 247)

> Societal expectations of corporate behavior: a behavior that is alleged by a stakeholder to be expected by society or morally required and is therefore justifiably demanded of a business. (Whetten *et al.*, 2002: 374)

> A commitment to improve community well being through discretionary business practices and contribution of corporate resources. (Kotler and Lee, 2005: 3)

> The commitment of business to contribute to sustainable economic development working with employees, their families, the local community and society at large to improve their quality of life. (World Business Council, 2005)

> A concept whereby companies integrate social and environmental concerns in their business operations and in their interactions with their stakeholders on a voluntary basis. (European Commission, 2005)

Some key themes can be discerned from these and other definitions of CSR. First, CSR implies some sort of commitment, through corporate policies and action. This operational view of CSR is reflected in a firm's social performance, which can be assessed by how a firm manages its societal relationships, its social impact and the outcomes of its CSR policies and actions (Wood, 1991). Social reporting and social audits are examples of how firms can assess their social

Table 2.1   Selected items from The Body Shop's stakeholder survey

---

I trust The Body Shop to provide honest information to its relevant
   stakeholder groups on social, environmental and animal protection
   agencies.

I trust The Body Shop to only sell products which comply with environmental
   guidelines.

I trust The Body Shop to stick to the principles they have stated.

I trust The Body Shop to always act ethically in business dealings.

I trust The Body Shop to check up on where their products come from.

I trust The Body Shop to be committed to social and environmental change.

The Body Shop does not test or commission tests on animals.

The Body Shop's business practices reflect a high standard of ethics.

The Body Shop takes active steps to make its business more environmentally
   responsible.

The Body Shop campaigns effectively on human rights.

The Body Shop trades fairly with producers in the Third World.

The Body Shop is committed to keeping the work environment free from all
   forms of discrimination.

---

performance. The Body Shop is an example of a company with a high CSR profile despite concerns about the veracity of some of its socially responsible practices (Entine, 1995). The Body Shop has been conducting social and environmental audits and reporting its social and environmental performance for more than a decade. The company's vision is the integration of 'economic success, stakeholder engagement and social and environmental change'. Its social audit report involved canvassing the views of a range of stakeholders on a variety of issues (see Table 2.1 for examples of statements for which respondents were asked to rate their perceptions on a four-point strongly agree–strongly disagree scale). The main stakeholders surveyed were employees and customers. It is important to realize that these surveys measured perceptions of stakeholders, not the company's actual social performance as such. Even the independent auditor of this report commented on the appropriateness of the methodology employed in collecting responses rather than determining whether the company actually did all the things it claimed to do or describing the actual impact of the social and environmental policies of the company. How much of CSR is reputation or impression management and how much is actually translated into positive social outcomes is open to debate.

Second, according to these definitions CSR activities should go beyond the law and exceed its 'minimum obligations'. Thus, a corporation that meets environmental legal requirements in terms of its emissions is not necessarily a socially responsible corporation because it is merely abiding by the law. If, however, it contributes corporate resources to promote community welfare such as providing free day care for its employees or lowering its emissions beyond the legal requirement then these actions can be termed socially responsible.

Third, CSR activities are discretionary and cannot be enforced in any court of law. Corporations that embrace CSR do so by means of voluntary codes of conduct at local, regional, national and international levels but these are not legally binding in any way. And finally, conceptualizations of 'society' and the 'social', which were central to CSR in the 1970s, appear to have been narrowed in subsequent years to 'stakeholders' under the assumption that stakeholders would represent societal interests and demand that corporations respond to these interests. Although this narrower focus makes CSR more tangible and 'practical' for managers it poses new sets of problems as we shall see in the next chapter.

A host of models, categories and taxonomies have been developed in an attempt to define CSR. Carroll (1979) described three elements that constitute a model of 'corporate social performance': a basic definition of CSR, the range of social areas for which corporations have a responsibility and the range of corporate responses to social issues. Carroll's (1979) categories of CSR as consisting of economic, legal, ethical and discretionary responsibilities have been influential in understanding the nature and type of obligations that business has to society. These categories were not mutually exclusive and neither were they located on a social–economic responsibility continuum. According to Carroll (1979: 500) the categories of CSR were based on their 'fundamental role in the evolution of importance'. The fundamental social responsibility for any business firm in this framework is its economic responsibility – 'to produce goods and services that society wants and to sell them for a profit'. Other responsibilities and roles are framed from this fundamental assumption – corporations are expected to follow all necessary laws while seeking to make profits and they are expected to behave ethically in areas that are not codified by law. While economic and legal responsibilities are clear-cut, ethical and discretionary responsibilities are not well defined and opinions on the appropriateness of the latter two responsibilities are divided, ranging from being 'subversive', as Milton Friedman would call them, to being those required of a corporate citizen.

Klaus Leisinger (2005: 583), CEO of Novartis, described his company's approach to CSR in a similar fashion: CSR in the pharmaceutical industry involved different degrees of obligations: the 'must do' (practices that are 'required of business by society', for example providing quality products and services at reasonable prices, complying with regulations, making profits and providing fair wages and decent working conditions); the 'ought to do' (less binding than the 'must do' dimension but still aspects of 'good corporate citizenship', like going beyond compliance in environmental responsibility in regions where the regulatory structures do not meet 'enlightened standards', anti-bribery and anti-corruption policies, and respect for human rights); and the 'can do' (practices that are 'desired of business by society', for example corporate philanthropy, community development and volunteerism). According to Leisinger, corporations *should* go beyond the minimum expectations of society but they can do so only if there is 'sufficient corporate political will'. How sufficient political will is created is not discussed. The key question is: what structural changes are needed in the corporation and the broader political economy that enable integration of the 'can do' and 'should do' dimensions into the 'must do' dimension? Unfortunately, the vast literature on CSR and stakeholder theory does not offer much guidance. From the perspective of a CEO of a transnational pharmaceutical corporation, governments, NGOs and civil society need to do more. Corporations can *respect the right to health* by offering safe and fairly paid workplaces, preventing discrimination and reducing pollution. Corporations can also *protect the right to health* by ensuring they follow environmental and labor standards in all their international operations, even if other regions have lower standards. Beyond these 'rights' any call for corporations to fulfill the right to health of people not employed by the corporation is bound to receive a limited response.

After identifying the social responsibilities of business, Carroll's framework seeks to classify the range of social issues that business must address. Social issues differ for different firms and industries and change over time. Product safety, environmental conservation, community development, employee diversity and occupational health and safety are examples of social issues that have received varying degrees of attention over the years. A business cannot be expected to address the entire range of issues facing society but needs to identify the specific areas in which its different responsibilities have an impact. There is no universal agreement on what social issues need to be addressed by business. Leaving philanthropic and charitable activities aside (while these can produce positive social outcomes they are not the core business of profit-seeking firms) many large corporations appear to tackle social issues on the basis of 'enlightened self-interest', which is the assumption underlying theories of corporate social responsibility (Carroll, 1979; Wood, 1991). This is also the predominant practitioner view. A recent survey of social initiatives implemented by 23 companies found that, while the initiatives were targeted to communities, employees and customers, they were also related to the company's core business (Kotler and Lee, 2005). Some initiatives, such as corporate social marketing, were designed to deliver specific financial benefits to the company. For example, an insurance company developed, financed and implemented a comprehensive fire safety campaign with the assumption that it would increase profitability through reduced claims. Other initiatives included cause promotion, cause-related marketing, corporate philanthropy, community volunteering and 'socially responsible business practices'. Kotler and Lee (2005: 23) advocate corporate social marketing because 'the beauty of corporate social marketing is that the social good does not come at the expense of company objectives or vice versa. Rather, it does the greatest good it can possibly do for the cause while doing the most good for the company.'

In addition to identifying the range of social responsibilities and social issues facing the corporation, a firm has to decide on how it will address the issues arising from its responsibilities. Frederick (2006) distinguishes between CSR1 – corporate social responsibility – and CSR2 – corporate social responsiveness where responsiveness is defined as the 'capacity of a corporation to respond to social pressures'. While CSR1 has a normative basis (what a company should do), CSR2 provides a more strategic and managerial focus (what issues a company chooses to address and its policies and actions to address the issues). Corporate social responsiveness strategies can be reactive, defensive or responsive (Sethi, 1979). As Carroll (1979) points out, his model of corporate social performance does not prescribe how far a company should go to address social issues but by positioning ethical and discretionary obligations into a 'rational economic and legal framework' it allows managers to develop planning and diagnostic problem-solving tools. Subsequent development of Carroll's model involved identifying principles of corporate social responsibility, processes of corporate social responsiveness and outcomes of corporate behavior (Wartick and Cochran, 1985; Wood, 1991). Principles of corporate social responsibility can operate at different levels, institutional, organizational and managerial. At the institutional level CSR focuses on the legitimacy of business in society along with business obligations to society and sanctions that society can apply to business when it fails to live up to its obligations. According to the 'Iron Law of Responsibility', 'society grants legitimacy and power to business and in the long run, those who do not use power in a manner which society considers responsible will tend to lose it' (Davis, 1973: 314). However, this view is somewhat naïve because it does not acknowledge that defining the terms of legitimacy is a contested process and that the norms of legitimacy are an outcome of power relations. Economic systems, governments and institutions often determine what is 'legitimate' and this power to determine legitimacy cannot be easily lost. While customers, employees, shareholders and governments may be able to 'withdraw legitimacy', forcing a corporation to either change its approach or perish, the power of other stakeholders to do so is constrained. Ongoing conflicts between indigenous communities and multinational corporations over land and resource use in Africa, South America and Asia are an example of the contested nature of 'legitimate' forms of economic development. A uranium mine for example is a perfectly legitimate form of development according to the norms of a particular segment of society. Other groups may consider this particular form of economic development 'illegitimate' based on their cultural, economic and social norms (Banerjee, 2000). For instance, in many indigenous communities

Western rational categories of 'economic', 'social' or 'cultural' are sometimes incommensurable with indigenous ways of living and are the source of many conflicts between indigenous communities, governments and multinational corporations. The parameters that define legitimacy are sometimes determined by a system of rules and exclusions that do not address concerns of marginalized groups in society.

The principle of public responsibility operates at the organizational level where business firms are 'publicly responsible, for outcomes related to their primary and secondary areas of involvement with society' (Preston and Post, 1975; Wood, 1991). This principle of public responsibility is designed to make larger societal concerns more relevant by providing behavioral parameters for organizations based on issues relating to the firm's activities and interests. However, social responsibilities should be relevant to the 'organization's interests' (Wood, 1991) and therein lies the problem: these 'public' responsibilities are defined and framed by larger principles of legitimacy. What happens if organizational principles are in conflict with the principles of other groups in society? How should an organization manage such conflicts? The vast literature on CSR is strangely silent on the issues of power in framing institutional and organizational principles designed to address social issues.

At the managerial level the principle of managerial discretion focuses on strategic choices, options and personal responsibility of managers in achieving institutional and organizational social goals. According to Wood (1991: 698), 'managers are moral actors. Within every domain of corporate social responsibility, they are obliged to exercise such discretion as is available to them, toward socially responsible outcomes.' The fallacy of managers as 'moral actors' is easily revealed by the Foucauldian notion of subjectification, a mode that reveals how managers become constituted as subjects who secure their meaning and reality through identifying with a particular sense of their relationship with the firm (Knights, 1992). Individual managers' role in accommodating stakeholder interests is predefined at higher levels, and practices at this level are governed and organized by organizational and institutional discourses. Do managers really have genuine freedom to make socially responsible decisions?

Some writers distinguish between 'social' issues and 'stakeholder' issues. For example Baron (2001) differentiated between altruistic CSR which a company engaged in without expecting any financial return and 'strategic CSR', actions that resulted in beneficial outcomes for the company. In a study assessing the financial benefits of CSR, Hillman and Keim (2001) distinguished between 'stakeholder CSR' and 'social CSR'. In their study, stakeholder CSR was correlated with financial performance whereas social CSR was not. According to Clarkson (1995), a particular society determines what is a social issue and the representative government enacts appropriate legislation to protect social interests. Hence, a test whether an issue is social or not is the presence or absence of legislation. Thus, health and safety, equal opportunity and environmental issues are social issues because legislation exists. If there is no legislation, the issue becomes a 'stakeholder issue', which needs to be addressed at the corporate level (Clarkson, 1995). However, this is an unsatisfactory argument because it does not provide a strong enough rationale for why corporations address some social issues at the expense of others, and while it provides a descriptive approach for addressing social issues it provides neither a normative basis for social action nor a political and legal framework to monitor and enforce CSR. Efforts to develop a normative basis for social action are focused on identifying and meeting the needs of an organization's stakeholders. Organizational theorists have argued that a 'stakeholder view of the firm' can provide a theoretical and normative basis for CSR. Let us now examine the basic assumptions of stakeholder theory and its relationship with CSR.

3. The stakeholder theory of the firm: a critical perspective

> In the corporate economies of the contemporary West, the market is a passive
> institution. The active institution is the corporation ... an inherently narrow and
> shortsighted organization ... The corporation has evolved to serve the interests of
> whoever controls it, at the expense of whomever does not. (Duggar, 1989)

We have seen in Chapter 1 how the modern corporation evolved to its current
form as a nexus of contracts between private actors designed to enhance shareholder value. The conventional theory of the firm states that the management
function is to maximize profits under the assumption that maximizing total firm
value would maximize social welfare (Jensen, 1988). Various theories of the
firm have been proposed over the last 75 years that have sought to explain the
roles and functions of the business corporation. The neoclassical view of the
firm attempted to explain the economic principles of investment, production
and marketing decisions of firms operating in competitive markets. Cyert and
March (1963) proposed a behavioral theory of the firm that attempted to explain
how goals, expectations and differing choice sets influenced decision-making
processes in firms. Transaction cost theorists attempted to explain why firms
exist in terms of the efficiencies produced through coordinated action in formal
organizations versus the efficiencies of the market (Coase, 1937; Williamson
and Winter, 1991). The overarching theme of these theories is efficiency: agency
theory for instance argues that the structure of corporations is based on getting
the agents (managers) to look after the principal's (shareholder's) interests,
following the separation of ownership and control in the modern corporation.
Neoclassical economists like Friedman argue that CSR activities constitute an
agency problem because they are a 'theft' of shareholder-owned resources, resources that should be used to increase efficiency. A nexus-of-contracts theory
of the firm is inconsistent with CSR in the sense that managers could misap-
propriate firm resources to pursue CSR activities instead of using them to
generate value for the 'owners' of the resources. There is also the possibility of
misallocation of resources when resources that are best used for a particular
purpose are diverted to meet a 'social' goal for which the resources are ill suited
(Margolis and Walsh, 2003). Monitoring and measuring an agent's performance
is one way of reducing agency costs, and the easiest way to do this is to focus

on a firm's stock price as a measure of the agent's performance, which is the basis of the dominant theory of the firm. The focus is on developing institutions and governance structures that align incentives of managers with interests of shareholders in order to reduce opportunistic behaviors of managers. While this mechanism ensures shareholder primacy it provides less leeway for a firm to address the interests of non-shareholder groups in any meaningful way. And as we have seen earlier, there are no enforceable legal mechanisms designed to serve non-shareholder interests and, even in cases where directors are allowed to 'consider' interests of other constituencies, this consideration is still based on serving shareholder needs. Critics have also questioned the fundamental humanistic assumptions of agency theory where the individual is viewed as opportunistic and self-serving, assumptions that tend to become self-fulfilling prophecies (Ferraro *et al.*, 2005; Ghoshal and Moran, 1996; Roberts, 2003).

Some theorists challenge the shareholder primacy model of the firm, arguing that focusing purely on the economic function of the firm ignores the complexity that firms deal with along with related inefficiencies, information asymmetries and multiple incentive problems. They propose a stakeholder theory of the firm that broadens a firm's role to include other external and internal actors apart from shareholders (Donaldson and Preston, 1995; Freeman, 1984). The conventional view of the firm depicts it as a 'black box' that transforms inputs from suppliers, investors and employees into outputs for customers resulting in benefits to all providers of inputs, particularly to providers of scarce resources and skills who receive above normal 'rents'. Stakeholder theorists argue that the conventional input–output model fails to take into account the complex, two-way interactions between firms and 'legitimate groups'. They see the business firm as a 'constellation of cooperative and competitive interests possessing intrinsic value ... with no prima facie priority of one set of interests and benefits over another' (Donaldson and Preston, 1995: 66).

So how is a stakeholder defined and which groups are seen as legitimate stakeholders by the firm? In a review of the literature on stakeholder theory, Mitchell *et al.* (1997) collated 27 definitions of the term 'stakeholder'. Conceptualizations differed significantly based on whether theorists took a broad or narrow view of the role of the firm. The first reference to 'stakeholders' was attributed to an internal memo at the Stanford Research Institute in 1963 where stakeholders were defined as 'those groups without whose support the organization would cease to exist' (Freeman, 1984). Probably the most widely accepted definition is Freeman's notion of stakeholders whom he defined as 'any group or individual who can affect or is affected by the organization's objectives' (Freeman, 1984). This broad view is not without its problems: different stakeholders have differing stakes, and balancing the needs of competing stakeholders is not an easy task. A narrower definition of stakeholders focuses on the nature of risk borne by stakeholders. Clarkson (1995) for example classifies stakeholders into voluntary and involuntary risk bearers where the former group bears some kind of risk by investing capital and the latter group is at risk as a result of a firm's activities. Thus, legitimate stakeholders have a stake only if they bear some risk: if stakeholders do not bear any risk then they do not have any stake in the company. In a related argument, Post *et al.* (2002) defined stakeholders by their ability to contribute directly or indirectly to wealth creation or destruction in an organization. Broad and narrow views of stakeholders also rest on differing assumptions: proponents of the broad view of stakeholders base their claim on a moral argument where the focus is on building and maintaining 'moral relationships' or a firm 'fulfilling its affirmative duty to stakeholders' by ensuring that there is a just and fair distribution of the benefits and costs of the firm's actions (Mitchell *et al.*, 1997: 857). Theorists who favor a narrower view of stakeholders base their definition on pragmatic assumptions: if everybody is a real or potential stakeholder, managers simply do not have the time and resources to address all their claims and interests. Instead, legitimate stakeholders are the ones who are directly relevant to a firm's fundamental economic interest.

Donaldson and Preston (1995) identified three themes in their formulation of a stakeholder theory of the firm. First, stakeholder theory is *descriptive* in that it describes a corporation as interacting with a wide range of groups with different interests and demands. The question arises as to the descriptive accuracy of this model of the firm compared with other theories of the firm such as nexus of contracts or transaction costs or agency theory. Although the maxim of neoclassical economics constructs the firm as a profit-maximizing entity with a sole focus on enhancing shareholder value, most large corporations have some sort of community engagement or philanthropic program. Whether these are for strategic reasons or justified on 'moral' grounds is another matter. As Milton Friedman said famously, 'just as an artificial structure like a building cannot have moral opinions or social responsibility, an artificial legal structure like the corporation cannot have morals or social responsibility'. If an investment on a particular CSR issue results in enhancing shareholder value then according to the neoclassical theorists it is a sound fiduciary decision whose 'social' benefit is irrelevant.

Second, stakeholder theory is *instrumental* in that it provides a basis for exploring a relationship between a firm's CSR activities and other corporate performance parameters like profitability, revenue, return on investments, and so on. There is an assumption that a corporation that takes into account the needs of all its stakeholders will also be successful in traditional performance criteria. This is a proposition that has received mixed empirical support. Margolis and Walsh (2003) in a study of 127 empirical studies conducted during 1972–2002 measuring the relationship between corporate social performance and corporate financial performance found that about half the studies reported a positive relationship. The research findings are far from convincing, however, and recent reviews have pointed out serious shortcomings ranging across sampling problems, measurement issues, omission of controls and, more significantly, lack of explanatory theory linking CSR with financial performance (Margolis and Walsh, 2003; McWilliams and Siegel, 2000; Orlitzky *et al.*, 2003). However, the authors found little evidence of a *negative* relationship. In other words there is no evidence to state that corporate social responsibility can harm the wealth-generating ability of business firms, which should lead to alleviating concerns about diminishing shareholder value.

Third, stakeholder theory is *normative* in that it recognizes that groups other than shareholders, employees, suppliers and customers, who may not have contractual relationships with the firm, are also legitimate stakeholders. Donaldson and Preston (1995) argue that the interests of *all* stakeholders have 'intrinsic value' meriting consideration for their own sake and not just because of their ability to enhance or harm shareholder value. Normative justification of stakeholder theory is typically based on Western philosophical and moral traditions such as utilitarianism, social contracts, fairness and reciprocity, fundamental human rights, and respect for human beings. However, the notion that we should embrace stakeholder theory because the dominant theory of the shareholder value-maximizing firm is 'morally untenable' (Donaldson and Preston, 1995: 88) is problematic because a stakeholder approach does not automatically guarantee that managers will make decisions based on morality or favor groups other than shareholders (Thomas, 1999). Stakeholder theory is normative with moral overtones. It focuses on what a company 'should' do in order to fulfill its societal responsibilities. Critics of CSR like Milton Friedman and Peter Drucker also use a normative argument in labeling CSR as a 'dangerous distortion of business principles' because it deviates from the fiduciary responsibilities that managers have towards a firm's shareholders.

Although stakeholder theory is proposed as an alternate to other theories of the firm some scholars have attempted to integrate it with conventional theories of the firm. For instance, Hill and Jones (1992: 132) expanded agency theory, which described the relationship between shareholders and managers, to develop a 'stakeholder-agency theory' where 'managers can be seen as the agents of all other stakeholders'. Thus, the primary focus in stakeholder-agency theory is not about equilibrium in principal–agent relationships but the 'process, direction and speed of adaption in stakeholder–agent relationships' (Donaldson and Preston, 1995: 79). A stakeholder-agency approach does not imply a reduction in efficiency; rather stakeholders and managers form relationships to perform organizational tasks as efficiently as possible, which should result in enhanced organizational performance.

Stakeholder approaches have also been applied to the contractarian view of the firm in an attempt to conceptualize the firm as a 'set of multilateral contracts over time' (Freeman and Evan, 1990: 352) where multiparty arrangements exist between firms and stakeholders through 'implicit contracts'. Using the language of transaction costs, Freeman and Evan (1990) argue that managers administer contracts with not only shareholders but employees, suppliers, customers and the community, with each group possessing different degrees of asset specificity that can affect other groups. Managing a diverse range of asset-specific transactions with a variety of stakeholders implies that managers need to consider the interests of all parties, with the assumption that effective management of stakeholders will reduce transaction costs leading to improved organizational performance. Balancing conflicting goals of multiple stakeholders is seen as redefining the purpose of a firm where satisfying multiple stakeholder interests rather than meeting conventional financial criteria is seen as the 'ultimate test of corporate performance' (Donaldson and Preston, 1995: 80).

There is an underlying tension between the normative and instrumental approaches to stakeholder theory. Ultimately, though, instrumental consequences of stakeholder theory have prevailed. For instance, McWilliams and Siegel (2001) use the conventional input–output model of the firm to conceptualize CSR as a form of investment that allows a firm to differentiate its products and processes. Demand for products to have 'CSR attributes' (McWilliams and Siegel point to organic and pesticide-free produce and union labeling in clothing as examples) can come from customers as well as investors and employees. CSR can be a source of product innovation (biodegradable detergents for example) or process innovation (sweatshop-free labor or energy-efficient and low-emissions production processes for example). Thus, the demand factors of CSR assume that competing on price and CSR attributes is more effective than competing on price alone (Smith, 1994). Apart from demand factors, there is a supply side perspective on CSR from the resource-based view of the firm which requires a firm to allocate resources to meet the demand for CSR. McWilliams and Siegel (2001: 124) describe how different kinds of resources like capital, materials and labor can be 'CSR related', for example capital expenditure in cleaner production, socially responsible purchasing policies and 'progressive human resource management practices'. Thus, in their formulation of a stakeholder firm the primary managerial task of balancing stakeholder needs involves determining an 'appropriate level of CSR investment and making decisions about the optimal use of inputs and resources that generate CSR attributes'. The ultimate criterion for justifying any CSR investment is market demand.

Corporate rationality dictates the nature and scope of acceptable practices engineering the inevitable compromise of making a business case for corporate social responsibility. Thus, corporate social responsibility becomes a product or service strategy designed to sustain a competitive advantage (Martin, 2002; McWilliams and Siegel, 2001). However the limits of corporate rationality when applied to social issues are exposed if we take this argument further. If corporate social initiatives are indeed a competitive strategy, it is not a particularly valuable one in terms of its imitability: the very visible nature of these practices makes it easier for competitors to develop similar strategies. Research on environmental strategies has shown that, once all economic actors have realized the immediate benefits of environmental improvements, the 'low-hanging fruit' of cost savings and efficiency increases, every incremental environmental improvement now required a substantially larger level of investment with a much longer time horizon which few companies were willing to consider (Banerjee *et al.*, 2003; Sharma and Vredenburg, 1998). Corporate social responsibility in this framework is limited to win–win situations starting with the assumption that it makes good business sense and enhances shareholder value. Thus, as Margolis and Walsh (2003) point out, the entirety of empirical research on the economic performance–social performance link, and indeed all of the conceptual research on stakeholder theory, actually serves to authenticate the economic contractarian model because it accepts its assumptions and does not pose an alternate view.

The dominant instrumental approach to stakeholder theory accommodates the fundamental economic assumptions of the theory of the firm while ignoring many social and economic conflicts between corporations and some stakeholders. If stakeholder theory is to promote genuine social good it has to be accepted and widely applied on normative not instrumental terms, which requires a fundamental rethinking of the purpose of a corporation and a shift away from the primacy of shareholders. Perhaps a different view of social relations is needed if we are to envisage a corporation that can address social ills. The current neoliberal model with its economic assumptions of fundamentally competitive social relations (Granovetter and Swedberg, 2001) can only produce a narrow and self-serving view of social responsibility. As Roberts (2003: 251) points out, at best this can produce 'moments of calculated cooperation when reciprocal self-interests coincide and ethical justification can take the form only of an argument that ethics pays'. Commenting on the results of a meta-analysis of more than 25 years of empirical studies on the link between corporate economic and social performance, Orlitzky *et al.* (2003) claimed that the literature was 'over inclusive' in defining organizational stakeholders and called for a more 'restrictive' concept of stakeholders in order to establish a stronger link. This implies a focus on stakeholders who can influence the financial or competitive position of the firm, leaving few or no resources directed to serve the interests of marginalized stakeholder groups. While there are a few cases where shareholder activism has influenced corporate behavior these have focused on specific corporate abuses and not on promoting corporate social initiatives per se. It is unlikely that shareholder resolutions will compel corporations to address social issues like poverty, health and education unless this is part of a broader political movement with the backing of governments, international organizations and other agencies (Welsh, 1988).

However, despite the dismissal of stakeholder theory by some of the more fundamentalist economists, the fact remains that almost every large corporation today is engaged in some form of social initiative. Margolis and Walsh (2003) argue that the fact that corporations do address social issues challenges economic theory. But does it? One could argue that current social initiatives serve a purely instrumental purpose where the rationale is that they enhance the economic bottom line by delivering tangible and intangible benefits like enhanced reputation and image, increased employee morale, enhanced customer value, increased market access and competitive advantage (Center for Corporate Public Affairs, 2000). For example, corporate environmental efforts that go beyond the law can serve to anticipate and shape future legislation or even circumvent legislation through voluntary codes of conduct. This process, called 'regulatory capture' by economists, serves to control regulatory agencies through extensive lobbying and 'selective information sharing' (Bakan, 2004: 152). This process was evident in the negotiations during the Montreal Protocol that phased out production of chlorofluorocarbons because of the damage they caused to the ozone layer as well as during the negotiations leading up to the Kyoto Protocol on climate change. Corporations played a leading role in this process through lobbying, developing codes of conduct and disseminating their research findings on climate change (Buchholz, 1993; Levy and Egan, 2003). The decline in the regulatory enforcement power of the Environmental Protection Agency is another case in point: systematic budget cuts over the years resulted in severe understaffing coupled with a significant shift in focus from controller and enforcer of legislation to 'industry partner'. Whether this partnership approach will deliver significant environmental benefits to society remains to be seen. Other examples of business lobby groups that have lobbied against corporate regulation at a variety of international fora include the International Chamber of Commerce (lobbied against binding emission targets in the Kyoto Protocol, implementation of the Convention on Biological Diversity, and the Basel Convention on export of hazardous waste), the World Business Council for Sustainable Development (lobbied against binding international environmental regulation at the 2002 Johannesburg Earth Summit), the Confederation of British Industry and the United States Council of International Business (lobbied against UN norms on transnational corporations and human rights) (Corporate Watch, 2006).

To summarize, we can discern three approaches to stakeholder theory in the literature: the shareholder value perspective which sees stakeholder theory as a 'dangerous distortion of business principles', the stakeholder value perspective aimed at making corporations more socially responsible by balancing the needs of different stakeholders, and the managerial perspective, a 'middle way' that identifies salient stakeholders in order to manage them efficiently. Thus, the primary approach, despite some normative concessions, remains avowedly instrumental whereby theoretical approaches focus on reconciling corporate social initiatives with the economic view of the firm. Margolis and Walsh (2003: 284), while acknowledging this drawback, call for a normative theory of the firm, where the role of management scholars is to identify the 'principles and guidelines for managing tradeoffs, rather than assert, deny or reconcile competing legitimacy claims of stakeholders'. However, they do not address the political and power dynamics that govern the process of developing principles for managing tradeoffs. The normative core of stakeholder theory is said to be a driver of corporate social performance and, once managers accept their obligations to stakeholders and recognize their legitimacy, the corporation is well on its way to achieving its moral principles (Clarkson, 1995). This is a simplistic argument that fails to recognize the inability of a single universal framework to represent different realities and define terms of legitimacy and responsibility. Proponents of stakeholder theory claim that corporate social performance can be evaluated based on the management of a corporation's relationships with its stakeholders. The fact that social performance needs to be 'managed' implies that, as is done with business ethics, it is deployed as a strategy designed to benefit the corporation. Who decided what is socially appropriate? Who assesses it?

The search for a legitimate, normative core for stakeholder theory must therefore be treated with caution, with the understanding that this search, like any search, is predicated on institutional interests. In an attempt to identify which stakeholders really count, Mitchell *et al.* (1997) classified stakeholders based on their possession of three attributes: power (the stakeholder's power to influence the company), legitimacy (of the stakeholder's relationship with the company) and urgency (the extent to which the stakeholder's demands require immediate attention). Their analysis of power in the context of organization–stakeholder relationships, however, is fairly superficial and focuses mainly on structural forms of power like coercive and utilitarian power while ignoring the mechanisms and apparatus of discursive power that forms and transforms economic and social domains. We will revisit the notion of power in a later chapter, particularly Foucault's formulation of the discursive power of knowledge systems in examining how constructions of stakeholder legitimacy are a function of power/knowledge systems. An analysis of discursive power will allow us to explain how particular concepts of the social and economic are discursively produced at the political level, the practices and policies they shape and the kinds of legitimacy they construct.

According to Mitchell *et al.* (1997: 869), legitimacy is derived from 'some socially constructed system of norms, values, and beliefs' and can be achieved at individual, organizational and societal levels. Stakeholder legitimacy is a function of power relationships between different actors and the rationality that determines the legitimacy of a stakeholder arises from corporate and economic interests, not social. In the 1960s, environmental organizations or consumer groups opposing corporate actions were not seen by firms as legitimate stakeholders. As these groups grew in power, corporations were forced to take into account their claims to the extent that several such movements were co-opted into the economic rationalist framework. The green movement started out as a grassroots, anti-business movement: today the global environmental agenda is set by multinational corporations not grassroots environmental organizations.

Thus, one of the tasks of corporations is to prioritize stakeholders based on an analysis of the corporation–stakeholder relationship. Senior managers of corporations determine the salience of stakeholders and those deemed salient tend to receive management attention. Typically, corporations tend to focus on stakeholders with higher levels of power, legitimacy and urgency: the demands of these 'definitive' stakeholders (Mitchell *et al.*, 1997) normally get the attention of top management. Interestingly, Mitchell *et al.* (1997: 878) define the group of stakeholders who have urgency and power but 'lack' legitimacy as 'dangerous stakeholders' and deplore their actions as being 'outside the bounds of legitimacy, dangerous both to the stakeholder–manager relationship and to the individuals and entities involved'. They single out 'wildcat strikers' and 'coercive environmentalists' as examples of dangerous stakeholders. They feel duty bound to 'identify' dangerous stakeholders without 'acknowledging' them because they 'abhor their practices'. They argue that by refusing to acknowledge these dangerous stakeholders they are 'counteracting terror in all its forms (which) is an effective counteragent in the battle to maintain civility and civilization'. While these writers should be applauded for their virtuous stand on their abhorrence of violence, it must be remembered that there are very few theoretical frameworks in organization studies to understand the continuing violence that development and management theories perpetuate on marginalized and poor communities throughout the world. Their argument is both ill defined and insidious: there is no attempt to analyse the problematic notion of 'legitimacy' (apart from a passing remark that legitimacy is 'socially constructed') and the power dynamics involved in setting 'bounds of legitimacy'.

The stakeholder framework developed by Mitchell *et al.* (1997) is particularly problematic for marginalized groups trying to negotiate their survival with corporations and governments. Their example of portraying the African National Congress in South Africa as an 'urgent' stakeholder with no 'legitimacy given the ruling South African culture and government' is a case in point. The ANC was illegitimate for a ruling elite that had the power to make laws governing legitimacy. Mitchell *et al.* (1997) claim that the ANC moved from being a 'demanding' stakeholder (possessing urgency, but no legitimacy or power) to a 'dangerous' one by using coercive power. However, they argue that only by relinquishing coercive power and becoming a 'dependent' stakeholder could the ANC achieve success by acquiring the support of more salient stakeholders (such as international investors). The breathtaking arrogance of this position not only denies years of struggle against colonial domination, but also serves to justify the '(then) ruling South African culture and government' as legitimate, a flawed and ahistorical argument that displaces attention from the coercive power used by 'legitimate' governments to the coercive power used by the ANC in its resistance (the authors are silent on the former but, of course, abhor the latter).

Other attempts to develop stakeholder theory have followed similar lines and have used a range of relationships including explicit and implicit contracts and non-contractual relationships to explain how and why different stakeholders influence organizations, why some stakeholders have more influence than others, differences in legitimacy of stakeholders and how organization–stakeholder relationships change over time (Friedman and Miles, 2002). However, stakeholder theories of the firm have been unable to escape the chains of neoclassical economic thought with its assumptions of maximizing self-interest, rationality and equilibrium. That (perceived) integration of stakeholder needs might be an effective tool for a firm to enhance its image is probably true. However, for a critical understanding of stakeholder theory, this approach is unsatisfactory. Effective practices of 'managing' stakeholders and research aimed at generating 'knowledge' about stakeholders are less systems of truth than products of power applied by corporations, governments and business schools (Knights, 1992). As Willmott (1995) points out, the establishment of new organization theories is very much the outcome of the historical development of capitalism, and they create value only for particular people and institutions. A view of the full picture of the consequences of stakeholder theory and practice requires a stepping out of the frame. A more critical examination of stakeholder theory, for instance understanding that stakeholder relations are systematized and controlled by the imperatives of capital accumulation, may produce a very different picture. There is a need for more empirical research on stakeholder management practices to understand whether stakeholder management is about 'motivating stakeholders to act in ways which are beneficial to the corporation', as a popular strategy textbook describes it (Harrison and St John, 1994: xii), or about '*manipulating* stakeholders to act in ways which are beneficial to the organization', as some critics claim (Thomas, 1999). Attributes of power, legitimacy and urgency that determine stakeholder salience are ultimately a function of power discourses between institutional, state and corporate actors and the process of stakeholder integration tends to either disallow alternative practices or assimilate them. The difficulties in integrating stakeholder needs are compounded when particular stakeholder groups have profoundly different and often incompatible interests and needs. Stakeholder engagement in these cases becomes a form of stakeholder colonialism where marginalized communities who are legitimate stakeholders fight for their survival in conflicts with transnational corporations and nation states. Nowhere is this more apparent than in the numerous conflicts between indigenous communities and transnational corporations that have been taking place for more than 200 years and continue to this day. Let us examine some cases of these stakeholder conflicts and analyse the power dynamics that determine how these conflicts are resolved.

THE PRACTICE OF STAKEHOLDER COLONIALISM

The stakeholder salience framework is descriptive: while it tells us which groups of stakeholders will get the attention of managers it does not explain how and why certain stakeholders are more powerful and legitimate than others. In a business firm investors and shareholders are the only definitive stakeholders with high levels of power, legitimacy and urgency. In a stakeholder firm more than one stakeholder group has a 'definitive' status (Kochan and Rubinstein, 2000). Only primary stakeholders (employees, customers, investors) are salient in the current political economy, and an enabling condition for stakeholder salience is the possession of assets that are critical to a firm's success as well as power and influence to engage the firm in meeting the stakeholder's needs. Stakeholder firms can be 'sustainable' when stakeholders have a voice in leadership succession and corporate governance arrangements. Even in this formulation of stakeholder theory there are many disempowered and marginalized groups who are adversely affected by corporate activity yet unable to participate in any 'stakeholder dialogue'. Indigenous communities living in the poorer regions of the world for example face severe social and environmental problems arising from extractive industries in their lands. While no one can doubt these communities are legitimate stakeholders their ability to engage with corporations is severely constrained.

At one level, the reformist view argues that all stakeholders must be consulted, and the consultative process is the area that needs attention (Egri and Pinfield, 1996). At another level, identifying appropriate stakeholders and prioritizing their needs tend to be driven by corporate needs and, as noted by some critics, may limit the scope of reformist change (Banerjee, 2000; Thomas, 1999). However, defining the basis of stakeholder legitimacy is problematic and tends to be framed from the perspective of the business firm, which limits understanding of the more complex dynamics of organization–stakeholder relationships, especially if the stakeholder groups have very different social, cultural, political and economic agendas than industry. Indigenous communities all over the world constitute one such stakeholder group. Historically, these communities have had little say on the kind of development that has taken place in their traditional lands. Awareness and recognition of the rights of indigenous peoples all over the world have increased in recent years. The United Nations Declaration on the Rights of Indigenous Nations recognizes the 'urgent need to respect and promote the inherent rights and characteristics of Indigenous Nations, especially the right to lands, territories and resources which derive from each Nation's culture; aspects of which include spiritual traditions, histories, and philosophies as well as political, economic and social customs and cultures' (United Nations, 1994: 1).

However, the history of interactions between indigenous communities and the corporate sector, especially in the mining and resource industries, is marked with blood, violence, death and dispossession. Mining is a global industry with a handful of large transnational corporations controlling a major part of the metals and minerals market. In recent years, the industry has become even more concentrated as a result of several mergers and acquisitions. Without exception, the social, cultural, economic and environmental impacts on these communities have been devastating (Australian Institute of Aboriginal Studies, 1984; Denoon, 2000; Howitt and Douglas, 1983; Katona, 1998; Roberts, 1981). In many cases, traditional relations have broken down, sacred sites been destroyed, communities been displaced, and patterns of indigenous life been disrupted. Traditional means of sustenance were also irretrievably affected: hunting land was destroyed, water resources depleted and contaminated, and forests denuded.

A 1984 Australian government report on mining described its impact on indigenous communities in the Northern Territory:

> The current civic culture is one in which disunity, neurosis, a sense of struggle, drinking, stress, hostility, of being drowned by new laws, agencies, and agendas are major manifestations. Their defeat on initial opposition to mining, fresh negotiations, new sources of money, the influx of vehicles together have led the Project to an unhappy verdict: that this is a society in crisis. (Australian Institute of Aboriginal Studies, 1984: 299)

Indigenous leaders and NGO activists point out that 22 years after this report of 'a society in crisis' the stated recommendations in the report are yet to be implemented. Mining is a key industry in Australia, and mining operations have been taking place for nearly 150 years. Over 60 percent of Australia's commodity exports come from mining, accounting for over $36 billion of Australia's export earnings (Kauffman, 1998). The benefits reflected by the number of jobs and dollars in royalty payments that result from mining are of little use to indigenous communities in Australia who are impacted by mining (Katona, 1998). Health, education, life expectancy, essential services and housing for indigenous people continue to be the worst in the country, well below national averages. Mineral wealth extracted from indigenous lands in the Northern Territory has provided more than $10 billion in gross revenue since 1978; however, most indigenous communities in the area live in dire poverty with little scope to access resources for education and training or gain political power. A closer look at the alleged economic benefits of mining for indigenous communities reveals a somewhat less rosy picture of reality. Royalty payments are not the solution: several studies, by government and non-government agencies, have shown that royalty payments do not provide the benefits they were designed to, and the socio-economic condition of indigenous communities continues to stagnate. These payments do nothing to address the fundamental problems of poor health, lack of local infrastructure, absence of tertiary education and chronic unemployment. The rural indigenous median family income is $5256, which is 61 percent of the non-indigenous rural family median income after accounting for differences in family size. Unemployment among indigenous people is about 40 percent compared to Australia's total unemployment rate of 8 percent. Although indigenous people make up 25 percent of the population in the Northern Territory (a region where more than half of all mining in Australia is carried out), they make up only 7 percent of the workforce, mainly in minimum-wage casual jobs (Kauffman, 1998).

Mining development plans promised vast employment opportunities but the reality is very different. Indigenous employment in the companies that mine their land is minimal and is restricted to casual, unskilled, minimum-wage jobs. To ensure that multimillion-dollar projects are commissioned in the shortest time frame skilled workforces are flown in from outside. Social and cultural disruption generally followed the establishment of mines on indigenous lands. Most leading mining companies, while sometimes acknowledging the damages caused to indigenous communities, claim that the current challenge is how to proceed with mining without the damaging sociocultural consequences. Thus 'consultation' processes regarding mining are framed by questions that evaluate the conditions under which the project should proceed rather than whether it should proceed at all. As Tatz (1982: 176) points out, indigenous communities are the '*receivers of consultation*, that is, that Aboriginal people are from time to time *talked to* about the decisions *arrived* at' (original emphasis). Education, training and employment in indigenous communities suffer from a similar bias, and indigenous 'participation' often means a dilution of their land rights and a continuation of colonial control.

It makes little difference to indigenous communities whether corporations' stakeholder strategies are 'reactive', 'defensive', 'accommodating' or 'proactive' (Carroll, 1979) or follow any other typology: the right to say no to development on their land does not arise in any case. Roberts (1981) documented a wide range of strategies used by mining companies in Australia to negotiate mining leases on indigenous land. Some of these strategies include (1) ignore indigenous land councils wherever possible (or threaten to do so); (2) isolate any indigenous group or individual who is a 'traditional owner' and focus company efforts in making a deal with them; (3) discredit advisers used by indigenous groups and any scientific evidence produced by 'outsiders' or use the law to restrict access to the land; (4) invoke the national interest and economic security of Australia; and (5) offer to employ 'employable' Aborigines. Some of these strategies were used recently in Australia by both the government and the mining company in an attempt to deflect opposition to a uranium mine in the Northern Territory (Banerjee, 2000; Katona, 1998). However, the statements that appear in current community reports of leading mining companies certainly do not take this adversarial stance. It remains to be seen whether the 'partners in development' approach touted as best practice by the leading mining companies actually improves the socio-economic condition of indigenous communities impacted by mining.

There seems to be a public recognition by some mining companies that interactions with indigenous communities need to change. Essentially, this change involves recognizing the rights of indigenous communities as legitimate stakeholders in the business with whom continuous consultation is needed. Most transnational mining companies have policies for dealing with indigenous communities where the latter are not seen as obstacles to resource development but as 'partners' in resource development. The paradigm has allegedly 'shifted from indigenous participation in mining to mining company participation in the indigenous community' (ICME, 1999: iii). How much of this shift is rhetoric represented by glossy reports that hide the grim realities of mining is open to debate. For instance, the mining giant Rio Tinto has been under attack for decades by environmentalists, activists and indigenous groups for human rights violations in the Bougainville copper mine in Papua New Guinea (which was forcibly closed in 1989) and mining operations in Borneo. The company's community report policy affirms

> that every operation shall try to understand and interact positively and constructively with its local communities. We set out to build enduring relationships with our neighbors that are characterized by mutual respect, active partnership, and long-term commitment. Community relations are about working closely with our neighboring communities, to arrive at an understanding of what we can do for mutual benefit and then to secure implementation of agreed objectives. (Rio Tinto, 2007)

There are serious doubts about whether mining companies' 'participation' in indigenous communities achieves the stated goals. 'Partners' in resource development assumes two things: first, both parties are relatively equal in their power and access to resources and, second, all indigenous communities are in favor of mining on their lands. Neither assumption is valid in all cases. It is important to realize the diversity of indigenous communities in the world: they have different development needs and expectations depending on various sociocultural and geopolitical contexts.

This is not to say that all indigenous communities are 'anti-development'. Rather, it is the kind of development that takes place that is most important to these communities. Economic self-sufficiency and removal of welfare dependency are the aims of government and corporate policies toward indigenous communities. Again, while these goals are laudable, they obscure the fact that these communities were economically self-sufficient before colonization. There is also the assumption that the economic benefit of mining will not have negative social or cultural impacts despite substantial evidence to the contrary. Since the 1970s there have been more than a hundred government and corporate reports on the impact of mining on indigenous communities in Australia. 'Impact' is the key word: these reports are, without exception, post hoc studies that assess adverse social and environmental effects of mining in the community (Tatz, 1982). Not one of these reports ever discussed with Aboriginal people the possibility of securing an independent economic future without depending on mining (Banerjee, 2000).

Given the profound incommensurabilities between the needs of indigenous communities and those of corporations it is difficult to see how an inclusive stakeholder approach can address the needs of this stakeholder group. In some cases, admittedly a minority, indigenous stakeholders have been able to leverage resources from NGOs and build international networks to promote their cause. A recent case involves the construction of a uranium mine in Jabiluka in northern Australia where an indigenous community consisting of 24 people took on the might of the Australian state and federal governments as well as a transnational mining company and managed to stop construction of the mine. They were successful in their efforts by forming coalitions with a wide range of other stakeholder groups including international environmental organizations, community organizations, churches, activist groups, academics, lawyers and student organizations and lobbying international agencies like the UN and UNESCO as well as engaging in street protests and non-violent blockades of the mine site. Their actions and the wide publicity they received resulted in shareholders of the parent company calling an extraordinary meeting to question their company's involvement in the mine. Despite the indigenous people being legitimate stakeholders and holding 'assets' that were critical to the organization (although their 'ownership' of the land does not meet Western property rights criteria because Native Title in Australia imposes severe constraints on land use by its indigenous 'owners'), the worldview of indigenous stakeholders was not really a legitimate alternative to Western notions of progress and development. Thus while indigenous stakeholders are positioned as legitimate stakeholders whose needs will be 'constructively addressed', the stakes that are involved for Aboriginal communities affected by mining are somehow positioned as 'illegitimate' or against 'national interest'.

The principle of 'public responsibility' in CSR also fails to consider interests of marginalized stakeholders. The public debate in the Jabiluka case has focused on the corporation's environmental responsibility as well as its responsibility to indigenous stakeholders. However, social responsibilities should be relevant to the 'organization's interests' (Wood, 1991) and therein lies the problem: these 'public' responsibilities are defined and framed by Western principles of legitimacy, principles that are inimical to indigenous stakeholders in the first place. Thus, the parameters that define a 'social outcome' are determined by a system of rules and exclusions that do not address indigenous concerns. The public–private dichotomy of stakeholder representation does not legitimize indigenous interests; instead it serves to regulate indigenous ways of living. Who is seeking stakeholder input? For what purpose? Public interests are represented by government agencies that seek stakeholder input to obtain information designed to legitimize support for their decisions. The input from indigenous communities regarding mining on their land at Jabiluka was unequivocal: they did not want it. The agencies that sought this input admitted the adverse consequences that mining had on indigenous communities. The decision to mine was motivated by the economic gains to 'the nation' (at the cost of irreversible loss to indigenous nations) and legitimized by promoting indigenous participation in 'development' despite its deleterious effects.

Many other indigenous communities all over the world are fighting against economic, social and cultural marginalization at different levels, and their struggles are against their own governments, multinational and domestic corporations, international agencies and global organizations. The primary victims of the structural violence caused by mining and extractive industries are the poor of the world. As Farmer (2005: 50) points out, not only are the poor 'more likely to suffer, they are also less likely to have their suffering noted'. The Zapatista uprising in the Chiapas district of southern Mexico is one case where the suffering of the poor received worldwide media attention. Indigenous communities in Chiapas rose up against the Mexican government in an armed insurrection and temporarily took over the regional capital of San Cristobal. The Mexican government responded with military action and after several conflicts offered conditional pardon to the rebels. On 18 January 1994 Zapatista leaders responded to the Mexican government's offer of conditional pardon with the following letter, entitled 'Who must ask for pardon and who can grant it?', suggesting that the Mexican government ask the Chiapans for a pardon instead, which they would consider:

> Why do we have to be pardoned? What are we going to be pardoned for? Of not dying of hunger? Of not being silent in our misery? Of not humbly accepting our historic role of being the despised and the outcast? Of having demonstrated to the rest of the country and to the entire world that human dignity still lives, even among some of the world's poorest peoples? (Marcos, 1995)

In Chiapas, 14,500 people die every year, the highest death rate in the country. Most of these deaths are caused by curable diseases: respiratory infections, gastroenteritis, parasites, malaria, breakbone fever, tuberculosis, conjunctivitis, typhus, cholera and measles. While there are 7 hotel rooms for every 1000 tourists there are 0.3 hospital beds for every 1000 Chiapans (Farmer, 2005). Transnational corporations extract wealth from Chiapas by mining their land, felling their forests, and selling a tourist experience at the expense of local communities who have the misfortune of 'inhabiting' the region. One of the leaders of the movement, Subcomandante Marcos, described their struggle: 'When we rose up against a national government, we found that it did not exist. In reality we were up against financial capital, against speculation, which is what makes decisions in Mexico as well as in Europe, Asia, Africa, Oceania, North America, South America – everywhere' (*Zapatista*, 1998).

The story is depressingly familiar to indigenous communities all over the world. In this case, officials of the World Bank met in Geneva and decided to give a loan to Mexico on condition they export meat under the agreements laid down by the World Trade Organization. Land used by indigenous communities in Chiapas was now to be used to raise cattle for fast food markets in the US while locking out local communities from participating in the benefits (there is no McDonald's in Chiapas). This is an inherently undemocratic process where peasant populations do not have the right to decide how they want to live. The corporate response by a major financier in the restructuring of Mexico's economy was not very encouraging to the Zapatistas either: 'The government will need to eliminate the Zapatistas to demonstrate their effective control of the national territory and security policy' (Mexico, Political Update, Chase Manhattan Bank, *Zapatista*, 1998). If communities have to be 'eliminated' for economic development to occur one can only wonder what corporate social responsibility and stakeholder engagement mean in this context.

Thus, a more critical engagement with stakeholder theory goes beyond documenting 'best practice' or 'worst practice' in stakeholder management. It would involve examining how knowledge and theory development in the field constitutes social relations between different stakeholders and perhaps even set the ground for a different set of conditions, which in turn needs to be critiqued. It needs to go beyond structuralist notions of cause and effect. Thus, instead of asking the structuralist question – what are the general rules governing stakeholder relations determined in relation to other similar relations? – the question becomes poststructuralist: what gives this particular person the right or power to say this? Why this statement and not some other one? The poststructuralist question is thus more historical and less universalizing (Muecke, 1992). Popular representations of organizations and their accompanying notions of decentralization, diffusion, democracy, market, empowerment, flexibility, trust and collectivity also need to be critically examined and countered by investigating how these corporate objectives along with notions of 'values' and 'ethics' increasingly dominate all other 'social' agendas, giving rise to a new corporate colonialism (Goldsmith, 1997; Grice and Humphries, 1997). Some critics like

Thomas (1999) argue that stakeholder management can actually damage the interests of external stakeholders while portraying an image of stakeholder engagement because the normative justification of stakeholder theory masks the instrumental and economic approaches and, instead of challenging and changing power and control structures in corporations, stakeholder theory ends up reinforcing existing structures. Recent cases appear to indicate that corporations seem to gain more from CSR than society. Examples of high-profile CSR strategies like those of Nike, which transformed itself from a villain to CSR hero (Zadek, 2004), Shell's £20 million public relations campaign to restore its tarnished image after the Ken Saro Wiwa execution in Nigeria, and Rio Tinto's expansive and expensive community relations campaign beg the question whether corporations are engaging with community stakeholders or with the CSR industry. The 'crises' in these examples of conflict are portrayed as crises of corporate reputation that need to be addressed rather than the plight of the stakeholders who suffer the most damage (Lawrence, 2002). High-profile CSR companies are also profitable, which raises the question whether companies that are socially responsible do better financially or whether companies that *say* they are socially responsible do better financially.

The normative basis of stakeholder theory with its philosophical assumptions of utilitarianism, justice and ethics is also predicated on particular notions of citizenship. Citizenship evokes notions of inclusion (and exclusion), diversity, social justice, pluralism, representation of diverse interests, democracy and individual rights. While these are desirable attributes for any society the corporatization of citizenship raises some doubts whether a corporation is able to deliver these outcomes. I will explore the possibilities of corporate citizenship in the next chapter.

4. The problem with corporate citizenship

> I see in the near future a crisis approaching that unnerves me and causes me to tremble for the safety of my country ... corporations have been enthroned and an era of corruption in high places will follow, and the money power of the country will endeavor to prolong its reign by working upon the prejudices of the people until all wealth is aggregated in a few hands and the Republic is destroyed.
>
> (Abraham Lincoln, 21 November 1864)

A new term entered the lexicon in the late 1980s to add to the plethora of terms describing business–society relationships. 'Corporate citizenship' now appears regularly in the business and academic literatures and is the theme of several academic and practitioner conferences – an early example is the Conference on Corporate Citizenship held in 1996 in Washington DC where in his keynote then President Clinton identified family-friendly workplaces, employee health and retirement benefits, employee safety and security and 'employee participation in workplace productivity' and community welfare as the 'essential elements' of corporate citizenship (Hemphill, 2004). The primary focus on employees and the 'local community' where corporations operate is a much narrower focus than CSR where the notion of the 'social' was broadly defined, too broadly according to some. There also appears to be some disagreement about terminology: while some writers view corporate citizenship and corporate social responsibility as synonymous (Swanson and Niehoff, 2001; Waddock, 2001), others argue that corporate citizenship focuses more on internal organizational values as opposed to corporate social responsibility, which is more concerned about the negative externalities associated with corporate behavior (Birch, 2001; Wood and Logsdon, 2001). Some argue that the roots of the two discourses are also different: corporate citizenship is a more practitioner-based approach whereas the discourse of corporate social responsibility emerged from the academic community (Davenport, 2000). Proponents of corporate citizenship claim it can bridge the theory–practice divide that characterizes much of the research on corporate social responsibility. Today most large corporations publicize their commitments to corporate citizenship in their annual reports and corporate websites: ExxonMobil pledges to be a 'good corporate citizen' by maintaining the 'highest ethical standards', complying with 'all applicable laws and regulations', respecting 'local and national cultures' and running 'safe and environmentally responsible operations' (www.exxonmobil.com). Ford's commitment to corporate citizenship is demonstrated by 'how we conduct our business and how we take care of our employees, as well as how we interact with the world at large' (www.ford.com). Nike's vision is to be an 'inspirational global citizen' by driving 'responsible business practices that contribute to profitable and sustainable growth' (www.nike.com).

Corporate citizenship also implies a distinction between being a 'good' and 'bad' citizen. Socially responsible investment funds for example exclude 'bad' corporate citizens like tobacco companies, weapons manufacturers and environmental polluters. However, the fact that these companies regularly publish corporate citizenship and social performance reports tends to muddy the waters more than a little. For example, a recent report released by the Vice President, Corporate Affairs and Social Responsibility, of Philip Morris outlines their 'values-based culture' that demonstrates 'integrity, honesty, respect and tolerance' while promising 'transparency' and 'stakeholder engagement' (Philip Morris, 2002). How tobacco firms can use these concepts to produce 'socially responsible' cigarettes is of course another matter. Despite the stigma of tobacco and the industry's negative public image and high-liability risks, the tobacco industry continues to have a bright future. In 2001 Philip Morris changed its name to the Altria Group mainly to minimize reputational damage from being perceived solely as a cigarette manufacturer. The company diversified into the processed foods industry with the purchase of the high-profile Kraft Foods, the world's second largest food company. By 2007 the wheel appeared to have turned full circle: in January 2007 the company announced it was selling Kraft Foods and regaining its identity of being primarily a tobacco company. The response from capital markets was overwhelmingly positive: the company's share price rose 10 percent after the announcement to divest itself of Kraft Foods was made. Wall Street analysts claim that the positive response had less to do with Kraft shedding the taint of tobacco and more to do with investor perceptions of the profitability of the tobacco industry (Martin, 2007). One analyst remarked, 'Something that is forgotten in all of this is that people like to smoke. It's enjoyable and there's not an alternative product.' US tobacco stocks have consistently outperformed the Standard & Poor's 500 stock index over the last six years. Despite the social stigma of smoking, cigarettes have a competitive advantage over other products because they are addictive, are relatively inexpensive to manufacture and require minimal innovation and there is a global market. Most importantly cigarettes have inelastic demand – manufacturers can raise prices without suffering a drop in sales (Martin, 2007).

Terms like 'stakeholder engagement', 'integrity' and 'transparency' are echoed by CSR academics as well: for instance, Birch (2001: 59–60) in developing a conceptual framework of corporate citizenship outlines '12 generic principles of corporate citizenship' including 'making a difference, employee and stakeholder empowerment, transparency, accountability, sharing responsibility, inclusivity, sustainable capitalism, a triple bottom line, long-termism, communication, engagement and dialogue'. Waddock (2001: 28) argues that operating with 'integrity and mindfulness' is at the 'core of good corporate citizenship'. It is interesting to see how these theoretical principles are seamlessly integrated into corporate policy statements. Take, for example, the following excerpt from the annual report of a large multinational corporation:

> The principles that guide our behavior are based on our vision and values and include the following:
>
> - Respect: We will work to foster mutual respect with communities and stakeholders who are affected by our operations.
> - Integrity: We will examine the impacts, positive and negative, of our business on the environment, and on society, and will integrate human, health, social and environmental considerations into our internal management and value system.
> - Communication: We will strive to foster understanding and support our stakeholders and communities, as well as measure and communicate our performance.
> - Excellence: We will continue to improve our performance and will encourage our business partners and suppliers to adhere to the same standards.

This corporation, voted by *Fortune* magazine for six consecutive years as the most 'innovative company in North America' and for three consecutive years as one of the '100 best companies to work for in America', and that is on *Fortune* magazine's 'All star list of global most admired companies', is of course none other than Enron (Enron, 2002). Glossy corporate social responsibility reports are forms of greenwashing that often do not reveal the grim realities that lie behind them. To quote the words of a famous philosopher, Marx (Groucho, not Karl), 'The secrets of success in business are honesty and transparency. If you can fake that, you've got it made.' The reference to 'stakeholder engagement' and 'understanding and supporting stakeholders and communities' is also misleading in the sense that it does not tell us which stakeholders and which communities are being supported and which ones marginalized. In my own research on the impact of mining on indigenous communities in Australia I conducted an extensive analysis of stakeholder perceptions about the costs and benefits of mining, the stakeholder group being the indigenous communities most impacted by mining (Banerjee, 2000, 2001b). The view expressed by each and every respondent was the same: they were all opposed to any expansion of the mine. When I communicated these views to the mining company (a very, very, very large multinational corporation) their response was to hire an anthropologist who could work with the natives to find out under what circumstances mining could proceed. It was imperative for the company, as a 'good corporate citizen', to convince the communities about the benefits the new mine would bring despite past and current experience of severe social and environmental problems faced by the communities due to mining. As we have seen in the previous chapter the practice of stakeholder engagement is really about managing stakeholders – telling them what to do and how to behave and under what conditions they can engage with the company – rather than a meaningful attempt to build constructive relationships.

Attempts to distinguish between corporate citizenship and CSR do not make a particularly convincing case and appear to be more of an academic exercise in staking out territories. Carroll (1998) for example defines corporate citizenship as essentially having the same features of CSR: the 'four pillars' that are the foundation of CSR (economic, ethical, legal and philanthropic responsibilities) now become the 'four faces' of corporate citizenship. One could argue that the renewed academic focus on corporate citizenship is an opportunity to reposition older ideas about CSR and business–society relationships in a more accessible form for practitioners (Matten and Crane, 2005). Thus, earlier formulations of CSR with its different types of responsibilities, its relation to corporate social responsiveness and stakeholder engagement and its outcomes that determine corporate social performance are seamlessly integrated in creating the identity of a corporate citizen. Some writers (Munshi, 2004; Wood and Logsdon, 2001) argue that because corporate citizenship is limited and specific and is largely voluntary in its focus on local community welfare and philanthropy it is necessary to envision 'global business citizenship' to bring back issues of responsibility and duty. The applicability of American and European notions of CSR to different cultures was questionable and hence there was a need to develop a universal understanding of the responsibilities of business. The notion of a 'global business citizen' was particularly relevant for multinational corporations where traditional boundaries of the firm were more fluid and it was no longer possible to clearly delineate the behaviors of the company from those of its suppliers, subcontractors and customers. Multinational corporations are both local and global actors whose rights and responsibilities across national boundaries implied an 'analysis of hypernorms' (Wood and Logsdon, 2001: 87). The UN Global Compact where multinational corporations voluntarily commit to a set of principles in the areas of the environment, labor and human rights reflects a similar 'global' sensitivity in its acceptance of a 'global compact of shared values and principles' which gives a 'human face to the global market' and aspires to overcome 'imbalances between the economic, social, and political realms' (Annan, 2000). In a similar vein, Post and Berman (2001: 68) offer their definition of global corporate citizenship:

> Global corporate citizenship is the process of identifying, analyzing, and responding to the company's social, political, and economic responsibilities as defined through

law and public policy, stakeholder expectations, and voluntary acts flowing from corporate values and business strategies. Corporate citizenship involves actual results (what corporations *do*) and the processes through which they are achieved (*how* they do it). (original emphasis)

From the above definition it appears that the main elements of corporate citizenship are not very different from concepts of CSR discussed earlier: legal requirements, societal obligations, voluntary actions, values and ethics are integrated along with a stakeholder view of the firm although for some strange reason specific reference to environmental responsibility, which is a key theme of CSR and sustainability, is missing. The problems of implementing a consistent set of universal 'hypernorms' seem to be glossed over in the literature. A multinational corporation must be seen to be sensitive to local cultures. At the same time it is required to implement a universal code of conduct, the assumption being that the company can adapt its hypernorms to suit local customs without violating them (Munshi, 2004). How this strategy will help address environmental and social problems is not clear: for instance, a 'hypernorm' of being 'environmentally responsible' can simply be operationalized as complying with local regulation. If emission requirements differ across countries, for example, there is no global legally enforceable mechanism for a company to transfer its cleanest technology as required by law in one country to another country whose laws are less stringent. A good corporate citizen is obliged to do so but the obligation cannot be legally enforced. The absence of any enforcement or punitive mechanism to meet extra-juridical obligations is the fundamental shortcoming underlying theories and practices of CSR, corporate citizenship and voluntary CSR initiatives like the Global Compact. At a global level the complexities of legal systems also enable multinational corporations to develop innovative and creative accounting practices that, while being perfectly legal, have questionable social outcomes. Thus, companies like Chevron and Texaco that claim to be corporate citizens were able to avoid payment of corporate taxes in the US of more than $8.6 billion between 1964 and 2002 by following legal transfer pricing strategies (Gramlich and Wheeler, 2003).

Barring a few skeptical voices the term 'corporate citizenship' seems to sit quite comfortably across academic and practitioner milieus. The problematic nature of citizenship when applied to corporations needs to be interrogated. The use of the term 'citizen' to denote corporate identity is related to the legal notion of the corporation as a 'natural person'. The problem is that while the rights of the corporation are guaranteed and protected its responsibilities remain discretionary. The term 'corporate citizen' extends the legal fiction of corporate personhood even further because a corporation cannot satisfy key canons of citizenship such as voting or holding public office, which are inalienable rights, held by individuals. Discourses of corporate citizenship also do not provide a critical analysis of power dynamics between individuals, groups and corporations. Thus, while the citizenship rights of corporations limit certain activities like the right to voting, the enormous economic power of corporations to influence electoral results through campaign contributions cannot be overlooked. In the US where voter apathy is the norm, ballot box power is no match for boardroom power.

Contemporary notions of corporate citizenship that deploy the legal fiction argument of the corporation in order to create a 'soul' for the body corporate run the danger of conflating citizenship with personhood. A corporation cannot be a citizen in the same way a person can. A corporation can however be considered a person as far as its legal status is concerned. Current notions of corporate citizenship conflate citizen (which as Windsor (2001) argues a business corporation cannot be) and person (which a corporation can be but only as a 'legal fiction'). Thus, as Windsor (2001: 4) points out, 'fictional personhood is not a sound basis for artificial citizenship', and theories of corporate social responsibility that take the citizenship approach will tend to be limited in defining the scope of responsibility. The problem is compounded in the case of multinational firms where there is no constitutional or legal basis for TNCs to become 'world citizens'. The conflation of a corporation with an individual citizen obscures the gaps between individual citizens' rights and corporate rights and consequently deflects attention from the need for regulations to reduce these gaps. There is some concern that corporate citizenship discourses could have the effect of reducing governmental scrutiny of corporate practices because they promote a particular form of self-governance. Corporate strategies of responding to social and environmental concerns have led to a bewildering array of 'codes of conduct' on a variety of issues, none of which are legally enforceable. There are no legislative requirements that corporations serve the public interest, thus opening up what Alan Greenspan calls more 'pathways to greed', raising justifiable concerns about self-governance, given the enormous influence and power wielded by large multinational corporations.

There is a profound difference between a corporation and an individual citizen. The corporation may be an artificial person in the eyes of the law but the artifice is significant because of its economic power and resources that individual citizens do not and cannot possess – corporations 'can live forever, exist in many places, alter their identity by chopping off their arms and legs and transform themselves into entirely different persons, and sell themselves to new owners, both domestic and foreign' (Greider, 1996: 331). The concept of citizenship, as Matten and Crane (2005) point out, either has generally been used in a very limited way (for example, corporate philanthropy as enlightened self-interest) or is seen as equivalent to corporate social responsibility. A few scholars have attempted to integrate meanings of citizenship from political theory with a view to broaden the concept of corporate citizenship. Wood and Logsdon (2001) for example, drawing on concepts of citizenship developed by Marshall (1965) and

Parry (1991), distinguish between 'minimalist, communitarian and universal rights views of citizenship'. The minimalist view focuses on individual liberty and individual rights where corporate citizenship is a nexus of private contracts. The communitarian view, while not denying individual rights, assumes that rights are contingent on specific communities and focuses more on duties. A universal view of citizenship is reflected in the UN Declaration of Universal Human Rights, which assumes that corporations have 'hypernorms' that should not be violated but can be adapted to meet the needs of local cultures. In all these models however there is a continual slippage between notions of whether a corporation 'is a citizen', whether corporations are 'like citizens' or whether they 'can become citizens'. As we have seen earlier, a metaphorical extension of an already fictional personhood can be quite problematic: an entity that is really not a person (except legally) can have the same rights as other citizens. Moon *et al.* (2005) critique Wood and Logsdon for accepting simplistic dualisms between liberal and communitarian views of citizenship and not accounting for a normative basis of the social role of corporations. In an attempt to overcome the dichotomy of individual versus communitarian ideologies, Moon *et al.* (2005) discuss four models of democratic citizenship based on Stokes's (2002) notions of 'liberal minimalist', 'civic republicanism', 'developmental', and 'deliberative' citizenship. Corporate citizenship in each of these models is determined by the level of participation in social welfare – from avoidance in the minimalist model, indirect participation (through pressure groups and political lobbying for example) and direct participation.

The ultimate form of corporate citizenship takes either a 'universal rights view' (in Wood and Logsdon's formulation) or a 'deliberate democracy' perspective (Moon *et al.*, 2005). Thus, in the universal rights view corporate citizenship is based on a 'value for balancing freedom with social welfare' (Wood and Logsdon, 2001: 96) or 'free deliberation over public decisions in a community' in the case of deliberate democracy (Moon *et al.*, 2005: 447). The participation of corporations in 'civic deliberations as equals' becomes the normative basis for citizenship. The nature of the firm in the context of corporate citizenship or CSR is that it is one participant in a network of stakeholder relationships. In the stakeholder view of the firm the diversity and complexity of stakeholder relationships make it impossible to capture every single relationship through contracts. The ontological basis for the business firm is its ability to 'permit creation of surplus value, allowing people and societies to do more with resources' (Wood and Logsdon, 2001: 96). This is somewhat of a naïve view of the corporation, despite its noble intention of showing how corporations *can* be viewed as citizens. While the first part of this argument is accurate there are doubts about the corporation's ability to enhance social welfare by 'allowing people and societies to do more with resources'. Which people and what societies and communities are empowered and enabled by corporations to better utilize their resources is the key question. There are many, many communities, particularly in the poorer regions of the world, that are currently engaged in a variety of struggles with multinational corporations over resource use (Banerjee, 2003). Several indigenous communities all over the world for example have been systematically deprived of their ability to access resources on their lands as a result of corporate interests. While the surplus value generated by corporations by access to natural resources enhances the welfare of some segments of societies (stockholders, customers, employees and suppliers) the social and environmental effects on indigenous communities are in most cases extremely damaging. There are significant problems in accepting both the communitarian view where a business firm can be viewed as a corporate citizen and a universal rights view of business citizenship. In the former case, Wood and Logsdon (2001) argue that because a corporation is a member of the local community it is responsible for its actions to the local community. But there are different levels of responsibility: what happens to community responsibility when a corporation decides to relocate its operation to a different region in order to increase its surplus value and enhance shareholder value? In the extensive management literature on CSR and corporate citizenship there is so much emphasis on responsibility and rights that notions of corporate power and accountability recede to the background. Business–society relationships whether community based or multiple stakeholder based are framed by power differentials that are not adequately addressed in concepts of CSR or corporate citizenship.

It is important to explore theoretical and practical difficulties in using concepts of citizenship transplanted from political theory to theories of the firm. In particular, the normative basis for citizenship poses some problems. An examination of the literature indicates that the rationale and assumptions behind the corporate social responsibility discourse are: (1) corporations *should* think beyond making money and pay attention to social and environmental issues; (2) corporations *should* behave in an ethical manner and demonstrate the highest level of integrity and transparency in all their operations; (3) corporations *should* be involved with the community in which they operate in terms of enhancing their social welfare and providing community support through philanthropy or other means. These notions of corporate citizenship should be operationalized through engagement and dialogue with *stakeholders* (a term that seems to be unproblematically and uncritically accepted in the literature) and corporations should always engage their stakeholders and build relationships with them (Waddock, 2001). The normative core of this discourse is not hard to ascertain: the assumption is that corporations should do all these things because (1) good corporate citizenship is related to good financial performance (despite the dubious nature of empirical evidence of this relationship) and (2) if a corporation is a bad citizen then its license to operate will be revoked by 'society'. Both of these are simplistic assumptions with little theoretical or empirical support.

Large transnational corporations responsible for major environmental disasters and negative social impacts (Union Carbide, Nike, Exxon, Shell and Nestlé to name a few) rather than lose their license to operate have actually become stronger and more powerful through mergers, acquisitions, corporate restructuring and relentless public relations campaigns. Even during negative global media coverage of Nike's use of sweatshops and anti-Nike protests the company continued to stay profitable – as Zadek (2004: 130) points out, 'institutional investors have shown a startling disinterest in Nike's handling of labor standards'. There is also some doubt about the effectiveness of consumer boycotts – one motivating force that CSR advocates claim can compel companies to become more socially responsible. A study of consumer boycotts in the US found that targeted firms did not suffer any decline in shareholder value as a result of boycotts (Koku *et al.*, 1997).

The problem with any normative theory is its assumption of universality. The discourse of universal human rights for example with its focus on individual rights, while intuitively appealing, can sometimes be at odds with other worldviews, for example collective rights over common property resources. In these cases individual rights, informed by typically Western notions of what constitutes an individual, become positioned as opposed to collective rights. The ethnocentric bias inherent in constructing universal notions of human rights is rarely acknowledged in the management literature. Western discourses of (post)modernity universalize human subjectivity thus directing the ways that diverse populations are allowed to participate in the economy, as consumers for example, which ensures that individual rights can be protected while denying the collective rights of millions of people who live in 'subsistence' economies. Thus, the construction of universal 'hypernorms' is located in a specific cultural timespace with specific race, class and gender features that despite its universalistic claims obscures power differentials underlying the process in which individual human rights are created (Bunting, 1996; Peterson, 1990). And while the goals of universal human rights are laudable, there are significant problems and challenges in their practical application in different contexts. Take the example of child labor, a volatile and emotional issue effectively publicized by many NGO campaigns highlighting exploitation of children by sweatshops that service multinational corporations. Principle 5 of the UN Global Compact calls for the 'effective abolition of child labor'. In an ideal world no child should have to work but the reality in the poorer regions of the world is grimmer: children often have to work for their household to survive. A shift in the discussion on the conditions in which child labor can be allowed (proper schooling, recreation, occupational safety and access to health care for example) rather than a hypernorm of abolishing child labor may lead to more beneficial outcomes in some contexts. If education is a way out of poverty and current forms of child labor do not provide for education then corporate and government intervention might be better suited in specifying the conditions of child labor, for example making education mandatory, providing better working conditions, allowing for family and recreation time, providing vocational skills, and so on. Thus, the debate over child labor must go beyond the dichotomy between hypernorms that declare all child labor should be banned and local norms that allow certain forms of child labor. In an analysis of stakeholder relationships involving child labor in Bangladesh, Rahman (2002) showed how non-profit groups in the US successfully pressurized Bangladeshi garment manufacturers to discharge all their underage factory workers. While this can be seen as a case of successful stakeholder activism the outcomes for the family, who saw their main source of income disappear, were largely negative. How does corporate or stakeholder responsibility deal with this problematic outcome of a successful 'socially responsible' intervention?

Rather than uncritically apply concepts of citizenship to the business firm, it is important to contest current notions of corporate citizenship. Matten and Crane (2005) in recognizing the limitations of applying a superficial concept of citizenship to corporations attempt to develop a broader conceptualization of corporate citizenship based on notions of liberal citizenship in political science. They sidestep the normative hurdles of corporate citizenship and provide a descriptive perspective instead. Corporate citizenship becomes relevant in an era dominated by neoliberal doctrine because, while corporations may not be the same as individual citizens, they are increasingly taking over many of the roles and activities normally associated with government (Hertz, 2001). Globalization does not mark the death of the nation state; rather it is characterized by a shift in state power that favors the needs and interests of corporations rather than public interests (Bakan, 2004). When the state is not the sole guarantor of citizenship rights and corporations provide services that were previously the purview of governments then it becomes necessary to interrogate corporate roles in administering citizenship. Thus, in Matten and Crane's formulation corporate citizenship is about administering citizenship rights for individuals rather than about whether the corporation is or can be a citizen. Following from Marshall's (1965) formulation of liberal citizenship as comprising civil, social and political rights, Matten and Crane (2005) describe situations where corporations administer some of these rights, either by themselves or in partnership with government agencies and NGOs. Corporations already play a role in administering a wide range of social services – providing funds for improving schools, promoting cleaner neighborhoods, providing security services and funding health care clinics for example. The case of political and civil rights is murkier: corporate collusion with despotic governments and corporate political influence through lobbying and campaign contributions are coming under greater public scrutiny. Let us now examine some cases where the practice of corporate citizenship falls short and sometimes conflicts with theories of CSR and corporate citizenship.

5. The dilemmas of CSR and corporate citizenship

> Corporate social responsibility is a dangerous distortion of business principles. If you find an executive who wants to take on social responsibilities, fire him. Fast.
>
> (Peter Drucker, 2004)

Despite attempts to incorporate perspectives from citizenship theory, corporate citizenship remains first and foremost a managerial ideology, a strategic doctrine that ultimately 'crafts an instrumental, self-serving view of the relationship between business and society' (Windsor, 2001: 51). While there has been a shift from the almost tiresome Friedman cliché of 'the business of business is business' to a vastly more accommodating (although ultimately meaningless if taken to the extreme) stakeholder framework, the difference between rhetoric and reality remains, although the language has become more sophisticated. Corporate speak about CSR in the 1970s reveals a more pragmatic approach. In 1979 the editors of *Business and Society Review* invited a group of CEOs and business leaders to decide 'whether corporate social responsibility is even possible'. Their collective responses under the title 'Is corporate social responsibility a dead issue?' makes for some interesting reading, with opinions clearly divided on the social role of corporations. Some CEOs endorsed Milton Friedman's view of social responsibility as maximizing profits while others called for a broader role for the corporation.

For example, Henry Ford II, then chairman of the Ford Motor Company, stated in his response: 'The corporation is not an all purpose mechanism. It is a sophisticated instrument designed to serve the economic needs of society and is not well equipped to serve social needs unrelated to its business operations' (Ford, 1978: 5). Twenty years later another Ford was driving a different line: commenting on a $5 million grant from the Ford Motor Company to Princeton University as part of their joint project, the Carbon Mitigation Initiative, William Clay Ford, Jr, stated: 'I believe very strongly that corporations can and should be a major force for resolving social and environmental concerns in the 21st century. Not only do I think this is the right thing to do, I believe it is the best thing to do to achieve profitable, sustainable growth' (Ford, 2000). Some business leaders in the 1970s appeared to be more receptive to CSR. The Chairman of AT&T argued in his response that 'Business profits and responsible behavior enhance each other. Insufficient profits hinder a corporation's efforts at being fully responsive to social needs, while on the other hand, the failure of a business to accept its proper social responsibilities can endanger the investor's stake in the enterprise' (deButts, 1978: 7–8). W.F. Martin, then chairman of Phillips Petroleum, made a similar point, while Edward Harness, Procter & Gamble's chairman at the time, advocated a more cautionary position:

> Generally we feel that social welfare is primarily the domain of government. We do see the need however, to practice corporate 'citizenship' by participating to some degree in social and community affairs. This we do partly through civic and cultural contributions – both in terms of time and money – but more significantly by adhering to environmental standards, practicing energy conservation, and providing stable employment opportunities for our people. (Martin, 1978)

> The corporation is a paper citizen and every citizen has a responsibility to his fellow citizen. However, I take real issue with the critics when they propose that corporations should put their other citizenship responsibilities ahead of our responsibilities to earn a fair return for our owners. The only way we can carry our huge and increasing burden of obligations to society is for us to earn satisfactory profits. If we cannot earn a return on equity investment which is more attractive than other forms of investment, we die. I am not aware of any bankrupt corporations which are making important social contributions. (Harness, 1978)

Public perceptions of a corporation's role in society more than 20 years later seem to reflect a broader role for corporations. In a survey conducted in 2000 by *Business Week* magazine, 95 percent of respondents agreed with the statement 'US corporations should have more than one purpose. They also owe something to their workers and the communities in which they operate, and they should sometimes sacrifice some profit for the sake of making things better for their workers and communities.' In contrast only 4 percent of respondents agreed with the statement 'US corporations should have only one purpose – to make the most profit for their shareholders – and their pursuit of that goal will be best for Americans in the long run.' In the same survey, 72 percent of those polled agreed that 'business has gained too much power over too many aspects of American life' while 74 percent felt that big companies had 'too much power' in influencing government policy, politicians and policy makers in Washington (*Business Week*, 2000). Whether these perceptions have any material effect on CSR policies is of course another matter.

The problems faced by corporations in attempting to enhance social welfare are exacerbated in the case of TNCs operating in the poorer regions of the world, and recent years have seen a public backlash over corporate malpractices such as corruption, environmental destruction, use of sweatshop labor, dispossession of local communities, military involvement and complicity with repressive regimes. For instance, NGOs and community groups have raised serious allegations against Shell and other multinational oil corporations operating in Nigeria that focus on the damaging material effects on communities impacted by oil drilling and refining. There are ongoing disputes over appropriate compensation for environmental damage, appropriation of community resources, loss of livelihood and share of the profits. Corporate complicity in abusive governmental practices is a common criticism of oil companies operating in the region (Ramasastry, 2002).

The highly publicized case of Shell in Nigeria provides an insight into the difficulties faced by corporations in the area of political and civil rights. In the case of Shell, we have one company that generates 75 percent of the Nigerian government's revenues and nearly 35 percent of the country's GNP. Despite millions of dollars in royalties, local communities most affected by Shell's operations continue to suffer dire levels of poverty and have seen their traditional sources of livelihood disappear (Hertz, 2001). And while government corruption is a major cause of the problem, several environmental and human rights activists have questioned Shell's role and relationship with the government. In a public statement responding to allegations about the company's role in colluding with the government in its violent crackdown on the Ogoni people protesting loss of their land and livelihood due to oil operations in the region, Shell issued a statement declaring:

> We do support the statement of human rights in Nigeria's constitution and are concerned that all citizens possess such rights. However, we follow a set of business principles endeavoring always to act commercially and operating within the confines of existing national laws in a socially responsible manner. Debate about Nigeria's human rights record is in the political arena and we have neither the right nor the competence to get involved. (Human Rights Watch, 1999)

The assumption behind this statement is that despite Shell's 'hypernorm' of acting in a 'socially responsible manner' the company feels that the national laws of Nigeria 'confine' its activities. But despite the company's public affirmation that it does not play the role of governments, in practice Shell fulfills many of the roles traditionally performed by governments. Transnational mining companies operating in remote areas serve as de facto governments because mining townships are often run by both company and government representatives. Corporations often own all the utilities, telecommunications facilities, retail outlets, roads, housing and airports in the region (Banerjee, 2000). In Nigeria, Shell has contributed to building roads, schools, hospitals and power utilities in the Niger Delta where its main operations are based. As a Shell manager put it: 'Things are back to front here. The government's in the oil business and we are in local government' (Hertz, 2001: 173). However, the social outcomes for communities affected by Shell's operations continue to be problematic: a health clinic built by the company never commenced operations because Shell claimed its responsibility ended when it completed the construction of the building. The government claimed it had no money to pay for medicines or doctors to run the clinic. A water tower built by Shell never delivered any drinking water to local villagers because the company did not dig a well or connect it to the water system in its plant (Maas, 2005). And while the company's 1996 community development report claimed they had spent $7.4 billion on building roads, the report omitted to mention that these roads were used primarily by the company to get access to the oil fields as part of their regular operations and were of no benefit to the nearby villages (Frynas, 2001). This is another example where tradeoffs between economic and social good become complex as oil companies operating in the region find that the money they contribute to the local economy does not do any good to local communities. Responsibility can also become a double-edged sword: when a local village leader complaining about the clinic's inability to deliver health care in the village was told that Shell's executives were not responsible for his government's corruption, he asked, 'But is it Shell's responsibility to take our resources?' (Maas, 2005).

Other oil companies operating in the Niger Delta have faced similar protests from local communities. Asked in an interview why his company was not doing more for the community, the general manager of Chevron replied:

> We have a responsibility as a corporate citizen to ensure that communities in which we operate benefit from our presence, or at least are not damaged by our presence. It is not our responsibility to provide the basic fundamentals that are required for communities to thrive. It is not our mission as a corporation. It is not our identity as a corporation. (cited in Maas, 2005)

However, the corporation's website lists a wide range of community activities that it funds including investing $142 million in 'sustainable development activities' since 1994. According to its website, Chevron funds programs in health care, HIV/AIDS education and prevention, basic education, teacher training, vocational skills training, health clinics, infrastructural development projects, environmental restoration projects and wildlife reserves (Chevron, 2006). Its Nigerian company won the US State Department Award for Corporate Excellence in 2003 for being a 'good corporate citizen' with specific reference to the company's role in 'airlifting more than 2000 community members to safety in 2003 during inter-ethnic conflict in the Niger Delta'. However, the company is fighting lawsuits filed by Nigerian villagers alleging the company subsidiary's complicity with military attacks on protesters in the Niger Delta with a class action lawsuit set for trial in 2007 (Chea, 2006). Chevron is also facing a class action lawsuit in Ecuador from indigenous groups where plaintiffs allege that Texaco, which merged with Chevron in 2001, dumped 18.5 billion gallons of contaminated waste in the Amazon rainforest between 1972 and 1990 (Chea,

2006). The company has denied the allegation and claims that its state-owned partner, PetroEcuador, is responsible for any environmental remediation. Chevron's response is typical of that of other TNCs that are fighting similar legal and public relations battles with NGOs and community groups: counterattack claiming there is no scientific evidence regarding health concerns caused by any contamination, discredit key plaintiffs and shift responsibility to host governments. Even if liability is established, which is very difficult to do based on past cases involving TNCs operating in developing regions, compensation payments are unlikely to make a significant dent in the company's profitability, and the lawsuits and protests are 'nothing but background noise' according to an energy analyst (Chea, 2006).

Among the big oil companies that are regular targets of green groups and NGOs, BP is probably the company with the highest CSR profile. Several NGOs have publicly acknowledged BP for being one of the first TNCs to endorse a human rights policy and for its transparency in allowing public scrutiny of its operations and regular reporting of its social and environmental impact (Christianson, 2002). Other NGOs were less charitable: in 2002 CorpWatch and Friends of the Earth awarded BP the 'Best Greenwash Award' at the Greenwash Academy Award Programs. BP's charismatic and high-profile CEO, an in-demand speaker about CSR worldwide, explained BP's CSR philosophy:

> BP's social responsibility is good business, driven by practical commercial reality and hardheaded business logic. The company's good deeds are in our direct business interest, not acts of charity but of what could be called enlightened self-interest. The fundamental test for any company is performance. That is the imperative. (cited in Bakan, 2004: 44–5)

In 2000 the company strategically repositioned itself as a market leader in environmental and social responsibility, with a high-profile and hugely successful £135 million 'Beyond Petroleum' public relations campaign complete with a new logo of a green, white and yellow sunflower. But despite its green positioning, its exit from the Global Climate Coalition (now disbanded but at the time a powerful industry lobby group opposing emission restrictions) and its public backing for the Kyoto Protocol, BP's core business remains oil exploration and drilling. How a company that spends 0.4 percent of its annual expenditure on oil exploration and 0.02 percent of its net worth on solar energy investments (Driessen, 2003) can by any stretch of the imagination go 'beyond petroleum' beggars belief. Tongue barely in cheek, *Fortune* magazine commented, 'if the world's second largest oil company is beyond petroleum, *Fortune* is beyond words' (Murphy, 2002: 44). Between 1995 and 2001 the company spent a total of $200 million on solar power (which was less than the company's annual advertising budget) whereas in 2001 alone it spent $8.5 billion on fossil fuel exploration and development with another $15 billion to be invested in oil exploration and drilling in the Gulf of Mexico over the next ten years (Murphy, 2002).

BP hedged its bets in the highly emotive and political debate in the US about opening up the Arctic National Wildlife Refuge (ANWR) to oil drilling, stating publicly, 'if ANWR is opened for development, BP will make a decision about seeking access at that time in the light of the economic, environmental and social risks and when compared with other opportunities in our global portfolio' (Christianson, 2002). The company stands to make handsome profits if it is allowed to drill on the Arctic's coastal plane, despite the protestations of indigenous communities and environmentalists. As long as drilling is profitable the company has no option but to pursue this strategy (Bakan, 2004), especially if its competitors do so. The rhetoric of 'environmentally friendly drilling' aside, the only factors that can prevent oil companies from drilling in the Arctic are legislation and/or strong enough public pressure that has the potential to nullify whatever profit it earns from its Arctic operations. BP also publicly committed to reducing its greenhouse emissions by 10 percent in 2010 and reached this target nine years ahead of schedule. This was a win–win situation for BP because, while the emissions reductions project cost $20 million, the company achieved $650 million in cost savings arising from energy efficiencies and sales of natural gas (Vogel, 2005). However, subsequent emission reduction will involve significantly higher costs and will prove much more difficult. The company appears to have exhausted its win–win options in emissions reductions as it discontinued its internal emissions trading scheme in 2002. Also, BP's opportunity costs in implementing this environmental initiative may have prevented the company from taking advantage of more profitable projects – several BP managers claimed to be 'relieved' that the emissions trading scheme was discontinued because it distracted them from 'more pressing business opportunities' (Vogel, 2005: 125).

Another industry that is regularly in the public spotlight for its social and ethical practices is the pharmaceutical industry, especially 'Big Pharma', one of the most profitable industries in the world (see Appendix). Intellectual property rights and patents on drugs, especially life-saving drugs, is a much-debated issue in the public sphere. Trade disputes between rich and poor countries at the World Trade Organization over patent protection have resulted in breakdowns at nearly every WTO meeting. The passage of the controversial trade-related intellectual property rights (TRIPS) legislation deepened the North–South divide and has been criticized by many environmental and community groups for depriving poor populations of affordable drugs. Proponents of TRIPS (mainly pharmaceutical corporations) argue that patent protection provides the necessary conditions for innovation and offsets some of the risks involved in developing new drugs. Industry leaders routinely cite high R&D investment as the main reason for patent protection. Selective amnesia seems to be operating in the pharmaceutical industry, because Big Pharma spends two to three times more on marketing than R&D while routinely overestimating R&D costs (Joseph, 2003). Moreover, the claim that a pharmaceutical corporation privately bears all R&D costs is a myth: much of the R&D that goes into creating a new drug occurs at public expense, not to mention the generous tax concessions and deductions for R&D granted to pharmaceutical corporations. If R&D costs were really the reason why drug prices were high and why patent protection was needed then it is a mystery why the pharmaceutical industry is so secretive about how much it actually spends on R&D. In fact, the industry fought and won a nine-year battle in the US Supreme Court to prevent disclosure of its R&D costs to congressional investigators (*Bowsher v. Merck & Co.*, 1983, cited in Joseph, 2003).

Pressure from activist groups and developing countries resulted in amendments to WTO provisions that allowed countries to suspend patent laws in emergency situations in order to produce cheaper drugs. The industry suffered a major public relations setback when 39 pharmaceutical corporations (whose combined profits far exceeded the GDP of South Africa) sued South Africa over violating WTO patent laws by producing cheap generic life-saving drugs. A public outcry resulted and the lawsuit was dropped (de George, 2005). In recent years public pressure has compelled many pharmaceutical corporations to provide drugs at low cost or free of charge to regions facing serious public health issues. And the cost difference is enormous: in 2001 the Indian generic drug manufacturer CIPLA offered to supply copies of patented anti-HIV drugs at less than 10 percent of their cost. It is difficult to believe that R&D costs would warrant a 1000 percent markup in prices (Gathii, 2001; Joseph, 2003).

Hank Mitchell, the CEO of Pfizer, a company which has a high CSR profile in the industry and is the only signatory from the pharmaceutical industry to the Global Compact, recently created some consternation in the industry with some candid confessions in his book *A Call to Action: Taking Back Healthcare for Future Generations*. While calling for stricter patent laws to ensure competitiveness, Mitchell admitted that the high prices of drugs in the United States have nothing to do with R&D expenses:

> It is a fallacy to suggest that our industry, or any industry, prices a product to recapture the R&D budget spent in development. Drugs are basically priced the same way as a car or an appliance. It is the anticipated income stream, rather than repayment of sunk costs that is the primary determinant of price. While income funds new R&D … if we generate more income … the price of our stock goes up. (Mitchell, 2005: 47)

Pfizer offers a free drug program in some African countries for treatment of trachoma. Mitchell described Pfizer's free drug program as a 'classic case of doing well by doing good' enabling the company to 'meet the needs of both our shareholders and the world's poor' (McKinnell, cited in Bakan, 2004: 48). The benefits of the program to the company are immense: enhanced corporate reputation and image, improved relations to the community, increased employee morale and increased customer goodwill. The costs are also negligible according to the CEO: 'the marginal cost of our drugs is very low, so if we give away a drug to somebody who wouldn't otherwise buy it, the profit impact of that action on us is just about zero' (cited in Bakan, 2004: 47). But why should a company's motive matter as long as its actions produce some social good? The problem is how long a particular initiative can be sustained and what the effects are on the communities it was designed to help. If the company decides to discontinue its free drug program because of shifting priorities what happens to the communities that benefited from the program? It is probably because of the long-term need for trachoma treatment that the NGO and government agency that ran the program declined Pfizer's offer for free drugs and imported a generic version instead (Bakan, 2004). From a profitability perspective, it would be difficult for any pharmaceutical corporation to justify developing drugs for treating malaria and tuberculosis, the leading cause of death in the poorer regions of the world, despite the enormous social benefits such a strategy would produce, because of the high cost of producing these drugs, especially when profit margins for drugs to treat baldness and impotence in affluent market segments are significantly higher.

For instance, in March 2005 the Indian government, in order to conform with WTO rules on patent protection, passed a law that would forbid the manufacture of cheap generic drugs by Indian pharmaceutical companies. Critics of the new law argue that these drugs have saved thousands of lives in developing countries whose poorer populations would now be deprived of cheaper drugs (Chadha, 2005). While non-governmental organizations like Médicins Sans Frontières have criticized the passage of the law, multinational corporations welcomed the decision because, as the managing director of Novartis India stated, 'it will move India toward the patent mainstream and support and encourage innovation and investment in research and development in India'. The new law is also expected to adversely affect smaller, local drug companies whose main purpose was manufacturing low-cost generic drugs. Whether such innovation and research will benefit the poorer segments of society who have limited or no access to medicine is a debatable point. As Margolis and Walsh (2003) point out there is very little research that describes what corporate social initiatives actually achieve for society in the long run because the primary focus in the literature is on the financial impact of these initiatives on the company. One survey of 'socially innovative' businesses found that in every case companies reverted to their conventional practice after a period of implementing socially innovative practices (Quarter, 2000). 'Structural problems', 'rising costs' and 'market forces' were some of the stated reasons. The zone of corporate social initiatives that can produce 'combined social and economic benefits' remains quite narrowly defined by business interests.

While corporate codes of conduct, ethical trading practices and social and environmental policies are aimed at enhancing a company's social performance there is considerable evidence that shows that poorer communities in developing countries do not benefit from economic activity on their lands. Newell (2005) argues that poor, marginalized communities are often excluded from processes of drafting codes of conduct (which are non-legally binding in any case) although they are supposed to be the intended beneficiaries. While high-profile international NGOs and unions often get the attention of transnational corporations, there is some doubt whether these bodies adequately represent the interests of poorer communities adversely impacted by economic activity. Resource extractive industries are often located in poor countries, and the benefits tend to flow to elite groups in these regions while further marginalizing poor communities who depend on the land for their survival and who become the victims of development by bearing the brunt of negative environmental and social impacts. Case studies of hazardous waste disposal indicate that there is an intersection of race and class when it comes to deciding on where disposal sites are to be located: in what could be called environmental racism, toxic waste is often dumped on poorer communities of color who are often underrepresented in political processes in their countries and are unable to leverage the resources of international NGOs and activist groups (Cole and Foster, 2001; Newell, 2005). Hazardous electronic waste arising from the disposal of appliances and computers, for example, is exported to Asian countries like China, India and Pakistan in the guise of 'recycling', leading to serious health hazards for communities that bear the brunt of open burning, acid baths and toxic dumping that poison the land, water and air (Puckett and Smith, 2002). International treaties like the Basel Convention ban the export of hazardous waste to poor countries but, while the European Union has signed the agreement, the world's biggest polluter and exporter of hazardous waste, the United States, remains the only developed country not to have ratified the Basel Convention. In fact, US government policies actively promote the export of hazardous waste to Asian and African countries by exempting electronic waste in the Resource Conservation and Recovery Act from the minimal laws that do exist in developing countries requiring prior notification of toxic waste shipments. Environmental justice programs in developed countries are often implemented by promoting environmental injustice in the poorer countries of the world: it is difficult to see how voluntary corporate social responsibility initiatives can work when it is ten times cheaper to ship used cathode ray tube computer monitors to China than recycle them in the US (Cole and Foster, 2001).

CORPORATE LIABILITY AND THE LIMITS OF CORPORATE CITIZENSHIP

All the theories and concepts of CSR and corporate citizenship suffer from a fundamental limitation: the absence of a clear political and legal framework for coordinating citizenship rights and responsibilities. This is the basis of the conundrum: the universality of normative theories are suspect (Whose norms? Why those norms and not any other?) and while descriptive theories describe the citizenship activities and responsibilities of corporations they do not provide a basis for monitoring accountability. An emphasis on the theoretical and practical basis of responsibility can lead to a situation where a corporation is responsible for everything and accountable for nothing. Governments, as key providers of citizenship rights, are accountable in the sense that they can be dismissed by a voting public. Corporations cannot be easily disbanded or dismissed when they fail to be accountable for their actions. For instance, several TNC operations in Latin America, Africa and Asia have resulted in human rights violations including use of forced labor, forced displacement of local communities, and violent reprisals including killings and torture by government security forces protecting TNC assets and project sites (Ramasastry, 2002). While corporations can face legal and financial sanctions for blatant violations of the law they often escape any punitive action or liability for complicity with repressive regimes involving human rights violations. The degree and type of corporate complicity vary depending on the political context: corporations can be directly complicit with repressive regimes resulting in human rights abuses, they can be indirectly complicit or their mere presence in a repressive region can mean complicity 'through silence or inaction' (Ramasastry, 2002: 101).

Direct complicity occurs when corporations knowingly participate in regimes that abuse human rights. Soon after World War II the United States Military Tribunal prosecuted three German industrialists for using forced labor during the Holocaust.[1] One of the first legal cases of corporate complicity involved the indictment in 1947 of 23 employees and five directors of I.G. Farben, a German chemical company. Because the Tribunal did not have jurisdiction over corporate entities the corporation itself escaped indictment but its employees and directors were prosecuted for 'acting through the instrumentality of Farben' to commit the crimes for which they were indicted, including 'plunder, slavery and mass murder'. During the Nazi regime the corporation 'acquired' factories and properties in countries under German occupation, which constituted a violation of the Hague Convention. The Tribunal specifically referred to the legal personality of the corporation, ruling that 'private individuals, including *juristic persons*', can violate international law by unlawfully acquiring property. Farben was also directly involved in war crimes as the corporation 'financed and owned Auschwitz' and hence was held responsible for the mistreatment and death of workers in the concentration camp. In a subsequent case, Farben opposed restitution claims in a lawsuit filed by a former Auschwitz laborer, arguing that the responsibility for damages lay with the SS, the Nazi Party and the German state and claiming that the inmates would have been killed sooner had the company not used them for labor. The German court found the company liable for its 'negligence in failing to protect the life, body and health of the plaintiff' and the company settled for a DM30 million compensation for using forced labor.

In another case of direct complicity, the Tribunal prosecuted 12 defendants from the German steel maker and weapons manufacturer Krupp for 'commission of war crimes and crimes against humanity with respect to plunder and spoliation of civilian property and factories in occupied territories and also in the deportation and use of prisoners of war and concentration camp inmates as forced laborers' in the company's factories in Germany. Direct complicity was established because the defendants 'exploited as principals and accessories, in consequence of a deliberate design and policy, territories occupied by German armed forces in a ruthless way, far beyond the needs of the army of occupation and in disregard of the needs of the local economy'. Eleven defendants were convicted for 'deportation, exploitation and abuse of slave labor' and the company was held liable because it specifically requested concentration camp labor when many other weapons manufacturers refused to use inmates from concentration camps. The Tribunal concluded that Krupp displayed an 'ardent desire' to employ slave labor, thus attributing specific intent to both the corporation and individual defendants. As Ramasastry (2002) argues, the legal interpretation of the Tribunal's ruling was that a corporation could plan and execute criminal acts and hence both its employees and the corporation could be held liable. However, there are complex legal difficulties in assigning liability between corporate actors, private individuals as employees of corporate actors and state actors. While employees of Farben and Krupp were prosecuted for their use of slave labor during World War II, the Chairman of Dresden Bank, known to be the major financier of the Third Reich, escaped prosecution because the Tribunal ruled that providing financing for criminal activity did not violate customary international law even if the financier had prior knowledge of the nature of the activity. In another World War II human rights abuse case involving corporations, eight employees of Nippon Mining Company were found guilty and convicted of using forced labor and mistreating POWs in Formosa during the war. In this case the British military court ruled that the defendants engaged in human rights violations not as private individuals but as employees of the mining company. During the trial both the corporation and the Japanese army blamed each other for mistreatment of prisoners, with army officials claiming that the responsibility for the safety of the laborers lay with the company since it was the company that allocated work hours, tasks and equipment to the POWs.

While direct complicity may be easier to prove if evidence is available, identifying and apportioning liability between repressive governments and corporations present a challenge in proving indirect corporate complicity. Understanding how liability was established in clear-cut cases of human rights abuses during the Nazi era might allow us to understand contemporary cases of TNC complicity with repressive regimes in perpetrating human rights abuses. Current debates in legal theory focus on whether TNCs that have benefited from using forced labor provided by a host government can be liable for prosecution. The issue of criminal liability for using forced labor becomes muddied outside the context of war. Recent federal cases in the US have ruled that knowingly accepting the benefits of forced labor is not a sufficient condition to establish liability. What happens when TNCs knowingly partner with repressive governments and obtain economic benefits on an ongoing basis as a result of human rights abuses perpetrated by government forces? Some legal theorists argue that, if repression and human rights abuses are a condition for a profitable return on investment, then the TNC should be liable. Others disagree, claiming that the host governments are the guilty parties and should be prosecuted under international law. And as we have seen earlier this is the same position taken by oil companies operating in Africa, where the strategy is to shift responsibility to the host governments because human rights are 'in the political arena' where business should not be involved, as Shell has described its situation in Nigeria.

While no universally accepted legal mechanism exists to enforce international customary law, federal courts in the United States have used the Alien Tort Claims Act (ATCA) to extend rulings from the war crimes tribunals established after World War II to contemporary cases on TNC complicity in human rights abuses. The ATCA allows victims of human rights abuses from other countries to sue their perpetrators in US courts for violations of the 'law of nations'. While the focus in the war crimes tribunals was on establishing the liability of individual defendants, more recent cases have attempted to impose liability on corporations based on their identity as legal persons. The slave labor issue in World War II re-emerged in 1999 when a series of cases were filed against German, Austrian and American corporations and their subsidiaries that had used and benefited from slave labor in the 1940s using the ATCA as the legal basis for such cases. Over 400 German corporations were alleged to have used slave labor during the war and during the case hearings the German government and the corporations each claimed the other party was responsible for any reparations. The corporations claimed that the German government as legal successors to the Third Reich were responsible for reparations while the government insisted that it was the corporations that should pay restitution because they had benefited from the use of slave labor.

For instance, in 1998 the Ford Motor Company was named as a defendant in a case involving slave labor because its subsidiary Ford Werke AG in Nazi

Germany 'knowingly earned enormous profits from the aggressive use of forced labor under inhumane conditions'. According to the complaint between 25 and 50 percent of Ford Werke's workforce consisted of unpaid slave labor during 1943–45, contributing to the company doubling its annual profits in 1943. The lawsuit was dismissed by the District of New Jersey on the grounds of 'nonjusticiability and international comity' and expiration of the statute of limitations. The issue of nonjusticiability refers to the inappropriateness of a judicial ruling over a political issue. Significantly, however, the court ruled that Ford's use of unpaid forced labor was a violation of customary international law and as a result the court did have 'subject matter jurisdiction' under the ATCA. Violation of international law was applicable to private actors like Ford and other corporations because they were legal persons. Other slave labor cases involving the German corporations Degussa and Siemens were dismissed by the federal court on similar grounds despite finding both corporations guilty of using slave labor. Some legal theorists argue that in the contemporary context of TNCs and the use of forced labor the issue is not about whether a TNC can be sued 'but rather what factual circumstances will give rise to liability' (Ramasastry, 2002: 121). The Nuremberg trials while finding individual defendants guilty of using forced labor did not indict the corporations, but the rulings of the 1990s extended the possibility of liability to corporations because of their identity as legal persons. Complicity with nation states did not diminish the responsibility of the TNCs; however, 'private' violations of international law can be resolved through governmental agreements and treaties.

Legal arguments about the liability of TNCs in contemporary circumstances outside the context of law focus around the complicity of TNCs with repressive regimes. The notion of *beneficiary complicity* can apply when a TNC initiates and maintains a business relationship with a repressive host government despite having prior knowledge about ongoing human rights violations (Clapman and Jerbi, 2001). If it can be established that the violations are linked in any way to TNC operations or investment then the corporation becomes an accomplice to human rights violations and if it benefits in any way as a result of these violations the corporation should be liable. In a recent case involving a joint venture between multinational oil companies and the Myanmar government, the Unocal corporation and its president and CEO were named as defendants accused of human rights violations on Burmese citizens who allegedly suffered 'torture, assault, rape, loss of homes and properties, and forced labor'. Two conflicting judgments resulted, with one court ruling that knowingly accepting the benefits of forced labor was 'actionable as a violation of international law' and the other court ruling that Unocal could not be held liable 'solely for knowing about the Burmese government's use of forced labor'. The Unocal case set a legal precedent by extending the scope of the ATCA to private corporations. The case was allowed to be heard in the courts because the corporation was alleged to have benefited from the use of forced labor. However, a later ruling in 2000 dismissed the case against Unocal because the company did not directly carry out human rights abuses despite having knowledge that forced labor was involved and benefiting from its use. 'Mere knowledge' that another party (the Myanmar government) was committing human rights abuses was insufficient grounds to hold the corporation liable: corporate liability could only be established if the company took 'active steps in cooperating or participating in forced labor activities' (Ramasastry, 2002: 137). There was no evidence to suggest that Unocal 'controlled' the military government's decision to commit human rights abuses. Some legal theorists have questioned this judgment, arguing that an ongoing relationship with a repressive government resulting in a 'conscious acceptance of economic benefit over an extended period of time' constitutes 'active participation' in forced labor and that beneficiary complicity over an extended period of time should result in liability. The plaintiffs appealed the court decision and Unocal settled out of court for an undisclosed amount, agreeing to compensate villagers and provide money to 'develop programs to improve living conditions, healthcare and education and protect the rights of people from the pipeline region' (Lifsher, 2005). While the out of court settlement meant that the matter of corporate liability remained unresolved, a host of TNCs are fighting similar lawsuits including ExxonMobil Corporation in Indonesia, Fresh Del Monte Produce Inc. in Guatemala, ChevronTexaco Corporation in Nigeria, and Occidental Petroleum Corporation, Coca-Cola Co. and coal miner Drummond Co. in Colombia (Lifsher, 2005).

Despite these legal precedents there are significant problems in establishing TNC liability for human rights abuses. International law, which historically applied to nation states, has been extended to non-state entities. While corporations are expected to comply with international standards there are no international legally binding mechanisms to hold them accountable. The US Alien Tort Claims Act is a US law and is not binding on other countries. Although some legal theorists have attempted to extend its purview from nation states to include liability of multinational corporations, this process continues to be contested, with critics arguing that such 'judicial activism' interferes with US foreign policy decisions. The United Nations is in the process of drafting a human rights code for companies but if the code is to have any meaningful value it has to be legally binding and ratified by states. However, advances in communication technologies have created networks of non-governmental organizations and community groups leading to increased scrutiny of corporate behavior. Corporate misdeeds are regularly publicized on the internet and many corporations have been forced to respond to these allegations. While cynics like Baron Thurlow may feel that corporations can never develop a conscience because they have 'no soul to be damned and no body to be kicked', perhaps increased public scrutiny may force corporations to exercise some degree of social and environmental prudence leading to the creation of at least a pragmatic conscience – 'an inner voice that warns them that someone may be looking', in the words of H.L. Mencken (Gibbons, 2007).

The cost of bringing lawsuits against powerful transnational corporations is prohibitive and in many cases beyond the resources of communities that are negatively impacted by corporate activity. Without a legally binding mechanism, CSR and citizenship initiatives can only allow activities that benefit the corporation instead of addressing issues of global poverty and sustainable development. As Newell (2005) argues, mainstream CSR 'best practices' are context dependent: they may work for certain stakeholders in some places at different times but do not address the inherently political problem of community rights and participation. This raises questions about the sustainability of CSR activities and the contribution of CSR to the broader goal of sustainable development. I will examine current debates about sustainability in the next chapter.

NOTE

1.   The discussion on corporate complicity and liability is based on several sources and legal documents. Key sources include *Doe v. Unocal Corporation* (1997); Hayes (1987); *Iwanowa v. Ford Motor Company* (1999); Lippman (1995); Ramasastry (1998, 2002); Reich (2002); *United States v. Krauch* et al. (1952); *United States v. Krupp* (1952); *United States v. Von Weiszaecker* (1952); and Wiesen (2002).

6.   The perils of sustainability

The Law doth punish man or woman
Who steals the goose from off the common,
But lets the greater felon loose
Who steals the common from the goose.
(Anonymous, eighteenth-century England)

The modern environmental movement in the West can be traced back to 1962 with the publication of Rachel Carson's book *Silent Spring*. Carson (1962) documented the harmful effects of chemicals and pesticides and described how dangerous toxins were introduced into the food chain. Her book served as a wake-up call to US government officials, consumer advocates and citizens, resulting in a series of environmental laws such as the Clean Air Act, the Clean Water Act and the Resource Conservation and Recovery Act. The US's Environmental Protection Authority was created in 1970 to monitor the extent of industrial pollution. Similar governmental agencies and environmental laws were created in Europe as well. The counter-culture movement of the 1960s also saw the emergence of what were then called 'ecology action groups', the first environmental activists in the US. The first Earth Day was celebrated on 22 April 1970, as a day for reflection and discussion of environmental problems and to demonstrate North America's growing consciousness of the environment. One of the organizers, then Wisconsin senator Gaylord Nelson, commented that '[the growing consciousness of ecology] could kick off one of the toughest – and most expensive – political fights this country has ever seen'. Thirty years later, the fight is far from over, although battle lines have been redrawn and roles and interrelations of major protagonists have changed over the years as well. Politicians (with very few exceptions) and corporate representatives were conspicuous by their absence in the many nationwide events marking the first Earth Day. In fact, several large corporations were the targets of protests owing to their polluting activities. There must have been some consternation amongst the more diehard of the protesters who gathered to celebrate the twentieth anniversary of Earth Day in 1990 when, on their arrival, they were greeted by leading business executives from some of the world's biggest transnational corporate polluters appropriately attired in 'Save the Whale' or 'Save our Planet' T-shirts and handing out glossy brochures describing how their corporations were protecting the environment.

The concept of sustainable development emerged in the 1980s in an attempt to explore the relationship between development and the environment. Eagerly embraced by policy makers, governments, corporations, global organizations, NGOs and local and regional councils, sustainable development soon became the buzzword of the 1990s. The problem with buzzwords is they tend to become disengaged from their original context and their meanings become discursively contested and deployed by a variety of agents, institutions and texts. In 1992, there were more than 100 definitions of sustainable development (Holmberg and Sandbrook, 1992) and a few more have probably been invented since then. The most widely accepted definition is from the Brundtland Commission, which defines sustainable development as 'a process of change in which the exploitation of resources, direction of investments, orientation of technological development, and institutional change are made consistent with future as well as present needs' (WCED, 1987: 9). This broad definition is problematic and there is considerable disagreement among scholars in different disciplines on how this definition should be operationalized and how sustainability should be measured. The Brundtland definition is really not a definition; it is a slogan, and slogans, however pretty, do not make for good theory. As several authors have pointed out, the Brundtland definition does not elaborate on the notion of human needs and wants (Kirkby *et al.*, 1995; Redclift, 1987) and the concern for future generations is problematic as well in its operationalization. Given the scenario of limited resources, this assumption becomes a contradiction as most potential consumers (future generations) are unable to access the present market or, as Martinez-Alier (1987: 17) elegantly puts it, 'individuals not yet born have ontological difficulties in making their presence felt in today's market for exhaustible resources'.

Before we examine the basic assumptions of sustainable development it may be useful to trace the continuities and discontinuities of discourses of sustainable development within the broader development discourse. The modern use of the term 'development' inextricably linked it with the economic and was deployed as a desirable global agenda by US President Harry Truman who in his inaugural address in 1949 urged his fellow Americans to 'embark on a bold new program for making the benefits of our scientific advances and industrial progress available for the improvement and growth of underdeveloped areas ... The old imperialism – exploitation for foreign profit – has no place in our plans.' Development thus created the notion of 'underdevelopment', resulting in the subdivision of the world into developed, developing and underdeveloped regions. As Esteva (1992: 7) argues powerfully, the 'Third World' was created at that moment when suddenly over 2 billion people became underdeveloped and 'transmogrified into an inverted mirror of others' reality: a mirror that belittles them and sends them off to the end of the queue, a mirror that defines their identity, which is really that of a heterogeneous and diverse majority, simply in the terms of a homogenizing and narrow minority'. Third World countries have been playing 'catching up development' ever since. Truman's assertion of the end of imperialism also seemed a trifle premature – colonial modes of development are still dominant in many of the former colonies, which are forced to sell their natural resources to the industrialized countries at cheap prices and find themselves unable to escape the twin traps of debt and poverty. In the postcolonial era the colonizer–colonized relationships are played out in trade conflicts between the developed and under-developed countries, resulting in the so-called North–South divide, a divide that has left nearly every trade agreement meeting of the World Trade Organization unresolved since the organization's inception.

Perhaps an explanatory note on terminology is in order before we proceed further. One of the hallmarks of modernity was to divide the world into eco-nomic regions based on their 'development'. Thus, the world was divided into 'developed countries', 'developing countries' and 'less developed countries'. These terms along with other ways to describe the world such as 'First World', 'Third World', 'core', 'periphery', 'developed', 'underdeveloped', 'traditional', 'modern', 'colonizer', 'colonized' and 'North–South' are essentialist and reduce the many complexities and contradictions of globalization into binary categories. These terms gained currency in the development agenda and North–South de-bates during the 1950s through the 1980s but they do not reflect the complexities of uneven development and inequalities in an era of globalization. There are First Worlds within Third Worlds, Third Worlds within First Worlds, North in the South and South in the North. Everyday life for a certain class of African-Americans and Latin Americans in the First World of Los Angeles is little different from the lives of their counterparts in the 'Third World' of Mexico (Davis, 1990). The term 'West' for example cannot be tied too closely to its physical origins. As Moore points out, even in these categories there are move-ment and change. The 'West', then, operates not so much as a particular set of geographical locations, or indeed a specific collection of locationally defined peoples. It has now become 'a discursive space, a set of positionalities, a net-work of economic and power relations, a domain of material and discursive effects' (Moore, 1994, cited in Duncan, 1996: 38). It is in this epistemological space of 'the West' that discourses of globalization and international develop-ment discourses about the 'Third World' are created. 'Third World reality' is also constituted and represented by a particular set of discursive power relations that underlie the development discourse. As Escobar (1992: 25) argues, Third World reality 'is inscribed with precision and persistence by the discourses and practices of economists, planners, nutritionists, demographers and the like, making it difficult for people to define their own interests in their own terms – in many cases actually disabling them to do so'.

Power relations also define how categories and labels are deployed: while many of the Asian economies were 'developing' some of them were recently hit by 'crisis', Latin American countries experienced 'a lost decade of development', the Middle East is in a state of perpetual 'turmoil', Russian and Eastern European economies are 'in transition', and Africa as a continent remains 'marginalized'. The 'West' on the other hand continues to enhance its wealth and has progressed further than other areas of the world (Payne, 2005: 5). Globalization and inequalities are connected in profoundly complex ways and each shapes the path of the other. Whatever way we choose to describe the world the fact remains that 'zones of extreme poverty' still exist in the world economy. There remains considerable disagreement among academics, economists, planners and institutions about the causes of global poverty: for the neoliberals and other pundits of the World Bank, IMF and WTO, the causes are 'temporary misadaptation of markets' (Thérien, 1999: 732) or 'country specific imbalances, policy errors or political difficulties' (World Bank, 1995: 5). Others take a more critical stance and blame 'asymmetrical inequalities in the structure of the global political economy' and point to the 'global politics of uneven development' as exacerbating global poverty (Payne, 2005). In the current political economy however the former discourse is dominant, perhaps even hegemonic, as exemplified by the macroeconomic dictates of the World Bank and IMF that require a market economy, 'free' trade, privatization, reduced government spending on social services and attraction of foreign capital. Thus, 'structural adjustment' policies designed to rescue 'backward' economies through economic shock therapies (mainly involving plenty of shock and little or no therapy) have now become a necessary and permanent condition for 'Third World' countries. In recent years, the World Bank and IMF have softened their rhetoric on structural adjustment programs and have called for poor countries to develop their own 'poverty reduction strategies' to be eligible for loans. The borrowing conditions for debtor countries, however, continue to be coercive and involve opening up their economies to foreign banks and TNCs and minimizing state spending to the point that repayment of debt becomes the primary aim of state fiscal policies or, as a Bank official put it, a 'compulsory program so that those with the money can tell those without the money what they need in order to get the money' (cited in Monbiot, 2004: 152). It is ironic that the mission of the World Bank and IMF – 'Fighting poverty by promoting free market democracy' – profoundly undermines democracy in the regions they are supposed to democratize by promoting market fundamentalism as the only choice available to poor nations. Perhaps a more accurate mission statement of the World Bank and IMF would read 'Promoting debt through market fundamentalism (with totalitarian zeal)'.

In an insightful analysis of the development discourse, Escobar (1995) has demonstrated how development 'modernized' the poor into the 'assisted' and underdeveloped through the use of modern, capitalist indicators such as dollar income per capita, material possession, resource extraction, household consumption and market economies. Economic growth thus became interchangeable with development and was reflected in the development and lending policies of institutions like the World Bank and International Monetary Fund. During the late 1960s and early 1970s it was becoming clear to development planners that economic growth did not necessarily mean equity and that unbridled economic growth had several adverse social and environmental consequences. Income inequalities worsened considerably in the developmental era and the gap between rich and poor continued to widen: on a per capita income basis, the rich to poor ratio was 2:1 in 1800, 20:1 in 1945 and 40:1 by 1975. The richest 20 percent of the world accounted for 82.7 percent of global income while the poorest 20 percent of the world earned 1.6 percent of global income (Waters, 1995). In the newly industrializing countries, economic growth was inevitably accompanied by an increase in income disparity and social dislocations including unemployment, underemployment and environmental and habitat destruction. There was little recognition that some development programs actually led to poverty and social problems, resulting in a sort of 'global apartheid' that separated the world into people who participate in the global economy and others whose basic conditions for life have been destroyed (Beck, 2000; Shiva, 1993). 'Progress' indicators like GNP and GDP simply measure market transactions and do not reflect the social and environmental costs of economic growth. Other environmentally, socially and culturally damaging practices like destruction of old-growth forests through logging also show up as gains in income statements of countries, while non-market transactions such as the 'subsistence' economies of much of the world's poor are not just ignored but marginalized and do not appear in income statements. Instead, GNP figures count environmental destruction as a positive contribution to a nation's economy as long as it is a market transaction. For instance, one of the world's major environmental disasters, the *Exxon Valdez* oil spill in Alaska, actually showed up as an *increase* in the US's GNP because of the goods and services required to clean up the spill (Guha and Martinez-Alier, 1997). Destroying old-growth forests for their timber also contributes positively to a country's GNP; however, the permanent and irreversible effects of deforestation are not counted. The escalation of global environmental problems also led to the struggle for natural resources, resulting in a number of battles between poor farmers and peasant and indigenous populations on one side and corporate and government interests on the other. The notion of sustainable development was conceived in the midst of these struggles as NGOs, environmental organizations and various peasant and indigenous groups as well as international institutions like the United Nations called for a conceptual and political re-examination of development.

The goal of sustainable development is to maintain economic growth without environmental destruction. Exactly what is being sustained (economic growth or the global ecosystem, or both) is currently at the root of several debates, although many scholars argue that the apparent reconciliation of economic growth and the environment is simply a green sleight of hand that fails to address genuine environmental problems (Escobar, 1995; Redclift, 1987). In an attempt to address criticism of the vagueness in the definition of sustainable development, Karl-Henrik Robèrt, founder of the environmental organization The Natural Step, along with a group of 50 scientists sought to obtain a consensus on sustainability and developed four 'basic, non-negotiable system conditions for global sustainability' (Frankel, 1998). These include:

1. No systematic increase of substances from the earth's crust in the ecosphere. This condition implies a drastic reduction in the use of minerals, fossil fuels and non-renewable resources.
2. No systematic increase of substances produced by society in the ecosphere. This condition means that substances cannot be produced faster than they are broken down and degraded biologically. Therefore, the use of nonbiodegradable materials must be minimized.
3. No systematic diminishing of the physical basis for productivity and diversity of nature. This condition requires preservation of biodiversity, non-environmentally damaging land use practices and use of renewable resources.
4. Fair and efficient use of resources and social justice. This implies equitable access to and just distribution of resources.

While the above four conditions may provide a more precise definition than Brundtland's, problems of operationalizing remain: there is still considerable disagreement among the scientific community on evaluation of environmental impact of products and processes. There are also other practical issues: what is the baseline from which we can measure 'systematic increases'? Are goals of 'zero emissions' as stated in the environmental policy statements of several transnational firms mere feel-good statements or are they achievable? In an analysis of the impact of globalization on environmental sustainability using the Natural Step framework, Osland *et al.* (2002) found the evidence to be 'mixed'. They were being quite charitable in their overall assessment because while there were some positive examples of environmentally sustainable practices like energy efficiency, recycling and cleaner technologies there were more negative environmental effects like species and biodiversity depletion, soil erosion, deforestation and salinity, to name a few.

In a content analysis of different definitions of sustainable development, Gladwin *et al.* (1995) identified several themes including human development, inclusiveness (of ecological, economic, political, technological and social systems), connectivity (of sociopolitical, economic and environmental goals), equity (fair distribution of resources and property rights), prudence (avoiding irreversibilities and recognizing carrying capacities) and security (achieving a safe, healthy and high quality of life). However, the 'challenge of sustainability', at least in the policy documents of international institutions, the World Bank and WTO, continues to be framed by an economic lens. Thus, the challenge is to find new technologies and to expand the role of the market in allocating environmental resources, with the assumption that putting a price on the natural environment is the only way to protect it, unless degrading it becomes more profitable (Beder, 1994). Economic development remains a priority over the environment, and environmental protection simply becomes part and parcel of the development process. Thus, environmental protection measures must not interfere with or impede economic growth. If the concern was truly about environmental sustainability a reverse argument would be expected where environmental protection was accorded a higher priority because economic development can only occur within the constraints and limits of the biophysical environment. Rather than reshaping markets and production processes to fit the logic of nature, sustainable development uses the logic of markets and capitalist accumulation to determine the future of nature (Shiva, 1991). The language of capital is quite apparent in discourses of sustainable development.

For instance, Pearce *et al.* (1989) emphasize 'constancy of natural capital stock' as a necessary condition for sustainability. According to them changes in the stock of natural resources should be 'non-negative', and man-made capital (products and services as measured by traditional economics and accounting) should not be created at the expense of natural capital (including both renewable and non-renewable natural resources). Thus, growth or wealth must be created without resource depletion. Exactly how this is to be achieved remains a mystery. Essentially, conventional concepts of capital are prefixed with the terms 'sustainable' or 'natural' and we are thus left with terms such as 'sustainable cost', 'sustainable growth', 'natural capital' or even 'sustainable pollution'. There is limited awareness of the fact that traditional notions of capital, income and growth continue to inform this 'new' paradigm of sustainable development. Discourses of sustainable development ultimately require the capitalization of nature where previously 'uncapitalized' features of nature like air, water, the ozone layer and tropical rainforests now become critical 'natural assets' (O'Connor, 1994). The language of capital pervades the academic literature in the social sciences, the media, policy documents of international agencies, NGOs, governments, the World Bank, the United Nations, the World Trade Organization and the Convention on Biodiversity, as well as multilateral trade agreements like NAFTA and ASEAN. It seems that everything these days is just different forms of capital – nature has become natural capital, human beings have become human capital (or resources) and society is transformed into social capital. There seems to be little awareness that social capital is not always a universal or desirable good; often it is generated for one group of people at the expense of some other segment of society. The Mafia has considerable amounts of social capital. So has Al Qaeda. The uncritical acceptance of market-based environmental protection measures is also problematic: while markets may be efficient mechanisms to set prices they are incapable of reflecting true costs, such as the replacement costs of an old-growth tropical rainforest or the social costs of tobacco and liquor consumption (Hawken, 1995). There is also a cozy relationship between economic ideology and Western science; while admitting that traditional economic valuation methods almost always undervalue biological diversity, Wilson (1992: 271) calls for new ways to draw income from 'wildlands': 'the race is on to develop methods, to draw more income from the wildlands without killing them, and so to give the invisible hand of free-market economics a green thumb'.

One of the more profound consequences of the discourse of sustainable development is the reinvention of nature and its transformation into the 'environment'. Meanings and values assigned to nature reflected European notions of nature and modernity where a 'wild, untamed, often hostile nature' was made more 'manageable' and turned into 'environment'. Rather than transforming the relationship between humans and nature, dominating nature became a key indicator of human progress (Macnaghten and Urry, 1998). The transformation of nature also involves a type of environmental realism that privileged Western science and technology as the only means to research the environment, identify environmental problems and formulate appropriate solutions while subsuming other social and cultural practices of protecting the environment (Macnaghten and Urry, 1998). The universalization of environmental values through market preferences is problematic because it constructs a new meaning of biodiversity that focuses on commodifying and trading the benefits of biodiversity. For this to occur, privatization and ownership are necessary conditions (Redclift, 1987) where once again biodiversity becomes framed as market preferences resulting in the poor (but 'biodiversity rich' populations) sustaining the rich. The new language of sustainable development – 'scientific understanding', 'citizenship', 'species rights', 'intergenerational equity' – obscures the inequalities and cultural distinctions surrounding environmental resources. Assessing market preferences for nature is based on invalid assumptions; as McAfee (1999: 133) argues, 'contrary to the premise of the global economic paradigm there can be no universal metric for comparing and exchanging the real values of nature among different groups of people from different cultures, and with vastly different degrees of political and economic power'.

Apart from attempting to reconcile economic growth with environmental maintenance, the sustainable development agenda of Brundtland also focuses on social justice and human development within the framework of social equity and the equitable distribution and utilization of resources. Sustainability, as Redclift (1987) points out, means different things to different people. Although theories of sustainability sometimes stress the primacy of social justice, the position is often reversed where 'justice is looked upon as subordinate to sustainability, and since neither sustainability nor social justice has determinate meanings, this opens the way to legitimizing one of them in terms of the other' (Dobson, 1998: 242). Thus, the debate about resource scarcity, biodiversity, population and ecological limits is ultimately a debate about the 'preservation of a particular social order rather than a debate about the preservation of nature *per se*' (Harvey, 1996: 148). Critics argue that the reframing of the relationship between economic growth and environmental protection is simply an attempt to socialize environmental costs on a global scale that assumes equal responsibility for environmental degradation while obscuring significant differences and inequities in resource utilization between countries (McAfee, 1999). Sustainability of local cultures, especially peasant cultures, is not addressed; instead, global survival is problematized as sustainable development, an articulation that privileges Western notions of environmentalism and conservation.

Espoused as a solution to the environmental ills facing the planet, 'global' environmentalism remains firmly rooted in the tradition of Western economic thought and marginalizes the environmental traditions of non-Western cultures. Images of polluted 'Third World' cities abound in the media without acknowledgment of the corresponding responsibility of industrialized countries, which consume 80 percent of the world's aluminum, paper, iron and steel, 75 per cent of its energy, 75 percent of its fish resources, 70 percent of its ozone-destroying CFCs and 61 percent of its meat (Renner, 1997). The so-called 'greening' of industry in the 'First World' has, in many cases, been achieved at the expense of 'Third World' environments through the relocation of polluting industries to developing countries. The poorer regions of the world destroy or export their natural resources to meet the demands of the richer nations or to meet debt-servicing needs arising from the 'austerity' measures dictated by the World Bank. It is ironic to the point of absurdity that the poorer countries of the world have to be 'austere' in their development while the richer nations continue to enjoy standards of living that are dependent on the 'austerity' measures of the poorer nations. Neither the dangers of environmental destruction nor the benefits of environmental protection are equally distributed: protection measures continue to be dictated by the industrialized countries often at the expense of local rural communities. This perverse logic pervades notions of 'sustainable' growth. Consumer spending and 'confidence' are primary criteria for sustaining the socio-economic system while welfare policies for the poor are dismantled because they are a 'pernicious drain on growth' (Harvey, 1996). Thus, the 'teeming millions' in the 'Third World' are responsible for damage to the biosphere whereas conspicuous consumption in the 'First World' is a necessary condition for 'sustainable growth' (Harvey, 1996). The structural adjustment policies of the World Bank and IMF reflect this inverted reality: Joseph Stiglitz (1996) commenting on the IMF and World Bank policies during the Asian financial crisis asserted that 'we did manage to tighten the belts of the poor as we loosened those on the rich'.

The 'global sustainability' agenda is set by a handful of industrialized countries guided by their narrow interests that are defined by large corporations. Corporate-funded think tanks are not averse to trying to bribe scientists to challenge received knowledge on environmental problems. In their most comprehensive report on climate change, released in February 2007 by the United Nations Intergovern-mental Panel on Climate Change, an international panel representing more than 1000 scientists, the panel cited 'unequivocal' evidence that human activity through greenhouse gas emissions is causing global warming. The report was written by 600 climate scientists from more than 40 countries and was reviewed by some 620 other scientists and took three years to produce (Monastersky, 2007). The American Enterprise Institute, a think tank funded by ExxonMobil, described variously as 'having close ties to the Bush administration' or, as Greenpeace called them, the 'Bush administration's intellectual Cosa Nostra', offered pay-ment to scientists and economists to undermine the UN report (Sample, 2007). Many transnational corporations despite their glossy reports about sustainability continue to fund agencies to discredit mounting scientific evidence on climate change in order to neutralize the possibility of binding targets on emission reduc-tion. The rhetoric of democracy and participation in contemporary discourses of free markets and international fora on sustainable development also needs to be examined with a critical lens. At the 1992 Rio Summit there were open conflicts between corporations, their trade associations, NGOs and indigenous community leaders over environmental regulations. The demands of NGOs to discuss a multilateral agreement for corporate regulation and accountability were dismissed and a voluntary framework to promote 'best practice' developed by the Business Council for Sustainable Development (consisting of a number of transnational corporations) adopted instead in what was supposed to be a democratic process of developing an action plan for sustainable development (Hawken, 1995). While the policies from the Rio Earth Summit and the more recent Johannesburg Earth Summit (an even bigger failure according to many NGOs and environmentalists) stressed the role of transnational corporations in promoting sustainable develop-ment, they are silent about corporate responsibility and accountability for environmental destruction. Not one of several hundreds of United Nations projects has ever challenged economic growth-oriented solutions despite their rhetoric of 'empowering' rural communities. In the current political economy it is simply not possible to simultaneously empower rural communities and tran-snational corporations and, as we have seen earlier, any compromise tends to seriously disadvantage the former group.

The discussion thus far has focused on more macro and institutional dis-courses of sustainable development. Rather than representing a major paradigm shift, discourses of sustainable development are very much subsumed under the dominant economic paradigm. Given that business is one of the major causes of the environmental problems facing the planet, how has industry engaged with the challenges of sustainable development? In the next section I will analyse the corporate response to sustainable development.

SUSTAINABLE DEVELOPMENT AS CORPORATE SUSTAINABILITY

Environmental issues entered the corporate agenda in the late 1960s and early 1970s when the first environmental legislation was enacted in the US and Europe. Environmental responsibility was seen as one way for a corporation to espouse its social responsibility policies. Emission reduction, pollution prevention, recycling and energy efficiencies were some ways for a corporation to reduce its environmental impact. Environmental issues also began to enter the academic literature around the same time with early attempts to theorize environmental issues as part of a corporation's responsibility to society. Concepts like social marketing, socially responsible consumption and ecologically responsible consumers were developed in the marketing literature. A decade-long hiatus followed during the Thatcher–Reagan regime in the 1980s, and environmental issues returned to the corporate agenda in the 1990s albeit in a different form. While social responsibility and morality arguments continued to be used as normative justifications for corporate environmentalism there was a strategic shift in theory and practice. Environmental issues became 'strategic' because they had the potential to impact the financial performance of firms due to escalating costs of pollution control, environmental liability for damage caused by a firm's products and processes, stricter environmental legislation and increased consumer awareness of environmental issues. The relationship between a firm and the natural environment was seen both as a stakeholder issue involving an organization's social responsibility to a wide range of stakeholders and as a corporate and business strategy that provides long-term competitive advantage. The 1990s saw a minor explosion of articles dealing with corporate greening in the management literature. Much of this literature attempts to incorporate current notions of sustainable development into corporate strategy (see for example the 2000 special issue on the 'management of organizations in the natural environment' in the *Academy of Management Journal*, the 1995 special issue on 'ecologically sustainable organizations' in the *Academy of Management Review*, or the 1992 special issue on 'strategic management of the environment' in *Long Range Planning*) and discusses the emergence of corporate environmentalism and organizational processes of environmental management.

The underlying assumption in the environment-as-strategy theme is that corporate environmentalism can provide sustained competitive advantage. In an attempt to incorporate environmental considerations into management theory, Hart (1995) proposed a 'natural-resource-based view of the firm'. The traditional resource-based theory of the firm links available resources to firm capabilities and competitive advantage. A business firm's capabilities are based on the nature of its internal and external resources: the less imitable the resources are, the more unique the capabilities they can provide. An organization can develop strategic capabilities in different areas including technology, design, procurement and production. These unique capabilities create competitive advantage. Thus, managing 'core competencies' becomes a key strategic task for achieving competitive advantage (Prahalad and Hamel, 1990). From a resource-based perspective sustained competitive advantage can be gained by leveraging competencies that arise from resource characteristics. Thus, through the strategic management of resources, a firm can generate a competitive position based on cost reductions and/or product differentiation that would allow it to pre-empt potential competitors as well as consolidate its future competitive position.

Hart (1995) takes this argument a step further by stating that the constraints imposed by the biophysical environment will provide new capabilities for firms and that recognizing, managing and leveraging these (natural) resource constraints will ultimately lead to sustained competitive advantage. Environmental issues can provide the basis for three kinds of strategic capabilities: pollution prevention, product stewardship and sustainable development. Pollution prevention (rather than 'end-of-pipe' pollution controls involving clean-up technologies and processes) becomes a strategic capability that can lead to competitive advantage by lowering costs of compliance. Tools like total quality management (TQM) are modified into total quality environmental management (TQEM) where environmental improvements are seen as quality improvements. Just as TQM focuses on 'zero defects', the aim of TQEM is 'zero emissions'. Although achieving zero emissions is scientifically impossible (it contradicts the second law of thermodynamics) it provides a direction for managers to develop environmental strategy using zero emissions as a goal. In TQEM the conventional notion of quality is expanded to include environmental quality and is a process that examines all environmental costs involved in every stage of manufacturing, distribution, consumption, and disposal of products (GEMI, 1992). TQEM is a popular managerial tool because it delivers economic and environmental benefits to firms and it is easier to justify an investment if it improves the environment, enhances quality and reduces costs. The basic elements of TQEM are derived from TQM practices with its focus on customer identification, continuous environmental improvement and employing a systems approach. However, environmental improvements may or may not improve product quality. Procter & Gamble developed a pump-action hairspray to avoid using aerosol propellants.

While the product had a lower environmental impact, its sales were poor. Procter & Gamble's executives felt this was because customers felt that hand pumping was inconvenient and did not think the environmental tradeoff was worthwhile. A win–win situation in this case would involve redesigning the product or developing a less harmful substitute for aerosols that avoids trading off environmental protection for convenience. In other cases environmental improvements led to quality improvements, often inadvertently. A transnational computer equipment manufacturer changed its packaging from plastic to cardboard as an environmental improvement strategy. Apart from saving costs, it also led to quality improvements because damage to the product was reduced since the plastic package had higher breakage rates than cardboard. It was an environmental improvement as well since it reduced material usage, was recyclable and was made from recycled materials to begin with (Banerjee, 2001a). Polaroid Corporation had a similar experience. New environmental legislation in Germany required less material to be used in packing their cameras. Trials of the new package showed that product breakage rates were higher due to the resulting diminished protective capacity of the new package. The TQEM process Polaroid had in place led to a shift in their approach to problem solving from the package to the product. Polaroid scientists increased the durability of their cameras to withstand damage during shipping with the lighter package and, as a result, breakage rates not only went down, but also were better than what they were in the older, heavier package (Banerjee, 1998).

Product stewardship involves internalizing the environmental impacts of products following a 'cradle-to-grave' approach that assesses environmental impacts beginning from raw material procurement, through production processes, usage and product disposal. Life cycle assessment (LCA) considers the environmental impact of a firm's upstream and downstream activities, covering raw material procurement (including assessing the environmental performance of suppliers and the environmental impact of raw materials used to make other raw materials), manufacturing process design, product and package design, and environmental impact of transporting, consuming and disposing of the product. The LCA process involves three stages: a life cycle inventory, where environmental inputs and outputs are quantified; impact analysis, where the environmental impacts of each element are assessed; and improvement analysis, which is a systematic evaluation of strategies to reduce environmental impacts (Frankel, 1998). While not yet an exact science, life cycle assessment attempts to quantify as many areas of environmental impact as possible and sometimes throws up interesting results. For example, after conducting a life cycle assessment of its dishwashers, the German appliance maker Bosch-Siemens Hausergäte found that the manufacture of dishwashers accounted for only 2 percent of the product's lifetime energy and material utilization. Product use accounted for 96 percent of energy and material use. Designing dishwashers that use less energy and water is an obvious environmental strategy for manufacturers because these products would have a lower environmental impact than existing products. The total systems approach used in LCA also found that carbon dioxide emissions from daily car trips to work by its employees was 10 percent greater than from the lifetime energy consumption of one dishwasher (DeSimone and Popoff, 1997). Car pooling and using public transport to reduce the environmental impact of a dishwasher is not a connection managers would normally make. A similar analysis conducted by Procter & Gamble of their compact powdered detergents found that the product used less energy and less materials and produced less waste than traditional powders. If a product uses fewer raw materials and less packaging, there are significant upstream effects involving fewer raw materials being mined, processed and transported, resulting in less energy use and less waste.

A second tool to promote product stewardship is design for environment (DFE). As the name suggests, DFE aims to integrate environmental concerns into the product design process. As the practice of recycling increased in a variety of industries, products were designed to make their dismantling easier for recycling. Automobile manufacturers, appliance manufacturers, electronics manufacturers, computer manufacturers and consumer product firms regularly use DFE principles in designing new products or modifying existing ones. IBM's PS/2E computer (the 'E' stands for 'environment') was designed to reduce environmental impact: it had more recycled components, was more energy efficient, and was designed for easier disassembly so that parts could be reused or recycled. The Dutch electronics giant Philips developed a range of products ranging from TV sets to imaging systems, lighting tubes and packages based on DFE principles of energy efficiency in the manufacture and lifetime use of the product, recyclability, hazardous waste production, durability and repairability (DeSimone and Popoff, 1997). Both life cycle assessment and design for environment converge in corporate environmental strategies of new product development.

While pollution prevention and product stewardship are 'win–win' ways that can reduce a firm's environmental impact and provide financial benefits, the third strategic capability of 'sustainable development' is not clearly developed in Hart's natural-resource-based view of the firm. A sustainable development strategy, according to Hart (1995: 996), 'dictates that effort be made to sever the negative links between environment and economic activity in the developing countries of the South'. Developing a sustainable development strategy implies a recognition that material consumption in the developed countries is linked to environmental destruction in developing countries, from which most of the raw materials are sourced. A sustainable development strategy also involves building new markets in developing countries without the corresponding environmental damage that inevitably accompanies increased economic activity. However, details on how this particular miracle is to be achieved are fairly sketchy and involve a few win–win situations that fail to address the complexities of social and environmental problems faced by the poorer regions of the world. For instance, Hawken (1995: 11) suggests an 'economy of restoration' as a solution to the global environmental crisis, where corporations 'compete to conserve and increase resources rather than deplete them'. Hawken (1995: 211) proposes three ways by which this can be achieved: eliminate waste from all industrial production; change our energy use from a carbon-based economy to a solar- and hydrogen-based economy; and create feedback and accountability systems that reward restorative behavior. These solutions are informed by environmental realism and idealism and assume there is both a scientific solution and a collective will of consumers in the affluent countries to 'serve and nurture the aspirations of the poor and uneducated' (Hawken, 1995: 214).

Hart's example of genetically engineered insecticides as an example of a sustainable development strategy because the product does not involve dangerous synthetic chemicals is particularly disingenuous. There are significant concerns about the so-called environmental benefits of genetically engineered products. The world's largest selling herbicide, Monsanto's Roundup (whose patent expired in 2000), is an example. Through biotechnology, Monsanto developed a new strain of soyabean that was genetically engineered to resist Roundup and promoted a new farming technique for genetically engineered soyabean that involves spraying the entire field with Roundup, which destroys the weeds without harming the soyabean crop but which also requires a package of chemical inputs for the new strain to work (Monbiot, 1997). Buoyed by the success of their Roundup product, Monsanto, along with several other transnational chemical and pharmaceutical corporations, embarked on an ambitious program of acquisitions of seed and biotechnology companies. These corporations now control over 70 percent of the world's seed markets. Exactly how this is supposed to empower rural populations in the poorer regions of the world remains a mystery. The development of the 'terminator seed', genetically engineered to produce sterile seeds (a particularly perverse and obscene oxymoron if there was ever one), also violates a timeless cultural and economic tradition – a farmer's right to grow seeds. Monsanto's permission to use their products comes with the company's right to inspect farmers' fields whenever the company desires. Worldwide protests by NGOs and farmers compelled Monsanto to withdraw introduction of the terminator seed and marked a victory (for the present at least) for small farmers everywhere.

In general, the business case for sustainability focuses solely on win–win situations. While there is an almost bewildering array of environmental codes of conduct, standards and certification systems they are all voluntary and not legally binding. The effects of voluntary environmental standards are also not uniformly beneficial for the environment. In his analysis of voluntary codes in forestry as developed by the Forest Stewardship Council (FSC), Vogel (2005) found that timber certification schemes produced mixed results. Created primarily as a result of NGO pressures in North America and Europe, the FSC is one of more than 50 different private forest certification schemes in the world. The FSC certifies forestry products to ensure they are 'sustainably harvested' and do not come from felling of old-growth forests. However, the scale of these so-called sustainable operations is minuscule: in the US only 7 percent of total forested area is under FSC certification (compared to 30 percent in Europe) and FSC certified wood products account for 1 percent of total sales of wood and wood products in the US (5 percent in Europe). While these standards have had a 'measurable impact' in preserving old-growth forests in North America and Europe, the rate of tropical forest destruction and loss of biodiversity continues unabated in the poorer regions of the world and has accelerated instead of declined in recent years, which raises questions about the effectiveness of voluntary standards for sustainable development.

In an attempt to make environmental management systems consistent worldwide, the International Standards Organization established the ISO 14001 series as international standards for environmental management systems. Based on the principles of TQEM and international standards on quality management (the ISO 9000 series), ISO 14001 aims at implementing a total environmental management and control system designed to measure, manage and improve a firm's environmental performance. To gain ISO certification, every manufacturing facility of a company is assessed on several key areas including environmental policy setting, environmental impact assessment, setting specific and measurable objectives and targets, implementing the total environmental management system, and environmental monitoring as well as auditing and conducting regular management reviews of the system. While certification does not come cheap (estimated certification costs for large firms range from $100,000 to $1 million per plant and between $100,000 and $200,000 for smaller firms), there is potential for cost and energy savings as well as enhanced environmental education of employees, customers and suppliers. Some transnational corporations require their suppliers and retailers to be ISO 14001 certified, which could result in both upstream and downstream environmental improvements. However, it is important to note that the ISO standards are process standards not performance standards. They do not prescribe acceptable levels of pollution or industry standards. A simple statement such as 'We will comply with all relevant environmental legislation' is adequate as a goal and a system is set up accordingly. The environmental benefits of these standards are therefore limited given the varying degrees of legislation that exist across the world. A firm can relocate to a country that has much weaker environmental legislation, set up a plant and apply for certification without making any significant environmental improvement, but taking advantage of a friendlier regulatory climate instead.

   The empirical academic literature on corporate greening is, not surprisingly, focused entirely on win–win situations and identifying the economic and financial benefits of environmental strategies. For example, in a study of the Canadian oil and gas industry, Sharma and Vredenburg (1998) found that companies that were 'environmentally proactive' developed unique organizational capabilities. In particular, the proactive firms in their sample demonstrated capabilities for stakeholder integration, higher-order learning and continuous innovation. These capabilities were also associated with self-reported managerial perceptions of competitive advantage. However, the link between corporate environmentalism and financial performance is yet to be fully explored. A few studies show there is a positive relationship. Using stock prices as a firm performance measure and environmental awards and crises as proxy variables for corporate environmentalism, Klassen and McLaughlin (1996) found that market valuation of firms rose significantly in the period following announcement of an environmental award. The converse was also true: significant negative returns were demonstrated for firms that faced environmental crises. Russo and Fouts (1997) used return on assets as a measure of firm performance and environmental ratings of firms by an external agency as a measure of environmental performance and found that environmental performance and economic performance were positively related. However, this was true only for high-growth industries.

   Another study by Dean and Brown (1995) indicated that high levels of environmental regulation actually conferred an advantage on firms in a variety of manufacturing industries as these regulations served as barriers to new firm entry. Environmental legislation is typically framed as a threat to corporate competitiveness and profitability. However, some researchers, Michael Porter for example, argue that strict environmental standards make business more competitive in international markets because tough standards trigger innovation and quality improvement. Porter (1995) cites the case of Germany, which has among the world's toughest environmental regulations, and consequently is a world leader in developing and exporting air pollution and other environmental technologies.

   While the ability to successfully integrate environmental concerns becomes a strategic capability that can confer competitive advantage, caution must be used to advocate the 'It pays to be green' maxim to all firms and industries. Although significant cost advantages can accrue due to corporate environmentalism, the relationship between corporate environmentalism and economic performance is more complex and not always a win–win strategy (Hart and Ahuja, 1996; Walley and Whitehead, 1994). There is also the problem of measurement: while measuring the financial performance of a firm is easy, developing comparable indicators of environmental performance of different firms in a variety of industries is a complex and difficult task. How do we define environmental performance and how can we assess it? Judge and Douglas

(1998) defined environmental performance 'as a firm's effectiveness in meeting and exceeding society's expectations with respect to concern for the natural environment'. However, this definition is fairly broad and difficult to operationalize. In the studies described earlier, environmental performance was measured in a number of ways: self-reports, proxy measures (for example environmental awards) or environmental ratings provided by external agencies. Capability studies, environmental audits, environmental policy statements, future activity analysis, risk analysis and management, continuous improvement in emission levels, input measures, resource measures and efficiency measures have also been proposed to measure environmental performance. While objective environmental performance measures are needed to assess a firm's actual environmental impact, universal indicators can be quite difficult to develop as there is considerable disagreement among the scientific community on what constitutes environmental impact and how this is to be measured.

If integration of environmental concerns is the key to developing a 'sustainable' strategic capability, how is this to be done? How can a company develop a more proactive environmental strategy that can leverage competitive advantage and lead to enhanced environmental performance instead of merely reacting to environmental concerns by complying with existing legislation? Research indicates that companies that integrate environmental concerns at the corporate level develop more capabilities than those that follow a more functional approach to environmental strategy (Banerjee, 1998, 2001a). A variety of internal and external factors influences the level of integration of environmental issues into corporate strategy. Table 6.1 is a list of the driving forces and outcomes of corporate environmental strategies. In a survey of environmental strategies of 311 US companies, Banerjee *et al.* (2003) found that legislation had the greatest impact on a firm's environmental strategy, followed by public concern. While voluntary measures and stakeholder pressures to reduce environmental impact may have had some effect on improving environmental performance, government regulation has been much more influential in changing corporate practice in the US and Europe, and fewer companies would have developed voluntary environmental policies had there not been government regulation (Gunningham *et al.*, 2003; Lyon and Maxwell, 2004). Tougher legislation can affect a firm in two ways: first, the cost of compliance can become prohibitive. It is estimated that companies spend over $350 billion each year on environmental compliance. Given these legislative forces, many senior managers of firms perceive that a more effective strategy is to reduce emissions at the start instead of complying with clean-up and pollution control regulations. Second, legislation can require substantial changes in product or package design or distribution channels. For example, several leading automobile manufacturers have implemented design for environment to include disassembly as a factor in their product design process. Another example is the reformulation of perfumes and colognes that is

Table 6.1   Driving forces and outcomes of corporate environmentalism

Driving forces	Outcomes
Legislation	Higher levels of corporate environmentalism in firms operating in industries facing stricter legislation than firms in other industries. Corporate environmentalism integrated at higher levels of strategy (corporate or business strategy) leading to:
Corporate strategy	Greater levels of investment in environmental protection when corporate environmentalism is integrated at higher levels (corporate or business strategy). Green product positioning. Cost advantages arising from environmental considerations, such as energy and resource conservation.
Public concern	Higher levels of corporate environmentalism when organizational decision makers perceive their customers to be environmentally conscious. Negative public perceptions of a particular industry imply higher levels of corporate environmentalism among firms in these industries. Increased expenditure on green advertising emphasizing the environmental benefits of products/services and promoting a green corporate image.
Top management commitment	Higher levels of corporate environmentalism in firms where top management team is supportive of environmental initiatives. Members of the top management team will coordinate corporate environmental policies and programs.
Competitive advantage	Higher levels of corporate environmentalism in firms that have experienced cost savings due to environmental initiatives. New product development based on environmental considerations. Developing new markets for environmental goods and services.

Source: Banerjee (1999).

required to comply with new regulations proposed by the California Air Resources Board. In Germany regulation requires manufacturers of electronics to take back used equipment, and European Union directives require the recyclability of automobiles and electronic equipment.

Thus, the corporate response to calls for sustainability has focused primarily on environmental sustainability. Corporate environmentalism, environmental management, industrial ecology, pollution prevention, optimum resource utilization and energy conservation are some ways that business firms address environmental issues within the larger framework of sustainable development. Corporate environmentalism has become part of a broader strategy to integrate economic, social and environmental issues into organizational decision making. This is designed to broaden the parameters that measure organizational performance and reflect the 'triple bottom line of 21st century business' (Elkington, 1997). This 'triple bottom line' approach attempts to assess the social and environmental impacts of business, apart from its economic impact.

Elkington (1997) describes interactions between the environment, society and the economy as three 'shear zones' that produce a variety of opportunities and challenges for organizations. Many of the advances in cleaner technologies and emissions reductions have arisen from the economic–environment shear zone, which is an area that business corporations are most comfortable with since it delivers measurable benefits to them. Outcomes of the social–environment and social–economy shear zones are more ambiguous (for corporations at least), although the assumption here is that organizations need to integrate these as well in order to survive in the long term. Theoretical perspectives of the triple bottom line approach focus on maximizing sustainability opportunities (corporate social responsibility, stakeholder relations and corporate governance) while minimizing sustainability-related risks (corporate risk management, environmental, health and safety audits and reporting). Organizational efforts in environmental education are one outcome of the social–environmental shear zone, involving environmental literacy and training for employees, customers, shareholders and other stakeholders. Tensions between the social and environmental zones create new problems such as environmental refugees, communities that are forced to find other means of existence because they have lost their livelihood due to air or water pollution, deforestation or soil erosion. The intersection of the economic and the social zones results in a re-examination of corporate social responsibility, business ethics, human rights, diversity and social impact of investments.

Proponents of the triple bottom line claim that, by using these and other parameters, it is possible to map the environmental and social domains of sustainability and ultimately assess the performance of corporations on a triple bottom line. However, the concept is little more than an article of faith, and more research on the environmental and social dimensions of sustainability is required to assess its validity. The fundamental problems with the concept are the vagueness associated with defining the parameters of the bottom lines and the complexities (if not the impossibility) of calculating a universally accepted social bottom line. While policies on diversity, industrial relations, health and safety, and community development can reflect a company's 'social' strategy, how each indicator is measured, reported and compared with measures from the economic and environmental bottom lines is not at all clear (Norman and Macdonald, 2004). Although the triple bottom line approach is proving to be popular among large transnational corporations (not to mention the consultants who are avidly and profitably selling the concept to corporations), the impact on local communities is unclear. There is no common unit of currency to evaluate how 'good' or 'bad' a particular social outcome is. Norman and Macdonald (2004) describe a hypothetical example of a company that has a family-friendly work policy with generous maternity leave entitlements but also faces several sexual harassment claims; an 'ethical sourcing policy' but a bad industrial relations record; and annual donations to charity but a conviction for price fixing. How can each of these outcomes be aggregated to come up with a net profit or loss on the social bottom line? Is a donation to the Red Cross a better social good than a donation to an inner-city youth development program? There is no grand formula to assess and compare the tradeoffs associated with each positive or negative outcome. While the triple bottom line concept may be well intentioned it is ultimately misleading because it falsely assumes there is a clear and universally accepted methodology to calculate and compare a company's social bottom line. This lack of a universal metric enables companies to focus on the indicator of performance that is most easily measured and compared, which is the economic and financial bottom lines, while allowing them to portray a socially and environmentally responsible image by making vague claims about their social and environmental performance that are difficult to assess.

The same companies that are being targeted by NGOs and indigenous communities for their negative environmental and social impacts are the leaders in espousing triple bottom line principles, and it remains to be seen whether this approach can deliver real benefits to communities or becomes a more sophisticated form of greenwashing. There is a real danger that the glossy 'social performance' reports of transnational corporations can deflect attention from the grim realities of their environmental and social impacts. While we have seen several examples of corporate environmentalism, there are an equal if not greater number of cases of corporate 'anti-environmentalism'. There are many examples of this in the business world. The engineering giant Asea Brown Boveri (ABB), one of the 'founding fathers of corporate environmentalism', was, until recently, involved in a controversial hydroelectric project in Malaysia that almost every international environmental agency described as a 'social and environmental disaster'. This was despite ABB's environmental policy of 'promoting sustainable development, and playing its part in the transfer of environmentally sound technologies and methods to developing countries' (Frankel, 1998). Obviously, the company did not see any inconsistencies between its environmental policy and a project that will flood 1000 square kilometers of rainforest, increase greenhouse emissions and forcibly relocate over 10,000 indigenous people. The company's argument that it simply intended to carry out the wishes of the Malaysian government is also a bit hollow given the power of transnational corporations and their influence in economic and political affairs of developing countries.

There are similar contradictions in many such organizations that are 'environmental leaders'. General Motors, which has come up with several environmental innovations, has been criticized for making exaggerated claims about its environmental record and attempting to defeat electric vehicle incentives in the US. The company was for many years the automobile industry's leader in opposing environmental controls for cars. Its strategy of aggressively marketing light trucks that are less fuel-efficient than cars and its opposition to governmental interest in reducing greenhouse gas emissions are not the hallmarks of a leader in environmental responsibility. The US automobile industry's history on environmental and social issues is not particularly distinguished. US car-makers in Detroit spent a lot of money in the 1930s, 1940s and 1950s buying up public transport companies in order to shut them down so consumers would be more dependent on cars. The industry has consistently fought regulators and community and environmental groups on a number of safety and environmental initiatives, including mandatory seat belts, fuel-efficient engines and anti-lock brakes.

Ford's public attempt to gain green credentials suffered when faced with declining profits. In 2002 the company admitted that 'difficult business conditions made it harder to achieve the goals we set for ourselves in many areas, including corporate citizenship'. Perhaps that was the reason why the company successfully opposed a US Senate proposal that would have raised fuel economy standards (Vogel, 2005). As with other car manufacturers, Ford's largest selling vehicles are gas-guzzling SUVs and light trucks. The company has been under attack by several environmental groups, the Sierra Club in particular, which claimed that in 100 years of production, Ford's Model T with fuel consumption of 25 miles per gallon was more fuel efficient than the current Ford Explorer at 16 miles per gallon (Truby, 2003). However, market pressures dominate pressures from environmental stakeholders. As an industry analyst commented, 'you might irritate the environmentalists but you have three major constituencies. The consumers who are not particularly interested in fuel economy; the United Auto Workers union who are not particularly interested in fuel economy; and the shareholders who are not particularly interested in fuel economy' (cited in Vogel, 2005: 122). Thus, one of the problems with the practice of corporate environmentalism is the ambiguity around its outcomes: the same corporations that rate consistently high on CSR and environmental rankings are also involved in legal disputes and stakeholder conflicts about their negative social and environmental impacts. Alcoa's plans to build an aluminum smelting point in Iceland are being opposed by a variety of environmental groups because of concerns of flooding from a new hydroelectric dam (De Muth, 2003). Toyota, whose green image is based on its hybrid automobile Prius, also manufactures gas-guzzling SUVs which are the company's biggest sellers, massively outnumbering sales of its hybrid models – Prius sales are less than 3 percent of the company's total car sales, with SUV exports accounting for three times as much as hybrid exports (*International Herald Tribune*, 2005; Toyota, 2005).

Wal-Mart's much-publicized 'eco-store' is another case in point where the line between enlightened self-interest and genuine environmental responsibility begins to get blurred. These stores have several environmental innovations that minimize energy consumption, use recycled materials and promote recycling behavior. The relative environmental impacts however do not address the broader effects on communities. The environmental costs of building these gigantic stores are high, no matter how 'green' the construction is. More people now need to shop in one place, which increases driving distances. Community leaders and non-profit institutes agree that the Wal-Mart strategy of selecting a small town that can only economically sustain one megastore tends to undermine community development. With the company's financial and retail muscle, these megastores drive out small local businesses and it is doubtful that the attraction of lower prices makes up for the social and environmental costs (Frankel, 1998). Thus, despite the rhetoric of triple bottom line it is the economic bottom line that determines how much corporations with 'invest' in social and environmental issues.

However, it is important to point out that becoming environmentally sustainable is a very complex task, and environmental problems can rarely be laid out as a series of neatly packaged alternatives. At the same time, there is a need to separate green hype from grim reality in corporate environmentalism. Environmental issues, like many other things in life, are not all win–win situations despite corporate rhetoric to the contrary. There is some evidence to suggest that the cost savings resulting from environmental improvements may be leveling off. The initial high-return/low-investment period of environmental improvement has come to an end for most industries, and managers are finding that additional environmental improvements often involve significant investment and, as a result, the company's environmental strategies hit a 'green wall' (Piasecki *et al.*, 1999). Not all environmental strategies can be justified based on benefits to the environment and costs (and benefits) to the company. For instance, Apple Computers recently disbanded its award-winning Advanced Environmental Technology Group as part of its corporate downsizing. Warner

Lambert is in the process of divesting itself of environmental packaging. Techniques such as life cycle assessment and design for the environment discussed earlier require significant amounts of time and money. Convincing product managers and marketing managers that these expensive and time-consuming processes will contribute to higher sales of their products is not an easy task.

While current corporate environmental practices might not be sustainable in the long term, the question is whether environmental management practices *could* be made sustainable. Several large transnational corporations are trying to define what sustainability means for them as individual corporations. The focus in all the discussions around sustainability, whether at the corporate or governmental level, is on win–win situations. However, this presents only a part of the solution, and restricts environmental problems to only those that can be solved by increasing corporate profit or competitiveness. Any radical notions of environmentalism or alternative theoretical viewpoints are dismissed as 'philosophical' or 'impractical', raising serious doubts about the limited efficacy of solutions that emerge from this problem misspecification. Environmental problem solving involves working with existing systems and providing technical solutions to problems with little chance of an alternative emerging from the outside or dismantling current unsustainable systems.

One consequence of the focus on win–win situations is a shift in the discourse from planetary sustainability to corporate sustainability. For example, Dow Jones launched its 'Sustainability Group Index' in 1999 that captured the leading 10 percent of the 2500 companies in the Dow Jones Global Index based on an assessment of corporate sustainability strategies. Their rationale was that investors were increasingly diversifying their portfolios by investing in companies that were world leaders in sustainability practices, the main assumption being that corporate sustainability increased long-term shareholder value. According to some analysts there exists a significant group of investors who feel that sustainability is a 'catalyst for enlightened and disciplined management' and is thus a crucial factor for business success. A sustainable corporation was defined as one 'that aims at increasing long-term shareholder value by integrating economic, environmental and social growth opportunities into its corporate and business strategies' (Dow Jones Sustainability Group Index, 2000). The rationale behind creating this index for investors is that corporations that are environmentally and socially responsible will provide long-term shareholder value and outperform corporations that do not address these issues. In a similar vein Zadek (2001: 9) proposed the notion of the 'civil corporation', which he defined as one that 'takes full advantage of opportunities for learning and action in building social and environmental objectives into its core business by effectively developing its internal values and competencies'. These opportunities are to be pursued 'within the limits imposed by the tenets of private enterprise', which raises doubts as to exactly what is being sustained. Acknowledging the limits of corporate sustainable development strategies, Zadek states that 'even the strongest and most progressive corporation, acting alone, will rarely be able to sustain significantly enhanced social and environmental performance for extended periods of time' (cited in Vogel, 2005).

'Green' investment funds have been around for more than 20 years, and some of these funds such as the Environmental Value Fund or the Dow Jones Sustainability Group rate companies on a 'sustainability' index. It is interesting to observe how notions of sustainability are constructed, manipulated and represented in both the popular business press and the academic literature. As evidence of the deleterious effects of development mounts, the discourse shifts from sustainable development to the more positive-sounding sustainability and then shifts the focus to corporate sustainability. Corporate discourses on sustainability produce an elision that displaces the focus from global planetary sustainability to sustaining the corporation through 'growth opportunities'. What happens if environmental and social issues do not result in growth opportunities remains unclear, the assumption being that global sustainability can be achieved only through market exchanges that are profitable for corporations. Despite framing sustainable development as a 'strategic discontinuity' that will change 'today's fundamental economics', corporate discourses on sustainable development, not surprisingly, promote the business-as-usual (except greener) line and do not describe any radical change in worldviews. As Monsanto's ex-CEO Robert Shapiro puts it, 'Far from being a soft issue grounded in emotion or ethics, sustainable development involves cold, rational business logic' (Magretta, 1997: 81). This conceptualization of sustainable development is consistent with Milton Friedman's reluctant acknowledgment of corporate social responsibility where CSR activities are legitimate only if they contribute to enhancing shareholder value. Public perceptions of environmental problems, and increased environmental legislation are two key reasons why the environment became an important issue for corporations, resulting in the need for companies to 'sell environmentalism' in order to be perceived as green (Banerjee, 2001a; Newton and Harte, 1997). Newton and Harte (1997: 91) argue that organizations also paint themselves green to avoid regulatory control: one of the aims of the 'Vision of Sustainable Development' promoted by the Business Council for Sustainable Development is to 'maintain entrepreneurial freedom through voluntary initiatives rather than regulatory coercion'. This is despite probably the only consistent finding of research on corporate environmentalism, which shows that government regulation is the most important predictor of corporate environmental performance. Even national governments and international organizations like the United Nations promote sustainability as a business case, a consequence of which is that business, not societal or ecological, interests define the parameters of sustainability. The relationship between business and government has undergone a qualitative change over the last two decades, and in an era of global neoliberalism the role of national governments seems to be more closely allied with business interests than ever before.

That corporations play a significant role in the path to sustainability (or unsustainability) is not in doubt. The question is, are current environmental practices compatible with notions of sustainability? Or are they mere 'greenwashing' exercises designed to ensure that the corporation maintains a positive public image? There is some disagreement among researchers about the relationship between sustainable development and corporate environmental practice. Some researchers caution that the greening of industry should not be confused with the notion of sustainable development (Pearce *et al.*, 1989; Schot *et al.*, 1997; Welford, 1997). While there have been significant advances in pollution control and emission reduction, this does not mean that current modes of development are sustainable for the planet as a whole. Most companies focus on operational issues when it comes to greening and lack a 'vision of sustainability' (Hart, 1997). In a recent 'Greening of Industry' conference, the proposed corporate strategy for sustainable development had no surprises: the focus was on 'scientific innovation, public service and turning the world populations into active consumers of its new products, and expanding global business into the less affluent segments of the world's population' (Rossi *et al.*, 2000: 275). Despite calls for a 'fundamental revision of organization studies concepts and theories' (Shrivastava, 1994) there are no explanations as to how this will occur. It is unclear how 'alternate conceptualizations of an organization's environment' (Shrivastava, 1994) or 'a complete moral transformation within the corporation' (Crane, 2000: 673) will take place or why this transformation will 'naturally' lead to social justice and a more equitable distribution of resources. Fundamental changes in organizations cannot occur unless there are corresponding shifts in the larger political economy and fundamental questions regarding the role of a corporation and its license to operate in society are addressed.

Critical arguments that question the sustainability of current economic systems are rarely found in the literature and much of the theorizing on green business is what Newton and Harte (1997) call 'technicist kitsch', laced with liberal doses of evangelical rhetoric. As long as conceptions of sustainable development continue to be driven solely by rationalizations of competitive advantage, no paradigmatic shift in worldviews of nature and sustainability can take place. 'Green consumption' will not save the world because, rather than attempting to reconstitute politically the mode of modern production to meet ecological constraints, it advocates 'nonpolitical, nonsocial, noninstitutional solutions to environmental problems' (Luke, 1993: 158). Corporate green marketing strategies continue to focus on the economic bottom line at the organizational level (Banerjee, 1999) without addressing the macro-level implications of the relationships between technological, political and economic institutions and their role in environmental decline (Kilbourne *et al.*, 1997). All the exhortations of green organization theorists do not begin to address the tremendous impediments involved in restructuring the political economy and abandoning conventional notions of competition and consumption (Newton and Harte, 1997).

Sustainable development is to be managed in the same way development was managed: through ethnocentric, capitalist notions of managerial efficiency. The macroeconomic criteria of sustainable development have now become corporatized: it is sustainable only if it is profitable; it is sustainable only if it can be transacted through the market. This notion of sustainable development is packaged and sold by international agencies, governments and transnational corporations. As Visvanathan (1991: 380) points out, the Brundtland report, *Our Common Future*, focuses on uniformity and order, organizing the future into resources, energy, populations, cities and towns with little place for plurality, difference or multiplicity. There is still a belief that better technology and management and better and more 'inclusive' procedures by international institutions like the World Bank and the World Trade Organization can save the planet. Eco-efficiency, green marketing and eco-modernization will not save the planet. Current discourses on sustainability ensure that economic rationality determines ecological rationality, resulting in even further erosion of alternate cultural and social values assigned to nature. Consequently, it effectively extinguishes the very cultural and social forces from which possible solutions out of the present crisis might emerge. There is a danger that current discourses of sustainability with their focus on what is sustainable and how it is measured can lose their radical and political edge (Redclift, 1987). Perhaps sustainable development will follow the fate of the modern environmental movement, which is being increasingly depoliticized by environmental policies that translate environmental choices into market preferences. If visions of sustainable development are to have an emancipatory goal, there needs to be a reconceptualization of current notions of progress and development. An unpacking of the notion of development is required, and concepts of sustainability must go beyond seeking a compromise between environmental protection and economic growth. It involves reversing the industrial appropriation of nature as well as recognizing the structural and natural limits of sustainable development (Redclift, 1987). The current focus on capital and markets to achieve sustainable development is restrictive and disallows alternate ways of thinking and knowing. Sustainable development is not just about managerial efficiency (although that has a part to play); it is about rethinking human–nature relationships, re-examining current doctrines of progress and modernity and privileging alternate visions of the world. Contemporary notions of sustainable development are embedded in the development discourse that requires the death of nature and the rise of environment. Alternate visions can be imagined only by rescuing sustainable development from this dichotomy.

If organizational analysis involves understanding the processes of how organizations are produced in particular societal contexts (Leflaive, 1996) and how 'external constraints of the environment are translated into organizational imperatives' (Knights and Morgan, 1993: 212) then a critique of contemporary notions of sustainable development should allow us to examine corporate strategies of co-optation and 'management' of the environment as well as strategies of resistance of the numerous grassroots organizations and NGOs that are at loggerheads with corporations. Such a critique also enables us to examine the structures and processes that discursively produce 'external environmental constraints' and how social and cultural relations are changed by organizations. The critique should allow us to broaden the debate to include the political economy and alternative approaches to addressing environmental problems, something that the current 'environmental management' discourse fails to address (Levy, 1997). It should also allow us to see how nation states, international organizations and transnational corporations support the needs of international capital by placing a critique of capital and capitalisms firmly at the center of the debate rather than the uneasy invisible position it currently occupies in most organizational theories (Pitelis, 1993).

More recent institutional and corporate efforts to broaden the role of corporations in society have followed a 'human development' approach. Clean air, water and access to natural resources, essential to maintain livelihoods, are increasingly positioned as a 'human rights' issue and there were pressures from NGOs and activist groups for corporations to integrate human rights into their policies and strategies. Let us now turn to the question of human rights and analyse its relationship with CSR and assess its potential for addressing the world's social ills.

7. The business of human rights

> If one really wants to see how justice is administered in a country one does not question the policeman, the judges, or the protected members of the middle class. One goes to the unprotected – those, precisely who need the law's protection most – and listens to their testimony. (James Baldwin)

If we want to examine social justice in the contemporary political economy we might find it useful to follow James Baldwin's advice and turn our attention away from CEOs, managers, employees, customers and shareholders of corporations and focus instead on the effects of corporate activity on marginalized and vulnerable populations of the world. We have seen in previous chapters some of the humanitarian problems faced by indigenous communities in their conflicts with governments and transnational corporations over land and resource rights. Watts (1999) has documented numerous cases of what he calls 'petro-violence': violence that often accompanies the extraction of oil leading to both ecological destruction and social and cultural dislocation in communities for whom oil has turned out to be a curse rather than a blessing. Oil extraction has a long and bloody history throughout the world involving dispossession, colonial conquest, military coups, wars, corruption, global politics and power. Oil has been the cause of civil conflict and war in so many regions of the world, with ongoing conflicts in Nigeria, Ecuador, Colombia, Myanmar and the Caspian basin, where petroleum has become central to what the Azerbaijani president calls 'armed conflict, aggressive separatism and nationalism' (Watts, 1999: 1). Transnational oil companies, governments and private security forces are all key actors in these zones of violence, and the communities most affected by this violence are forced to give up their sovereignty, autonomy and traditions in exchange for modernity and economic development which continue to elude them. Nearly all of the transnational oil companies have been accused of human rights violations through their use of private and state military forces in Africa, Asia and Latin America (Abrahamsen and Williams, 2005).

Discourses of human rights are playing an increasingly important role in corporate social responsibility. Whereas a globally acceptable framework of human rights was developed in 1948 and enshrined as the Universal Declaration of Human Rights (UDHR), debates about the responsibilities of corporations and business in protecting human rights began in the 1990s. The UDHR declaration specified civil and political rights as well as rights to health, housing and education. For instance, Articles 23 to 25 of the UDHR state:

> Article 23 (3): Everyone who works has the right to just and favorable remuneration ensuring for himself and his family an existence worthy of human dignity, and supplemented, if necessary, by other means of social protection.
> Article 24: Everyone has the right to rest and leisure, including reasonable limitation of working hours and periodic holidays with pay.
> Article 25 (1): Everyone has the right to a standard of living adequate for the health and well-being of himself and his family, including food, clothing, housing and medical care and necessary social services, and the right to security in the event of unemployment, sickness, disability, widowhood, old age or other lack of livelihood in circumstances beyond his control.

It is doubtful whether even a quarter of the world's population enjoys these rights nearly 60 years after their formulation. The UDHR exists as a resolution of the United Nations General Assembly and as such is not legally binding. However, the UDHR is the basis for subsequent treaties and conventions that signatories are expected to follow such as the 1966 International Covenant on Civil and Political Rights (which involves the right to life, freedom from torture, freedom from arbitrary arrest and detention, and freedom of association) and the 1966 International Covenant on Economic, Social and Cultural Rights (which involve the right to work, rights to fair wages, freedom from child labor and forced labor, the right to education, the right to join trade unions, and the right to occupational health and safety) as well as the core conventions of the International Labour Organization.

Nation states and governments were until recently seen to be the sole arbitrators of human rights. Several high-profile cases of human rights violations by governments and transnational corporations resulted in the recognition of the responsibilities of non-state actors in protecting human rights in the form of various human rights codes guidelines developed by NGOs like Amnesty International. Examples include the OECD's Guidelines for Multinational Enterprises, adapted in 1976 and revised in 2000, the ILO's Tripartite Declaration of Principles Concerning Multinational Enterprises and Social Policy, adopted in 1977, and the UN Global Compact, which was launched following the Davos World Economic Forum in 1999. In addition there is a plethora of corporate and industry codes of conduct and several other codes developed by NGOs. In the mid-1990s, a UN Sub-commission on Human Rights began drafting an instrument on 'Companies and human rights', the most recent draft of which is called the 'Draft norms on responsibilities of transnational corporations and other business enterprises with regard to human rights' (United Nations, 2002). The preamble to the draft norms justified the role of corporations in ensuring human rights: 'Even though States have the primary responsibility to promote and protect human rights, transnational corporations and other business enterprises, as organs of society, are also responsible for promoting and securing the human rights set forth in the Universal Declaration of Human Rights.' The draft norms for TNCs covered civil and political rights as well as economic, social and cultural rights. These rights include:

- The right to equal treatment.
- The right of security of persons as concerns business engagement in or benefit from war crimes, crimes against humanity, genocide, torture, forced disappearance, forced or compulsory labor, hostage taking, other violations of humanitarian law and other international crimes against the human person as defined by international law.
- Rights of workers, in particular the prohibition of forced or compulsory labor, the rights of children to be protected against economic exploitation and freedom of association.
- Respect for other civil and political rights, such as freedom of movement, freedom of thought, conscience and religion, and freedom of opinion and expression.
- The provision of a safe and healthy working environment.
- Compensation of workers with remuneration that ensures an adequate standard of living for them and their families.
- Protection of collective bargaining.
- Respect for the social, economic and cultural policies of the countries in which companies operate, including transparency, accountability and prohibition of corruption.
- Respect for the rights to health, adequate food and adequate housing, adequate drinking water, the highest attainable standard of physical and mental health, adequate education ... and refrain from actions which obstruct the realization of those rights. (Muchlinski, 2003)

At the present time there is no mechanism for monitoring or enforcement of these rights. While corporate complicity in human rights abuses has been established, in some cases as we have seen in Chapter 5 through the US Alien Tort Claims Act, these cases are few and far between and no corporation has been successfully prosecuted. The legal status of the draft norms for TNCs is still in question: at best they can be used to develop more codes of conduct and rules of engagement, none of which are legally binding. The draft norms could also open the door for more transparency as NGOs can pressurize corporations to report their human rights performance. It may be possible to bring private lawsuits against companies that violate these norms but such a process is expensive and requires constant monitoring of corporate activity by NGOs and other agencies. In a bid to operationalize draft norms of TNCs and human rights and obtain wider support from corporations, the United Nations Global Compact was launched amidst plenty of publicity and fanfare in 1999. Let us examine the key substantive elements of the Global Compact and the opportunities and challenges it presents.

THE UN GLOBAL COMPACT: TOWARD A VOLUNTARY APPROACH TO HUMAN RIGHTS

Launching the Global Compact after the Davos World Economic Forum in January 1999, Kofi Annan, then secretary general of the United Nations, challenged business leaders to 'join a global compact of shared values and principles' that would 'provide globalization a human face' (Williams, 2004: 755). The operational phase of the Global Compact was launched in June 2000 at the UN headquarters in New York. The Global Compact was designed as a collaborative effort between corporations, UN agencies, NGOs, labor organizations and civil society to support universal environmental and social principles. It asked corporations to 'embrace, support and enact within their sphere of influence', a set of core values in the areas of human rights, labor standards, environment and anti-corruption. The core values were represented by ten principles derived from the Universal Declaration of Human Rights, the ILO's Declaration on Fundamental Principles and Rights at Work, the Rio Declaration on Environment and Development and the United Nations Convention against Corruption. The ten principles are listed below (United Nations, 2006):

Human rights
- Principle 1: Businesses should support and respect the protection of internationally proclaimed human rights; and
- Principle 2: make sure that they are not complicit in human rights abuses.

Labor standards
- Principle 3: Businesses should uphold the freedom of association and the effective recognition of the right to collective bargaining;
- Principle 4: the elimination of all forms of forced and compulsory labor;
- Principle 5: the effective abolition of child labor; and
- Principle 6: the elimination of discrimination in respect of employment and occupation.

Environment
- Principle 7: Businesses should support a precautionary approach to environmental challenges;
- Principle 8: undertake initiatives to promote greater environmental responsibility; and
- Principle 9: encourage the development and diffusion of environmentally friendly technologies.

Anti-corruption
- Principle 10: Businesses should work against all forms of corruption, including extortion and bribery.

The Global Compact is a purely voluntary initiative designed to support UN goals of sustainable development and social justice by integrating the ten principles listed above with corporate policy. The principles of the Global Compact are not legally binding and the UN does not monitor, measure or enforce the principles but relies 'on public accountability, transparency and the enlightened self-interest of companies, labor and civil society' (United Nations, 2006). Designed as a complementary instrument to government regulation rather than a substitute, the Compact is supposed to 'help establish the business case for doing the right thing' (Kell, 2003: 41). Participating companies are required to provide written support for the Global Compact's ten principles, integrate the principles within corporate strategy and day-to-day operations, publicly advocate support for the principles in corporate communication and publish an annual report describing the ways the company has enacted the principles. Failure to submit this report results in removal from the Compact. The mechanisms for integrating the Compact's principles include 'leadership (initiating change through CEO commitment to the principles); dialogue (including a multi-stakeholder approach to identify problems and find solutions); learning (reinforcing dialogue through examples and identifying what works); and outreach/networks (providing frameworks for action at the country, regional or sectoral level)' (Kell, 2003: 37). Multi-stakeholder dialogue is a key mechanism of the Compact designed to establish relationships between business, labor and NGOs. Whether this dialogue can promote meaningful social change or enable corporations to neutralize demands of NGOs remains to be seen. If the objective of the multi-stakeholder dialogue is to 'both influence policy making and the behavior of all stakeholders' (Kell, 2003: 39), one would hope that the direction of influence and behavior change produces beneficial outcomes for society rather than change the behavior of stakeholders to produce beneficial outcomes for corporations. The learning approach to corporate citizenship involves UN sponsorship of 'learning forums' where academics, corporate executives, NGOs and government representatives discuss opportunities and challenges of global CSR. An outcome of the learning forum is a repository of case studies and projects that could increase transparency of corporate activities and provide a database for future projects and partnerships.

The Global Compact is the largest voluntary corporate citizenship network in the world, with 1366 corporate participants. More than half are European corporations and only 8 percent of participating firms are North American corporations. The main reasons why North American firms have not embraced the Global Compact are fear of liabilities, concern over aspects of the labor rights in the Compact and a general 'low opinion of the UN' (Vogel, 2005). Given the litigious nature of US society, corporate fear of lawsuits is perhaps justified. A 2002 California court decision allowed activists to sue a corporation if the latter 'falsely colored its social image' (Williams, 2004). In *Marc Kasky v. Nike*, the

Californian Supreme Court ruled that claims about safe working conditions are 'commercial speech' that requires the company to defend these claims in court if challenged. This particular case was settled out of court with Nike agreeing to pay $1.5 million to the Fair Labor Association if the claimant withdrew the lawsuit. Corporations had differing motives for signing up to the Global Compact: some joined as a result of pressures from NGOs and activist groups, which also exerted similar pressures on the firms' competitors. Other firms were from developing countries where CSR initiatives were limited and the Compact provided opportunities to explore public–private partnerships. Another motive was to work with international organizations and other UN agencies to develop future public–private initiatives (Vogel, 2005).

Criticisms of the Compact include its inability to enforce the principles it espouses and a lack of accountability among participating corporations. Although about half the signatory companies claim that they have changed some CSR policies based on the Compact's principles, 86 percent of the Compact's signatories had not attended any international learning fora (Vogel, 2005). While the Global Compact does not mark a radical reconceptualization of CSR it has resulted in increased partnerships between the corporate sector and international agencies. Monitoring and assessment of these partnerships are required to see if they produce meaningful social outcomes or whether participation in the Global Compact is a form of 'bluewashing' where corporations wrap their credentials in the blue UN flag to escape scrutiny of their actions at the global level. The lack of accountability, monitoring and enforcement mechanisms is a fundamental problem with the plethora of human rights declarations, codes of conduct, standards, compacts, policies, statements and reports. We will explore the limits of corporate efforts to address human rights in the next section.

CORPORATIONS AND HUMAN RIGHTS: AN UNEASY RELATIONSHIP

While governments have an overall responsibility to protect the rights of their citizens, transnational corporations have the 'obligation to respect, ensure respect for, prevent abuses of, and promote human rights recognized in national and international law within their respective spheres of activity and influence' (United Nations, 2006). Corporate 'spheres of activity and influence' extend far beyond their immediate operations, as we have seen in earlier chapters. Apart from direct effects on human rights, labor standards and anti-discrimination policies of transnational corporations have both upstream and downstream impacts based on corporations' relationship with suppliers, subcontractors, retailers and business partners, which can also have implications for human rights. The use of sweatshop labor by several transnational corporations is a well-publicized example. Transnational corporations can also partner with repressive regimes, as we have seen in the case of Myanmar and Unocal, which while providing economic benefits to certain segments of the population can cause suffering and harm human welfare in other segments. If a government misuses tax or royalty revenues generated by transnational corporations who is responsible? As an increasing number of corporations are finding out, pointing the finger at corrupt governments does not seem to convince NGOs and activist groups any longer. Thus, TNCs are expected to take responsibility albeit indirectly for human rights violations committed by host governments, bribery and corruption, as well as misuse of corporate tax revenues and economic inequality. This may seem to be far removed from a corporation's purpose and beyond its capabilities. As Klaus Leisinger (2005: 585), CEO of Novartis, points out, 'bringing human and social values into decisions of the economic subsystem will ultimately lead to a shift from market mechanisms to political mechanisms'. In developing Novartis's CSR policy, managers agreed that the company must not profit from the use of slave labor and child labor, or from lax environmental standards and regulations. Neither should the company 'lobby for such deficient standards'. However, it was not possible for transnational corporations as 'ambassadors of human rights to criticize government decisions in individual countries or even become publicly engaged against these governments' (Leisinger, 2003: 123). Despite acknowledging that silence in the face of gross human rights violations could be seen as complicity and that 'silence was not neutral', it was 'not decided that there was a corporate duty to engage in political resistance'. Corporate commitment to 'political neutrality' is the reason given by many companies for their unwillingness to include human rights in their corporate policies. This commitment to neutrality must be treated with a great deal of skepticism, however, given the impressive record of corporate complicity with corrupt governments in carrying out human rights abuses, aggressive political lobbying in their home countries, political activity to influence the outcome of international trade negotiations, and bribes and kickbacks to foreign government agents.

The oil and mining industries in particular have a long history of human rights abuses in the Third World along with the active participation of their 'partners in development' – repressive and corrupt governments. TNCs in these industries have been accused of using government and privatized military forces to protect Western investment in the Third World, which has led to the deaths of hundreds if not thousands of innocent civilians, mainly indigenous communities (Abrahamsen and Williams, 2005; Collier, 2000; Dosal, 1993; Grandin, 2006; Marcos, 1995; Ong, 2005; Watts, 1999). Attempting to respond to public criticism about their actions in developing countries, several TNCs, NGOs and representatives of the US and British governments developed a set of 'Voluntary principles on security and human rights'. These principles were operationalized into codes of conduct that were designed to prevent human rights abuses in corporate security policies through corporate relationships with state and private security forces (Vogel, 2005). TNCs that endorsed these principles included Chevron-Texaco, Conoco, BP, Shell, Rio Tinto, Freeport McMoran, Occidental Petroleum, Newmont Mining and ExxonMobil, all of which were accused of human rights violations as a result of their relationship with private and state militaries. However, as with most codes of conduct they are not legally enforceable and there are no monitoring or reporting mechanisms either. It is difficult for these mechanisms to have any real impact on the social and economic conditions of communities that are most impacted by extractive industries: there is a long history of conflicts and ethnic tensions between indigenous communities and their own governments. Corporations are ill suited to address these conflicts. As a result, violent clashes between indigenous communities and security forces employed by TNCs continue to occur despite the industry's principles on security and human rights. Similar problems arise in corporate principles on corruption and bribery – despite several TNCs signing a 'zero tolerance' policy on bribery there is no mechanism to monitor or enforce this policy (Vogel, 2005).

The 'business case' for human rights is similar to that for CSR: companies that adhere to human rights principles are alleged to have a 'better reputation and image, gain competitive advantage, improve recruitment and staff loyalty, foster greater productivity, secure and maintain a license to operate, reduce cost burdens, ensure active stakeholder engagement and meet investor expectations' (Amis *et al.*, 2005: 1). Similarly, the UN Global Compact claims that participating companies can reap the following benefits (United Nations, 2006):

- Demonstrating leadership by advancing responsible corporate citizenship.
- Producing practical solutions to contemporary problems related to globalization, sustainable development and corporate responsibility in a multi-stakeholder context.
- Managing risks by taking a proactive stance on critical issues.
- Leveraging the UN's global reach and convening power with governments, business, civil society and other stakeholders.
- Sharing good practices and learnings.
- Accessing the UN's broad knowledge in development issues.
- Improving corporate/brand management, employee morale and productivity, and operational efficiencies.

There is little if any empirical evidence if these benefits indeed accrue to companies that have a good record on human rights or that companies with a bad record on human rights are economically disadvantaged. Moreover, while a company may choose not to enter a country because of its repressive governments and human rights abuses, once it has started operations it is difficult to justify an exit strategy while the company continues to make a profit on its investment. The financial and business risks of violating human rights may be outweighed by the benefits of investments in corrupt regions and there is no evidence to suggest that corporations are being punished financially by investors or markets based on their human rights record. In fact, the opposite might be true in some cases: divesting from South Africa during that country's repressive apartheid regime led to a competitive disadvantage for some American firms while Levi Strauss's much publicized efforts to phase out production in China because of that country's human rights record were 'quietly reversed' as the company faced declining sales. Despite the company's unconvincing claims that China's human rights performance had improved, 'commercial considerations' were the driving force behind the decision according to the company's president, who commented: 'The company had no choice but to engage itself more fully in China or risk losing out in the competitive game of the global apparel business. You're nowhere in Asia without being in China' (Schoenberger, 2000: 125). Thus, in the 'competitive game of the global apparel business' the main players continue to do business as usual while human rights become silent spectators. As Kennedy (2002) argues, human rights solutions treat symptoms not problems and tend to excuse violations rather than provide remedies for prevention. Signing up to a code of human rights becomes a substitute for ending human rights violations without questioning the dynamics of power that create the space for violations.

Human rights occupy an uneasy position in the policies of global organizations like the World Trade Organization and in the politics of global trade agreements. Although terms like 'sustainable development' and 'environmental protection' appear in WTO policy documents, it is apparent from their various rulings that human rights have little if any part in trade law (Kinley and McBeth, 2003). There is no doubt that international trade can and does violate human rights in some areas but WTO advocates argue that trade law cannot and should not be used to prevent such abuses because it would 'too easily destroy the fundamentals of the trading system' (Wolf, 2001: 201). National environmental legislation, safety regulations, social welfare nets and ethical buying policies are all examples of 'unfair trade practices' according to recent WTO rulings. For instance, in 1996, the state of Massachusetts ruled that companies operating in Burma would not receive any government contracts because of the country's brutal human rights record. As a result of corporate lobbying, the European Union threatened to take the case to the WTO, arguing that the ban was an unfair trade practice. The courts ruled in favor of the corporations. Lawyers representing Massachusetts argued that Nelson Mandela 'would still be in prison had current trade rules been in force in the 1980s' (Hertz, 2001: 78).

While labor and human rights are not on the WTO agenda, the only rights that the WTO actively promoted despite strong objections from developing countries were intellectual property rights. Article 15(1)(C) of the International Covenant on Economic, Social and Cultural Rights recognizes and protects the right to 'benefit from the protection of the moral and material interests resulting from any scientific, literary or artistic production of which he is the author'. Thus, individual intellectual property rights were recognized as human rights. While WTO agreements are between member states, the Agreement on Trade-Related Aspects of Intellectual Property Rights (TRIPS) recognizes and protects the rights of persons including corporations by virtue of their 'artificial person-hood'. Thus, corporations emerged as the major beneficiaries of TRIPS, which was finally signed by WTO member states during the Doha meetings in 2001 after years of protests by developing countries, wheeling and dealing by corporate lobbyists, political pressures, threats of sanctions and secret 'green room' meetings. The arguments used for excluding trade-related labor rights or other human rights while including intellectual property rights were disingenuous to say the least. Currently existing human rights treaties and other international laws that nation states have to abide by were the main reasons given for excluding human rights from WTO agreements to avoid 'unnecessary duplication'. However, the same argument was not applied to intellectual property rights despite the existence of intellectual property regimes that operated side by side with international trade laws and were in place more than 100 years before the formation of the WTO (Kinley and McBeth, 2003). If the existence of the ILO and the United Nations, which are the protectors and enforcers of human rights in the international system, precluded human rights in WTO agreements then why did the presence of the World Intellectual Property Organization not preclude the inclusion of intellectual property rights? Why was protection of civil, political, economic, social and cultural rights not made an exception just as protection of intellectual property rights was? Because both the exclusion of human rights and the inclusion of intellectual property rights served the interests of powerful transnational corporations in the chemicals, pharmaceuticals and information technology industries and these powerful interests influenced the outcome of WTO negotiations.

The purpose of any intellectual property rights regime is to find a proper balance between protecting the private rights of inventors and the public good that new inventions and information access. The debate about providing low-cost life-saving drugs to poor countries is also very much a part of the TRIPS legislation. Most people living in poor countries simply cannot afford to buy patented drugs. A patent on a life-saving drug which protects the property rights of the corporation appears to breach Article 6 (the right to life) of the International Covenant on Civil and Political Rights (ICCPR, 1976) as well as Article 12 of the International Covenant on Economic, Social and Cultural Rights (ICESCR,

1976), which guarantees the right to 'the highest attainable standard of physical and mental health'. If the right to property is a human right it must be balanced with other rights and should not outweigh the right to life or health. If it does, then enforcement of patents on life-saving drugs constitutes a breach of human rights. Pressure by developing countries to offer affordable anti-HIV drugs to their citizens resulted in the inclusion of a 'compulsory licensing' clause in TRIPS that allowed WTO member states to manufacture generic versions of a patented drug at times of 'public health crises'. The blatant hypocrisy in the way First World countries enforce TRIPS and whose interests TRIPS really serves was evident in the diametrically different approaches taken during two public health crises: the AIDS crisis in Africa and the post-9-11 anthrax scare in North America. While US and European pharmaceutical corporations sued the government of South Africa for manufacturing generic copies of patented anti-HIV drugs, the response of the United States government to the anthrax scare post-9-11 was very different: citing the public health crisis of anthrax, the US and Canadian governments forced the German company Bayer to sell its patented anti-anthrax drug at heavily discounted prices, threatening to invoke compulsory licensing laws if the company did not comply. Suddenly, the high profit margins of Bayer and other pharmaceutical corporations became a major media story in North America. The US and Canadian governments were able to challenge Bayer's patent remarkably easily on the basis of their 'public health crisis', which resulted in a grand total of 13 anthrax cases in the US and three deaths, with no anthrax cases detected in Canada. The millions of dead children, women and men in the Third World as a result of HIV/AIDS however was not enough of a public health crisis to warrant a breach of patent; in fact a group of pharmaceutical corporations sued the South African government for manufacturing generic anti-HIV drugs in breach of patent laws (Joseph, 2003).

Thus, the system of rights and obligations that is enforceable by TRIPS legislation serves the interests of the industrialized countries at the expense of the developing world. The obligations of developing countries to 'harmonize' their national intellectual property rights laws with TRIPS requirements are enforceable through WTO mechanisms, as are the property rights of patent holders in the industrialized countries. However, the developing countries' right to economic development and the obligations of developed countries to assist in the development process through technology transfers are not enforceable (Wade, 2003). The evidence that intellectual property rights regimes promote innovation and lead to economic development is also questionable; in fact there is convincing evidence that intellectual property rights regimes have detrimental consequences on economic development in the poorer countries of the world (May and Sell, 2006). Research on the economic development experiences of Japan, Taiwan and Korea also suggests that weak or nonexistent intellectual property rights regimes were instrumental in their success and that former 'pirate activity' contributed to infrastructure development and technological capabilities (Brenner-Beck, 1992). The costs of developing a framework for protecting and enforcing national intellectual property rights for the poorer countries are also very high. World Bank figures reveal that there is a significant net outflow of funds from the poorer to the richer countries: whereas the United States received annualized payments of $19 billion in 2002, annual outflows from Brazil were $530 million, China $5.1 billion and India $903 million (World Bank, 2002a). According to another study, only six countries (the United States, Germany, France, Switzerland, Italy and Sweden) gained from international patent protection while all other countries experienced different degrees of net loss (McCalman, 2001). Rent-seeking behavior rather than technology transfer or economic development is the primary outcome of global intellectual property rights regimes. While the motive of enforcing TRIPS was to reduce rampant piracy in the music, video and software industries, the application of intellectual property rights regimes on life forms such as genetically engineered plants and organisms threatened the livelihoods of farmers and indigenous communities in the poorer regions of the world. Critics argue that TRIPS as it related to agriculture protected the rights of corporations while denying the rights of farmers (Blakeney, 1997; Rifkin, 1999; Mooney, 2000; Shiva, 2001). Let us examine some of these criticisms and explore the implications of biotechnology and intellectual property rights regimes on human rights.

BIOTECHNOLOGY, BIODIVERSITY, INTELLECTUAL PROPERTY RIGHTS REGIMES AND HUMAN RIGHTS

The loss of biodiversity due to industrial agriculture involving heavy chemical inputs is recognized as a global environmental problem. The solution proposed by the scientific and business community is a new revolution: biotechnology. This new revolution of biotechnology is simply a logical continuation from the 'chemical revolution' in agriculture of the 1950s and not only serves to sustain corporate and scientific structures of power by creating an intellectual property rights regime on life forms but also threatens to colonize life forms and recolonize spaces in the developing world, a region that contains two-thirds of the world's plant species. Technocentric definitions of nature and life forms enabled the transformation of genetic material in plants and animals through biotechnology into 'new knowledge' and 'intellectual property' belonging to corporations. The fact that this 'knowledge' existed and has been used by indigenous communities for thousands of years is somehow not relevant: it is either dismissed as a 'philosophical' issue or incorporated into the Western environmental discourse as 'traditional ecological knowledge' that needs protection because of its 'world heritage' value. Laws governing protection of intellectual property

are governed by Western technocentric notions that are biased against indigenous communities (Blakeney, 1997). Under existing laws, patents are granted
for inventions that must be 'novel', and the rights of the creator of this novelty
are protected. Novelty is assessed by reference to prior technological use. There
are millions of people in the world who do not fit this model, indigenous custodians of medical knowledge and peasant cultivators of seeds for example, and
who are denied intellectual property protection. Thus, if intellectual property is
indeed a human right as defined under Article 15(1)(C) of the International
Covenant of Economic, Social and Cultural Rights, national and international
legislation such as TRIPS appears to privilege some humans over others – in
this case the rights of corporations as artificial persons seem to trump the rights
of real human beings, mainly indigenous communities.

Patents and intellectual property laws on genetic resources such as seeds
protect and serve corporate and institutional interests of developed countries
while violating peasants' and farmers' rights in the poorer regions of the world.
Medicinal plants, cared for and sustained by indigenous cultures, were appropriated by pharmaceutical companies without any payment and later used to
develop profitable drugs that were protected by patents and trademarks. The
knowledge of indigenous cultures in recognizing and using the medicinal properties of these plants is positioned as 'traditional' and not 'novel' and hence can
be obtained without payment, while the 'knowledge' of pharmaceutical companies requires protection. Indigenous knowledge does not fit into the current
intellectual property framework, and their knowledge by itself has no 'economic
value' unless it is commodified for the purposes of the market. Only then can
it be assigned 'value' and be eligible for protection, which explains the current
alacrity with which chemical and pharmaceutical corporations are investing in
genetic engineering and biotechnology.

Peasant struggles to control seeds and medicinal plants are being fought in
many countries, and several social movements in Mexico, Latin America and
Asia have raised these issues at international conventions of the United Nations
Economic Program. The International Convention on Biodiversity was established at Rio de Janeiro in 1992 to address the implications of biodiversity
conservation and use. However, as Shiva (1993: 151) argues, the Convention
on Biodiversity (CBD) was primarily 'an initiative of the North to globalize the
control, management and ownership of biological diversity ... so as to ensure
free access to the biological resources which are needed as "raw material" for
the biotechnology industry'. The biodiversity 'crisis' arose because of rampant
industrialization and unbridled economic growth resulting in habitat destruction
and the replacement of diversity with homogeneity in agriculture and forestry
(Shiva, 1993). This crisis is almost always represented as a 'Third World' phenomenon, and the solution developed and applied by the North is to conserve
biodiversity in the South. Evidence of this can be seen in policy documents of

the World Bank and United Nations Environmental Program as well as in scientific texts. For instance, in his popular book *The Diversity of Life*, Edward Wilson describes in detail the biological history of the planet and the negative human impact on biodiversity. While acknowledging that richer countries dictate the rules of international trade, Wilson claims that it is their responsibility to 'use this power wisely'. In providing some solutions to the biodiversity problem, Wilson advocates promoting sustainable development – for the 'striving billions of rural poor in the Third World'. Almost nothing is said about the corresponding responsibility of the striving millions of urban rich in the First World. A similar slippage can be observed in CBD policies: their 'action plan' for sustainability involves 'enabling the poor to achieve sustainable livelihoods' (Hawken, 1995: 216) without any mention of the unsustainable livelihoods of the rich that do not allow the poor to achieve sustainable livelihoods. Thus, sustainable development proceeds the same way as development did – the problems are located in the South, the solutions in the North – and continues to obscure how the political economy of the process destroys biological diversity (Shiva, 1991).

Despite using the right phrases – 'sustainable', 'inclusiveness', 'local custodians' – the CBD is very much a top-down process imposed on local communities, similarly to the way the 'Green Revolution' was orchestrated. The CBD negotiations took place after years of North–South conflicts over resources and rising environmental concern. The initial position was that genetic resources were a 'common heritage to man' (Downes, 1996: 171) and 'biodiversity information belonged to no one and could be exchanged freely among the countries of the world'. Developing countries, justifiably suspicious of the price they will pay for this 'free exchange' of information, supported the current view as expressed in Article 15 of the CBD that provided national sovereignty over genetic resources, 'combined with an obligation to facilitate access by other countries' (Bugge and Tvedt, 2000). This 'obligation' is to be operationalized through the granting of individual permits to interested parties, raising an interesting question: while 'sovereignty' over genetic resources is now clearly established, there is no mention in the CBD about ownership of the resources, whether by the state, private landowners or indigenous communities through common property rights. Conflicting interests over resources between nation states probably resulted in the 'constructed ambiguity' of many of the articles in the CBD that do not provide legal rights to any party in particular.

The CBD is essentially a compromise agreement between conflicting North–South interests. While 172 countries have ratified the CBD, the United States, not unsurprisingly, refused to ratify the convention on the grounds that it would pose a threat to the US biotechnology industry. Although the CBD was a first step in addressing issues of biodiversity and conservation, it did very little in real terms for indigenous and peasant communities who were protesting the violation of their rights. Interestingly, at the Rio Summit in 1992, then President

George Bush used a similar rights-based argument to justify his decision not to ratify the CBD saying 'it is important to protect our rights, our business rights'. Technocentric notions strongly informed strategies of biodiversity conservation and the CBD concentrated too heavily on issues of financing, access of business corporations to genetic diversity, and technology transfer rather than on peasant and indigenous peoples' rights. Critics point out that the CBD placed too much faith on biotechnology and technological fixes to prevent loss of biodiversity, creating 'a reliance on the diversity created through technology which would replace the respect for the diversity found in nature' (Munson, 1995).

Article 2 of the CBD gives states the 'sovereign right to exploit their own resources pursuant to their own environmental and developmental policies' along with the responsibility to ensure that these activities 'do not cause damage to the environment beyond the areas of national jurisdiction' (Hallman, 1995). While this might appear to be a victory for Third World nations over developed countries, there are grave doubts whether the ownership of genetic resources by states will help the rural poor or indigenous communities (Guha and Martinez-Alier, 1997). The imposition of market economies on transactions that were out of the market, such as the 'subsistence' economies of peasant populations or genetic resources used by them, confers a value and a price based on an external political economy, a price that is bound to be very low because these communities are poor to begin with. As McAfee (1999) argues, if the distribution of the benefits of biodiversity is to be determined by market forces, then the world's economic elites will benefit disproportionately. Compensation based on market mechanisms will simply serve to further disempower and impoverish the rural poor. Several farmers' organizations, indigenous groups and NGOs are fighting this battle at different levels, and the fight to maintain possession of land and resources is not just an economic struggle; it is a cultural struggle fought by communities to ensure their survival. While their efforts have contributed to the recognition at the Rio Convention that indigenous peoples have used and conserved genetic resources for thousands of years, the CBD does not ensure their ownership and management rights to these resources. Allowing these rights to be legislated by nation states is also problematic given the nexus between governments, corporations and international trade institutions, none of which represent the interests of indigenous or peasant communities.

For example, several indigenous groups, developing country governments and NGOs have raised concerns about the apparent incompatibility between the CBD and the Agreement on Trade-Related Aspects of Intellectual Property Rights (TRIPS) developed by the World Trade Organization (WTO). Article 8 (j) of the CBD declares that a state should:

> [s]ubject to its national legislation, respect, preserve and maintain knowledge, innovations and practices of indigenous and local communities embodying traditional

lifestyles relevant for the conservation and sustainable use of biological diversity and promote their wider application with the approval and involvement of the holders of such knowledge, innovations and practices and encourage equitable sharing of the benefits arising from the utilization of such knowledge, innovations and practices.

Article 27.3 (b) of the TRIPS agreement states:

> Members may also exclude from patentability plants and animals other than micro-organisms, and essentially biological processes for the production of plants or animals other than non-biological and microbiological processes. However, Members shall provide for the protection of plant varieties either by patents or by an effective sui generis system or by any combination thereof. (World Trade Organization, 2000)

Dawkins (1997: 27) provides a clearer interpretation of the above clause: 'this means that anything that can be genetically manipulated can be patented and monopolized as the private property of transnational agricultural and pharmaceutical corporations'. While the CBD calls to 'respect, preserve and maintain' the traditional knowledge of indigenous communities the TRIPS agreement legitimizes private property rights through intellectual property over life forms. These rights are for individuals, states and corporations, not for indigenous peoples and local communities. In effect, governments are asked to change their national intellectual property rights laws to allow patenting of 'microorganisms, non-biological and microbiological processes'. A 'sui generis' system applies to countries that do not have well-developed patent protection systems at the national level, and the WTO TRIPS agreement allows them to develop their own system based on international guidelines. The TRIPS agreement resulted in mass protests by indigenous and peasant communities along with NGOs in Asia, Africa and South America that continue to this day. A globally enforceable intellectual property rights regime such as TRIPS when applied to agricultural resources raises conflicting demands between breeders' rights and farmers' rights while protecting the interests of agribusiness. Advances in biotechnology have resulted in creating faster and more diverse options for breeding plant varieties. Current intellectual property rights regimes tend to favor breeders' rights and the intellectual property rights of formal innovators, which are mainly private corporations, while diluting the protection of the rights of farmers, who are the 'informal' and typically poor innovators. Intellectual property rights regimes also do not take into account contextual factors in developing countries where much of agricultural research takes place in public institutions and where the farmer/breeder dichotomy is less prevalent since farmers are also breeders individually and collectively conserving and producing genetic resources and seeds (Randeria, 2007).

There are two related problems that arise from imposing a regime of intellectual property rights on indigenous knowledge. First, 'traditional' knowledge belongs to the indigenous community rather than to specific individuals. Access to seeds, plants and animals to ensure the sustainability of indigenous communities has less to do with individual human rights and more to do with collective rights and common property resources. Second, as indigenous communities all over the world have discovered, national governments are increasingly employing neoliberal agendas (some willingly, a majority through coercion) that have adverse impacts on their livelihoods because of restricted community access to natural resources. 'Equitable' sharing of commercial benefits through mutually beneficial contracts between indigenous groups and transnational corporations are unlikely to occur given the disparities in resources and capacities to monitor or enforce the terms of any contract. TRIPS laws protect the rights of corporations that are 'bioprospectors' because they consider the manipulation of genetic resources that exist in nature as deserving of intellectual property rights protection. Thus, a foreign corporation can claim exclusive rights to the use of a gene extracted from germplasm found in another country.

Take for example the much-publicized bioprospecting agreement with Merck and the Instituto Nacional de Biodiversidad (INBio) of Costa Rica, touted as a 'model' agreement under the Convention on Biological Diversity. Under the terms of this agreement, INBio agreed to provide Merck with chemical extracts from 'wild' plants in exchange for an undisclosed share of royalties from any resulting commercial products (Mooney, 2000). INBio also agreed to allocate 50 percent of any royalties it may receive to the Costa Rica National Park Fund. Although it was hailed by corporations, governments and several environmental organizations as a 'model' agreement, the rights of indigenous communities did not appear to play any part in the process. Biodiversity was being 'conserved' by national institutions for transnational corporations and their customers at a bargain price for the company (not to mention the enormous public relations boost for the company). How a national organization like INBio can be counted on to protect indigenous interests is doubtful given that its central activity is 'the generation, organization and dissemination of biodiversity knowledge and rational use of it at the national and international level' (Mateo, 2000: 46). There seems to be a curious silence on its role or impact at the local level, especially the acknowledgment that local communities have always 'generated, organized and disseminated' biodiversity knowledge in very 'rational' ways until this was appropriated without compensation. Royalties and compensation, however useful, still do not address the lack of local control of knowledge and its transfer to national and international institutions. Recognition of the 'national sovereignty' of Costa Rica over its biological diversity will be of little benefit to indigenous communities that have developed and sustained that biodiversity for thousands of years – in fact it marks a dilution of their rights over their resources. What happens when bioprospecting activities result in a valuable discovery? Who owns the discovery? The corporation that conducted bioprospecting? Local inhabitants who may have cultivated that particular plant variety for thousands of years? The government? What is an 'equitable' division among the claimants? In several other cases of bioprospecting, in Thailand, Malaysia and Africa, the outcomes for indigenous peoples have been the same, with hardly any compensation or 'technology transfers' as specified by the CBD. Thus, regardless of what terminology we use in this postmodern, postcolonial, globalized world, the fact remains that the 'Third World', the 'South', 'developing countries', or the 'least developed countries' possess most of the world's genetic resources. The 'developed countries', the 'First World' or the 'North' are the bioprospectors, searching for germplasm in the 'global commons'. These 'common genetic resources' are then privatized and the seeds of new varieties are protected by intellectual property rights and are sold for profit in both North and South. 'Biopiracy' is a more accurate description of this process than 'bioprospecting', albeit couched in the rhetoric of corporate citizenship and sustainable development, a rhetoric that obscures the reality of continuing colonial modes of development (Shiva, 1993).

The strong pressure from the World Trade Organization, transnational corporations and developed countries to establish a global intellectual property rights regime will ensure that the rights of the corporations at least are protected. The sovereign rights of local communities, whose cultural survival cannot be separated from the biodiversity of their environment, are not addressed by the CBD. Biotechnology impacts these communities in an irreversible way: biodiversity simply becomes raw material (information) for biotechnology. However, the products of biotechnology become genetically uniform substitutes of the original biodiversity used as raw material. Modern scientific notions of biodiversity conservation again misspecify the problem: rather than approach biodiversity conservation as a conservation of the 'means of production', they conceptualize the problem as conservation of 'raw material' (Shiva, 1991). Since the problem is articulated incorrectly, the solution that biotechnology will lead to biodiversity conservation is also wrong: it can produce a diverse range of commodity products but will breed uniformity in life with destructive effects on indigenous communities all over the world. As Shiva (1991) argues, global discourses of biodiversity fail to recognize that biodiversity is intimately linked with the survival of indigenous and local communities where farmers produce both the product and the means of production, not just 'raw material'. This free germplasm is used by corporations to produce genetically engineered non-generative seeds (a product that can be patented) and it is this shift 'from the ecological processes of reproduction to the technological processes of production that underlies both the problem of dispossession of farmers and tribals and the problem of erosion of biodiversity' (Shiva, 1991: 52). Thus, biotechnology, far from being the savior of biodiversity, is an inherently imperialistic narrative that produces a replication of uniformity and colonizes spaces and sites in the

'Third World', spaces that now need to be made 'efficient' because of the capitalization of nature.

The application of intellectual property rights to biodiversity conservation suffers from the same reductionist view of life. The emergence of the 'life sciences' industry marks the convergence of a number of industries including agriculture, chemicals, pharmaceuticals, food processing, cosmetics, computer hardware and software and energy (Enriquez and Goldberg, 2000). Technological and economic forces driving these changes are also reinventing conceptions of nature that mirror their relationships with the natural environment (Rifkin, 1999). Thus, nature itself is defined as 'the storage and transmission of information within a system' (Waddington, 1977: 145) where everything in nature is seen as genetic information that can be manipulated, controlled and organized, a process that is constituted and discoursed about as part of the 'natural' evolution of humanity itself, evolution that is, 'in the end, the process by which the creature modifies its information and acquires other information' (Grassé, 1977: 23). Everything becomes a series of information systems, including institutions, corporations and the natural world, where success and progress are assessed by the quality and speed of information processing. According to Robert Shapiro, Monsanto's ex-CEO, 'biotechnology is really a subset of information technology because it is about DNA-encoded information' (Magretta, 1997). These new concepts of nature, apart from assuming no material ecological impact, provide legitimacy for the dominant order and ruling elites. As Harvey (1996: 147) points out, notions of 'scarcity' and 'limits' in natural resources are also rooted in social systems where a natural resource becomes a 'cultural, technical and economic appraisal of elements and processes in nature that can be applied to fulfill social objectives and goals through specific material practices'. For example, the mechanisms of ensuring a 'free and fair' flow of information that are developed and proposed, such as intellectual property rights on genetically modified living organisms, serve to protect certain interests. The controversial Trade-Related Aspects of Intellectual Property Agreement (TRIPS) at the Uruguay Round of the GATT was developed 'in large part' by a committee called the Intellectual Property Committee (IPC) consisting of many transnational firms including Bristol Myers, Merck, Monsanto, Du Pont and Pfizer. Monsanto's representative described the TRIPS strategy:

> [We were able to] distill from the laws of the more advanced countries the fundamental principles for protecting all forms of intellectual property ... Besides selling our concept at home, we went to Geneva where we presented our document to the staff of the GATT Secretariat ... What I have described to you is absolutely unprecedented in GATT. Industry identified a major problem for international trade. It crafted a solution, reduced it to a concrete proposal, and sold it to our own and other governments ... the industries and traders of the world have played simultaneously the role of patients, the diagnosticians and the prescribing physicians. (cited in Rifkin, 1999: 52)

What are the economic, cultural, political and social consequences if the industries and traders of the world have monopolized the roles of key actors in the political economy? Who gets left out of the negotiation process and how does it impact the human rights of those populations who are unable to play the 'role of patients, the diagnosticians and the prescribing physicians'? Corporate power in the development of global trade negotiations determines who are the major beneficiaries of trade agreements. For example, in three of the main trade advisory committees of the US trade representative's office, representing a total of 111 members, 92 represented individual companies and 16 were trade industry associations (10 from the chemical industry). Two represented labor unions. More than a third of the member companies represented at these meetings had been fined by the Environmental Protection Agency for failure to comply with environmental regulations. Another third of member companies had actively lobbied state and federal governments opposing higher environmental standards (Korten, 1995). Most of these agreements are arrived at in so-called 'green room meetings' at WTO ministerial meetings which are essentially closed-door meetings with no access to the public. Many Third World governments have raised concerns about this process, and social and environmental activists have complained about the exclusionary nature of 'global' trade policy development. International trade regimes like the WTO despite using the rhetoric of promoting development and democratic participation have the opposite effect: their policies shrink the space for development, resulting in a 'democracy without choices' where citizens of sovereign states can use the ballot box to change ruling political parties but have no say in influencing public policies that erode their capabilities and rights (Krastev, 2002; Randeria, 2007).

Global trade environmental policy regimes, despite the rhetoric of inclusiveness, do little to address concerns of small farmers, peasants and indigenous peoples of the poorer regions of the world. At one of the many meetings during the development of the Kyoto Protocol the organizers, no doubt alarmed at the riots that derailed the 1999 WTO meeting in Seattle, decided to follow an inclusive approach and invited a diverse range of stakeholders to discuss a global forestry policy as a means to tackle climate change. Scientists, academics, policy makers, NGOs, environmental groups and politicians were invited to participate in developing a global forestry strategy. The only people the organizers omitted to invite were the people who currently bear the greatest burden of negative social, environmental and economic impacts: the forest dwellers, whose representatives organized their own forum at the Second International Indigenous Forum on Climate Change held at The Hague in November 2000. Of primary concern was the exclusion of indigenous peoples as participants in the development and the implementation of the Kyoto Protocol. The forum also professed concern that the measures to mitigate climate change currently being negotiated are based on a worldview of territory that reduces forests, lands, seas and sacred sites to only their carbon absorption capacity. This world view and its practices adversely affect the lives of Indigenous Peoples and violate our fundamental rights and liberties, particularly, our right to recuperate, maintain, control and administer our territories which are consecrated and established in instruments of the United Nations. (IIFC, 2000)

'Carbon absorption capacity' refers to forests as 'carbon sinks', which allows a system of tradeable emissions that credit countries for not reducing their emissions if they plant trees instead. This system can allow perverse outcomes to emerge where a country can get environmental 'credit' for (a) not reducing its emissions; (b) leveling old-growth forests; and (c) replanting trees to grow new forests, i.e. creating carbon sinks. This monocultural mindset of 'scientific' forestry does not recognize that forests are not just 'carbon sinks' or timber mines for local communities: they are their source of food, agriculture and medicine, in short, their entire livelihood. Carbon trading schemes also privatize the earth's capacity to absorb greenhouse gases by creating a system of property rights on emissions, valued at \$2.345 trillion (Victor, 2001). Critics of the scheme have raised serious doubts about the efficacy of planting trees to offset emissions because burning fossil fuels still depletes carbon reserves and it is impossible to verify whether a power plant's emission can be truly compensated by tree plantations (Lohman, 2005). At Kyoto, corporations and lobby groups were successful in opposing any socially equitable ways of reducing emissions (through regulation for example) because of the negative impact to the corporate financial bottom line.

Despite highlighting issues of poverty and equity, contemporary discourses of sustainable development do not critique the structural conditions that characterize the increasing intrusion of capital into the domain of nature resulting in the capitalization, expropriation, commodification and homogenization of nature. Thus, nature, once a commons and a resource, is now reinvented as a vast gene pool, inspiring 'today's molecular biologists and corporate entrepreneurs in their quest to capture and colonize the last frontier, the genetic commons that is the heart of the natural world' (Rifkin, 1999: 170). Some advocates argue that an IPR regime will help in conserving biodiversity, recognizing the 'essential value of biological diversity: its informational content' (Swanson, 1995: 169). The rationale is that 'human capital' does not produce all important and valuable information but there is a 'base biological dimension that generates information'. This 'base biological dimension' is the 'evolutionary process' and the task is to develop a fair and equitable system that can appropriate 'evolution's values'. Swanson (1995: 171) goes on to say:

> To a large extent, the extension of 'intellectual property' regimes to include natural resource-generated information simply levels the playing field between those societies

which are more heavily endowed with human capital and those that are more heavily endowed with natural forms of capital. It is a very rational approach to the resolution of the biodiversity problem.

The problem with this statement is the nature of the 'rational approach' and the framing of the 'biodiversity problem'. The valuation of biodiversity is based on its potential international economic value that ignores or underestimates the values ascribed to nature by peasant populations with negligible purchasing power in the global supermarket (McAfee, 1999). Far from 'leveling the playing field', the intellectual property rights regime constructs problems and applies solutions in a way that acknowledges 'diversity-rich but cash-poor' countries only if they accept privatization of their commons as well as their knowledge, leading to an erosion of the rights of indigenous communities and peasant populations who depend on the commons for their survival. This argument also resonates with other conservation strategies dictated by the 'First World', such as the creation of 'national' parks based on a vision of pristine, unspoiled, intact nature. The problem, of course, is that indigenous inhabitants of these parks are also subsumed into the category of nature and conservation, denying them the right to determine what direction their future should take (Perera and Pugliese, 1998). There is an important distinction between what Dasmann (1988) calls 'biosphere people', those who have the entire biosphere at their disposal, and 'ecosystem people', the indigenous peoples whose subsistence is intimately linked with the ecosystems in which they live. As Dasmann (1988: 303) points out, 'the impact of biosphere people upon ecosystem people has usually been destructive ... Biosphere people create national parks. Ecosystem people have always lived in the equivalent of national parks.' For ecosystem people loss of commons is not just an 'environmental problem' but destroys their entire livelihood. Biodiversity conservation raises complex questions about human rights, questions that do not have easy answers because of profound differences in cultural, economic, social and political contexts between indigenous communities and the neoliberal markets system in which they are being interpellated in increasing numbers.

Scientists and business and government leaders often hail biotechnology as an advance that will end world hunger. The difficulty with this, of course, is a misspecification of the problem: that hunger exists because of a gap between food production and population. The reality is that in 2000 the world produced enough food to feed every child, woman and man, yet more than 800 million people, many of them living in food surplus countries, went hungry (World Development Report, 2001). More telling is a report from the Food and Agriculture Organization that estimates that 78 percent of all malnourished children in the developing world live in countries with food surpluses (Food and Agriculture Organization, 2000). The problem in developing countries, as Amartya

Sen (1999) points out, is not the production of food but access to income to buy food. A biotechnological food fix for world hunger is not a paradigm shift: it is a continuation of the (post)industrial model of agriculture that constructs problems of the poor and applies solutions developed by scientists and experts from the North without addressing fundamental inequalities in income and access to natural resources. This 'sustainable' form of development represents world hunger as a demand for genetically modified food rather than as an outcome of repressive conditions in the global social and political economy. It is possible that biotechnology could treble or quadruple food production in the next 50 years; however people would probably still go hungry.

Appropriating traditional ecological knowledge of indigenous peoples for the advancement of Western science and medicine through patents and intellectual property rights is simply another violation of indigenous rights. Saving seeds for future harvest is a timeless tradition among farmers and under a regime of intellectual property rights farmers have to pay transnational corporations for the right to do so. The novelty that is protected by intellectual property rights is an altered genetic sequence that reduces the total functionality of the seed. In the case of Monsanto's terminator seed the innovation was to genetically engineer a seed to make it sterile so farmers could not breed it, which was then sold back to the farmers as a package including the seed along with the biological and chemical supplements without which the seed could not function. The transnational corporation in the agricultural sector is thus 'in the business of manufacturing the chemicals necessary to compensate for the weakness it also manufactures' (Perriere and Seuret, 2000: 33). The recent battle over patenting extracts from the Neem tree (Azadirachta indicaa), known and used in India for its medicinal properties for thousands of years, is an example of biopiracy. Claiming intellectual property rights over Neem extracts is based on a system of multiple exclusions that denies indigenous knowledge and agricultural practices. The knowledge that these extracts could be used for medicinal purposes (contraception, and curing ulcers and skin disorders), pesticides, and body and teeth cleansing existed earlier and was 'in the prior public domain', which is what patenting laws seek to establish. If this knowledge had existed in the West, these patent applications would never have been considered. The fact that this prior knowledge existed in poor rural communities allowed a 'non-novel entity to be constructed as novel' and patented under current intellectual property rights legislation (Shiva, 1993: 115). Traditional ways of obtaining extracts were deemed 'obvious' and hence not eligible for intellectual property rights protection. NGOs and activists supporting poor farmers in India argue that the discovery of Neem's pesticidal and medicinal properties was by no means 'obvious' but evolved through extended systematic knowledge development. Just because this knowledge was not produced in Western laboratories by men in white coats and the active ingredient did not have a Latin name does not mean it is not knowledge. It took a five-year legal battle fought by NGOs (without the support of the state) for the European Patent Office to revoke the patent on Neem extracts. North–South conflicts between what constitutes an 'invention' and what is a 'discovery' are ongoing in intellectual property rights disputes with no clear resolution in sight. The struggle is far from over: legislative changes in the European Union recently allowed patents to cover life forms (Downes, 1996). The number of applications for genetic patents received in the United States rose from 4000 in 1991 to 500000 in 1996 (Enriquez and Goldberg, 2000). According to a recent World Bank report, in 1987 the six largest multinational corporations in the agricultural sector held 10 percent of biotechnology patents. Universities and public institutions held over 50 percent. By 1999, the figures were reversed: the 'Big Six' TNCs now held 70 percent of biotechnology patents with public institutions holding 10 percent (World Development Report, 2001). The World Trade Organization is also under pressure by the US to remove the exception it currently has on life forms and enforce patents on life forms.

The poorer countries of the world contend that the patent system restricts their ability to obtain access to sophisticated technology because they have to recognize the rights of foreign technology suppliers. 'Global' patent systems thus reward commercial breeders (mainly transnational corporations) and consolidate the power of a small number of technologically developed countries while discriminating against poor farmers because intellectual property regimes neither recognize the contributions of farmers and indigenous communities nor compensate them for taking their resources away. As Shiva (1993) points out, for a majority of poor farmers around the world the right to life cannot be separated from the right to livelihood. Any global trade regime that threatens the right to livelihood is a violation of the Declaration of Human Rights. There is a real danger that the TRIPS legislation by granting intellectual property rights to corporations at the expense of small farmers can result in an erosion of human rights. Although human rights are positioned as a universal discourse they are the product of a specific social, cultural, historical, political and economic context and this (Western) specificity cloaked in a universal vocabulary can produce disempowering effects when enforced in other contexts.

THE PROBLEM WITH THE HUMAN RIGHTS DISCOURSE

The discourse of human rights, though well intentioned, has significant problems in its applicability especially to the vast majority of the poorer populations of the world who are negatively impacted by corporate activity. While the onus of respecting human rights falls on state and non-state actors, governments, institutions and corporations, little effort is made to address the potential erosion of human rights due to the imposition of neoliberal economic regimes in the poorer regions of the world. Neoliberalism, to borrow a phrase from Polanyi (1944), 'confers rights and freedoms on those whose income, leisure and security needs no enhancing leaving a pittance for the rest'. The implications of a universal vocabulary of rights need to be carefully scrutinized before designing any global charter of human rights. Often a universal definition of a problem can in reality be a misspecification that disallows possible local solutions to emerge. As we have seen earlier in this chapter as well as in Chapter 6, the construction, deployment and proposed solutions of a global environmental problem can disempower already marginalized populations. While environmental harm can be framed as a human rights violation this should not preclude other ways of thinking about environmental protection depending on which constituencies are involved, for example environmental protection as a duty of care and collective commitment rather than solely as a right to a clean environment (Kennedy, 2002). A 'right to development' becomes a hegemonic discourse, which constructs particular notions of poverty as problems and privileges industrial economic growth as the only solution. Thus, within a discourse of human rights, international economic policy makers with a neoliberal agenda determine the parameters and solutions for global poverty without ever questioning the problematic nature of development. For instance, the 2003 World Development Report while acknowledging failure in tackling global poverty blamed 'poor implementation and not poor vision' and a general failure of governance. The problems of poor governance according to this report could be overcome by 'welcoming private actors' and a 'smooth evolution of property rights from communal to private' (World Development Report, 2003). Thus, a property rights regime that privileges the rights of private capital over the rights of local communities to access resources essential for the communities' survival is proposed as a just solution to conflicts over resources (Newell and Wheeler, 2006).

Also, while the focus on individual rights may be a good thing let us not forget that a corporation is legally a 'fictitious individual' protected by the same bill of rights. Focusing on the responsibilities of nation states and corporations to protect human rights elides the disempowering and disenfranchising effects that economic systems have on particular sections of the world's populations. For instance, damage caused by structural adjustment programs to a country's economy does not constitute a human rights violation even if the economic policies have resulted in people losing their livelihoods and lives and caused immense suffering (Asad, 2000). Responsibility for these outcomes lies with the governments, and human suffering is blamed on inefficient and corrupt Third World governments rather than the economic policies they have been forced to adopt by the IMF and World Bank. While the vocabulary of human rights has entered the policies of these global institutions the outcomes are far from emancipatory for the 'Third World' (Kennedy, 2002). Instead their policies serve to facilitate repression as states enforce harsh structural adjustment policies while co-opting local and international resistance through 'stakeholder management' practices and legitimizing the rationality and universality of neoliberal policies that serve narrow interests of the rich and powerful. In his analysis of the Asian financial crisis of the 1990s, Joseph Stiglitz (2000), then chief economist of the World Bank, commented:

> East Asian countries had liberalized their financial and capital markets not because they needed to attract more funds (savings were already 30 percent or more) but because of international pressure including some from the US Treasury Department. These changes provoked a flood of short-term capital … Unemployment soared, increasing as much as tenfold and real wages plummeted in countries with no basic safety nets. Not only was the IMF not restoring economic confidence in East Asia it was undermining the region's social fabric.

While trade liberalization and economic reform in China and India, for example, have created wealth for a large middle class, the economic, environmental and social conditions of the poorer segments in those societies who make up a majority of the populations have worsened (Kahn and Yardley, 2004). Extreme poverty creates social conditions that negate all human rights, regardless of how many declarations of human rights governments, institutions and corporations sign – as Muhammad Yunus (1998: 30), founder of the Grameen Bank, says, 'A poor person has no rights at all.' The suffering of the people in Iraq caused by UN sanctions was also positioned as ultimately being the responsibility of that country's dictatorial regime. When asked on US television if she thought that the death of half a million Iraqi children because of the sanctions against Iraq was a price worth paying, then US ambassador to the UN Madeline Albright replied: 'This is a very hard choice, but we think the price is worth it.' The 'we' of course excludes the dead children and their families, and refers to the 'international community', another fiction produced by the human rights discourse that creates a vision of a benevolent community that in reality is made up of what Kennedy (2002: 117) describes as a 'first world media audience of political elites, disconnected from economic actors and interests'.

In their vision for global economic development in 1951, a report from the United Nations Department of Economic Affairs (cited in Escobar, 1995) stated:

> There is a sense in which rapid economic progress is impossible without painful adjustments. Ancient philosophies have to be scrapped; old social institutions have to disintegrate; bonds of caste, creed and race have to burst; and large numbers of persons who cannot keep up with progress will have to have their expectations of a comfortable life frustrated.

The 'painful adjustments' for 'large numbers of persons' appear to continue unabated after more than 50 years of 'development'. The regime of development

makes large numbers of people invisible, mainly the poor, the disinherited and
the dispossessed. 'Development refugees' – poor people who are 'involuntarily
displaced' (often by force) and resettled to make way for the construction of
dams, roads, ports and other infrastructure projects – also suffer violations of
their human rights. The numbers are staggering: some reports claim more than
10 million people worldwide are forcibly displaced each year (McDowell,
2003). In a review conducted in 2000 of World Bank-funded projects another
report found that 2.6 million individuals were 'adversely affected' in ongoing
Bank projects. Roy (2001) estimates that 30 to 50 million people have lost their
traditional lands as a result of large-scale dam projects in India since the 1950s.
A single project, the Sardar Sarovar dam project, will displace 400 000 tribal
people once it is completed. A more conservative estimate puts the number of
people displaced in India as a result of development projects between 1951 and
1990 at 21.3 million people. Forty percent of 'displacees' were indigenous
peoples, who make up 8 percent of India's population, while another 40 percent
were from other rural poor communities (Fernandes, 2000). As is the case in all
developing countries the dispossessed poor do not participate in any of the
benefits: the electricity generated by the dams is for use by city dwellers and
the water for irrigating large industrial agriculture farms. As Randeria (2007:
8) observes, the Indian state 'is selectively strong in advancing the interests of
the privileged, but strategically weak in fulfilling even its constitutional duties
towards the poor … The privatization of the commons forces the poor to pay
the price for advancing the public good.'

And as for the 'bonds of caste, creed and race' having to burst, the opposite
is true: there is strong evidence that development projects are frequently used
by governments to deliberately target ethnic minorities and indigenous communities, especially in cases where there are existing conflicts between separatist
groups and governments. 'Development cleansing' or 'ethnic cleansing in dis-
guise' has been documented in Tibet, Colombia, Sudan, the Philippines and
Angola among other places (McDowell, 2003; Pettersson, 2002; Rajagopal,
2001). The international legal status of these 'internal refugees' is also in some
doubt: some researchers argue that development refugees face similar risks to
refugees escaping conflict zones (Cernea and McDowell, 2000) while others
claim that there are significant differences between the experiences of conflict
refugees and development refugees (Scudder, 1993; Turton, 1996). This distinction is not just academic: responsibilities for reparation and resettlement need
to be clarified and legal liabilities clearly established if the human rights for
displaced populations are to be protected. Exporting 'free market democracy'
has also led to social unrest and disruption in many parts of the world, accompanied by violence directed at ethnic groups, so-called 'market-dominant
minorities' in South East Asia, Latin America, Africa and post-Soviet Russia
(Chua, 2004). This 'subjective violence' tends to grab headline news with little

or no analysis of the structural violence of global capitalism that creates the conditions for subjective violence as well as vast numbers of excluded and dispensable people (Balibar, 1997, cited in Zizek, 2006). National and international efforts are made to make the agents of subjective violence accountable and brought to justice whereas agents of structural violence – global institutions, transnational corporations and governments – often escape scrutiny.

We have seen earlier in this chapter how privatization of the commons through corporate control of natural resources can destroy livelihoods. The collusion of local states is instrumental in the battle over natural resources. For instance, a 1975 Philippine government advertisement placed in *Fortune* magazine declared: 'To attract companies like yours ... we have felled mountains, razed jungles, filled swamps, moved rivers, relocated towns ... all to make it easier for you and your business to do business here' (cited in Korten, 1995). The effects of creating a business-friendly climate are often violent, leading to loss of life and livelihoods, which are fundamental human rights. For instance, a combination of trade liberalization in agriculture (agriculture is 'liberalized' in the poorer countries and protected in the richer countries) and the failure of genetically modified seeds have been linked to a 260 percent increase in suicide rates of farmers in India (Milmo, 2005). More than 4000 farmers have committed suicide in the southern state of Andhra Pradesh since the imposition of agricultural reforms. Roy (2001: 46) claims that:

> India's rural economy which supports 700 million people, is being garroted. Farmers who produce too much are in distress, farmers who produce too little are in distress, and landless agricultural laborers are out of work as big estates and farms lay off their workers. They're all flocking to already overcrowded cities in search of employment.

The imposition of neoliberal regimes in the 'Third World' allows people to enter political life only as consumers, often excluding the poor from participating in any benefits and leading to even more impoverishment of the rural poor as a result of environmental degradation and loss of access to natural resources. For instance, in a speech introducing economic reforms the then prime minister of India observed:

> The crust consists of about six crore [60 million] people, who do not need to be canvassed about economic reform. The next layer contains about 25–30 crore [250–300 million] people belonging to the middle class, who are beginning to appreciate the benefits of liberalization. It is the next segment, of 55–60 crore [550–600 million] of lower income and poor people who remain unappreciative of the changes in the economy. (Kothari, 1997: 51)

The 'unappreciative' people, making up the majority, are the rural and urban poor, tribals, traditional fisherfolk, artisans and small farmers. These reforms were also essentially undemocratic in the sense that parliamentary approval was sought for economic policies already in place, thus bypassing a majority of the population (Mitra and Singh, 1999). One of the consequences of these reforms was the displacement of rural communities and erosion of their rights to common property resources while securing the interests of foreign and domestic investors (Randeria, 2007). As Kothari (1997) argues, 'it is no longer the poor that are being taken for granted, but rather deliberately excluded and considered dispensable under a political and economic regime that legitimizes poverty and destitution'. Measurement of world poverty by global organizations like the World Bank and IMF do not take into account the effects of macroeconomic policies on poor communities. The obsession is with income poverty, how many billions or millions live on a dollar or two dollars a day. What is not addressed is the capability of the poor to escape the poverty trap by obtaining access to education, health care and housing. If poverty is a deprivation of basic capabilities, as Amartya Sen claims (1999), and capabilities are related to human rights (Sengupta, 2002) then destruction of capabilities whether as a result of structural adjustment programs or loss of livelihood by local villagers due to oil drilling and mining or displacement of communities as a result of infrastructure projects is a breach of human rights. The problem of course is that the chief guarantor of these rights, the state, is often responsible for violating them, along with the global organizations that drafted these rights and the corporations that are signatories to them.

The new economic doctrine in the postcolonial era also requires the complicity of the political elites in the former colonies. Ong (2005) develops the notion of 'graduated sovereignty' to describe how some countries in South East Asia, notably the so-called 'Asian tigers', embraced the global market with a combination of governmental political strategies and military repression. Her research on globalization in Indonesia and Malaysia showed that the interaction between states and transnational capital resulted in a differential state treatment of the population already fragmented by race, ethnicity, gender, class and region as well as a reconfiguration of power and authority in the hands of transnational corporations operating in special export processing zones. The neoliberal turn in these regions follows a different trajectory where the interplay of market versus state results in differing levels of sovereignty: some areas of the economy have a very strong state presence and, in other areas, markets and foreign capital rule. State sovereignty is dispersed because global markets and capital with the collusion of governments create states of exception where coercion, violence and killings occur. State repression against rebel populations and separatist movements is often influenced by market forces: as Ong (2005) argues, territories are cleared of rebels ('outlawed citizens') to make way for logging concessions, petroleum pipelines, mines and dams. Thus, 'democratic rights are confined to a political sphere' while there are continuing forms of domination, exploitation and violence in other domains (Wood, 2003: 80). Accountability, in this complex web of interrelationships between international organizations, transnational corporations, NGOs and nation states, becomes an illusory concept as different actors embedded in 'legal pluralities and overlapping sovereignties play an endless game of passing the blame' (Randeria, 2007: 1) in which states blame the draconian measures of the WTO/IMF/World Bank triad for unpopular economic policies, which in turn blame states for not implementing social safety nets, while transnational corporations grow from strength to strength as a result of international trade policies and agreements as well as weakened state control over resources.

High-profile protests by activist groups have forced international lenders to specify resettlement and displacement conditions that borrowing governments are supposed to follow, but monitoring the resettlement process is often left to local governments who more often than not ignore these conditions. Also, governments are increasingly looking to private investors or public–private partnerships to fund infrastructure projects, as the Indian government did when the World Bank withdrew funding from India's mega-dam project as a result of protests by NGOs and activist groups. Resettlement arrangements are not always mandatory in these privately funded projects although some transnational corporations are now taking direct responsibility for resettlement and rehabilitation of people who are directly impacted by their projects. And recent attempts by the World Bank and nation states to be more transparent and inclusive in the resettlement process by involving NGOs simply result in a diversion of responsibilities to NGOs, as has happened with the Bank-funded Mumbai Urban Transport Project where the responsibility to resettle 100 000 displaced people was shifted to NGOs, which bore the brunt of the criticism (Randeria, 2007). In general, displacement and resettlement whether conducted by governments or the private sector have resulted in an erosion of human rights, entrenched poverty and caused immense social and cultural dislocation. Compensation payments and rehabilitation programs have not addressed the problems created by displacement, and researchers have documented loss of land and livelihoods, education, declining mental and physical health, food insecurity, social dislocation and even premature death (Fernandes, 2000; Downing, 1996; McDowell, 2003; Scudder, 1993).

The actual social impact of corporate human rights policies is limited because of the vagueness in many of the aims, the lack of any credible enforceability mechanism, differing corporate priorities in addressing human rights, and the political, economic and social conditions in many Third World regions where TNCs operate. Typically, corporations tend to respond to human rights violations that draw media and public attention, often publicized by NGOs, or at least corporations are careful to be seen to address them while other corporate abuses escape scrutiny. Human rights discourses can at times only provide a restricted view of the problem and thus provide suboptimal solutions. Despite the focus on rights to life, livelihood, occupational health and safety, and social and cultural rights, the right to property remains paramount, which tends to restrict the range of socio-economic and political choices in developing countries, all in the name of 'rights' (Kennedy, 2002). Because states are the ultimate arbiters of human rights they sometimes use human rights discourse against their own citizens, a hangover from the old colonial days of 'civilizing the natives'. In analysing the Chiapas rebellion in Mexico, Speed and Collier (2000) describe how the Mexican government used human rights discourse to undermine indigenous efforts to gain autonomy. The government strategy of arresting indigenous leaders for allegedly violating human and constitutional rights of the community resembled earlier colonial modes of governance where 'repugnant' native practices were banned in the name of civilization. As a result human rights discourses can serve to insulate the economy without challenging the status quo and existing arrangements of wealth and power by focusing instead on the institutional processes and remedies for human rights violations. As Kennedy (2002: 109) states, 'however useful saying "that's my right" is in extracting things from the state, it is not good for extracting things from the economy, unless you are a property holder. Indeed, a practice of rights claims against the state may weaken the capacity of people to challenge economic arrangements.'

The Western liberal origins of the international human rights movement are part of the problem according to Kennedy because the problems of the liberal tradition are transposed on to the human rights movement. Western enlightenment notions that inform relationships between society, economy, polity and the law privilege a particular worldview that constrains political choices in other regions of the world to 'local/traditional' and 'international/modern' categories, which impoverishes local political discourse while selling the illusion that 'rights' can lead to emancipation. Kennedy (2002: 115) argues:

> Human rights encourages people to seek emancipation in the vocabularies of reason rather than faith, in public rather than private, in law rather than politics, in politics rather than economics ... Human rights is too quick to conclude that emancipation means progress forward from the natural passions of politics into the civilized reason of law. Work to develop law comes to be seen as an emancipatory end in itself leaving the human rights movement too ready to articulate problems in political terms and solutions in legal terms. Precisely the reverse would be more useful. The posture of human rights as an emancipatory political project ... repackaged as a form of knowledge delegitimizes other political voices and makes less visible the local cultural and political dimensions of the human rights movement itself.

In order to make visible the cultural and political dimensions a shift in the unit of analysis is required. It is unlikely that any radical revision of sustainable development or human rights will emerge from organizations given how this discourse is constructed at higher levels of the political economy. For any such rethinking to occur, a more critical approach to organization theory is required and new questions need to be raised not only about the ecological and social sustainability of business corporations but of the political economy. Corporations, governments and non-state entities do not exist in isolation but are actors in a much larger and more complex political economy. If corporations are to address social problems like poverty, health and education, current theoretical approaches like CSR and stakeholder theory still fall short because of the continued emphasis on the corporate bottom line. Focusing our analysis at the level of the individual corporation can only produce limited outcomes restricted to win–win situations. Perhaps structural changes are required at the level of the political economy to produce more comprehensive and sustainable social outcomes. If there is a normative basis for stakeholder theory then it becomes important to understand how societal norms are formed. The dynamics of power between corporations, governments, international institutions, NGOs and other societal interests produce a particular form of political economy as well as the conditions and norms for participating in that economy. We will explore in the next chapter the role of the economic in constructing the social and the inclusions and exclusions that result.

8. The political economy of CSR

At the level of people, the system isn't working. (James Wolfensohn, 1999, former President, World Bank)

Wolfensohn made this statement in the aftermath of the Seattle riots during the 1999 World Trade Organization meetings. It is a remarkable statement, especially coming from the leader of one of the most powerful global institutions that has set the development agenda for the globe for more than 50 years. The remark raises the obvious questions: what other level is there, apart from people? And if the 'system' is not working at the 'level of people', at what level and for whom is it working? The World Bank, along with other institutions like the International Monetary Fund and the World Trade Organization, has been accused of pursuing economic growth at the cost of social development in the 'Third World' by many community groups, governments, non-governmental organizations, environmental organizations, activists and even some economists (Adams, 1990; Escobar, 1995; Goldsmith, 1997; Guha and Martinez-Alier, 1997; Jacobs, 1994; Shiva, 1991). And, as Wolfensohn's statement indicates, there seems to be some recognition at the top echelons of the World Bank that the economic development agenda set by the industrialized regions of the world and the institutions they support has had severe social and environmental impacts in the developing world. 'Social development' goals are now de rigueur in all World Bank policies and in recent years it has promoted many international conferences on the topic, commissioned scores of reports on 'social capital' and 'social sustainability', and even withdrawn funding from mega-dam projects because of protests by social and environmental activists (Fine, 2001; Roy, 2001). It appears that the 'social' is making some sort of a comeback at the economic policy-making level, which can have repercussions at the institutional and organizational levels. From the 'growth at all costs' approach of the 1950s and 1960s, the World Bank's rhetoric and language have softened considerably in recent years. Their avowed mission today is to 'fight poverty by stimulating free market democracy' (Wolfensohn, 2002). The private sector has a key role to play in this fight according to Wolfensohn, because most of the infrastructure projects in developing countries (communications, water, energy, roads, housing) are increasingly moving from the public to the private sector. While acknowledging that the private sector does not make investments for 'social purposes', Wolfensohn (2002: 32) envisioned a 'new development regime' that requires 'true worldwide coalition built on the co-operation of the United Nations, governments, development organizations such as the World Bank, the private sector, and civil society' for the global fight against poverty. The neoliberal agenda has transformed notions of poverty from being an unjust outcome of 'the system' to an outcome of inefficiency (and corrupt governments). As Eduardo Galeano (1998: 32) puts it, 'poverty may arouse pity but it no longer causes indignation. People are poor by the law of chance or the hand of fate.' The danger of course is that in this scenario corporations, being more 'efficient' than the public sector, are asked to play the role of governments, which they cannot, given their narrow financial self-interest. Transnational corporations that have tried to do this have faced serious problems as we have seen in the case of the oil and mining industries.

Perhaps a critical look at 'the system' the former president of the World Bank mentions may reveal the limits of what corporations can or cannot do to address social ills. In other words we need to look at the political economy of CSR and examine the relationships between major actors and institutions as well as the structural and discursive mechanisms of power that underlie their relationships. However, I want to use a slightly different lens to examine the political economy of CSR, a more critical lens that goes beyond identifying and testing relationships between different variables in the political economy and instead locates power as the central unit of analysis. This lens will allow us to see that ultimately any discourse about political economy is about social relationships not just relationships between abstract 'variables' like wages, profits, inequalities, consumer spending and the like (Gibson, 1998). As Gibson (1998: 5) argues, to understand the relations of power in a community we need to ask a range of questions: who owns the means of production, the land and mineral rights?

> Who works and who is unemployed? Who distributes the goods? Who profits from production and distribution? Who makes the decisions in the land, the workplace, the school and the home? Who has the power to portray inequality as the natural order of things or socially necessary? Whose values are taken to be second nature, self-evident?

A critical analysis of political economy differs from the dominant discourse of mainstream liberal political economy by problematizing the issue of power and knowledge. It is critical in the sense that instead of describing the prevailing order of the world it seeks to reveal how that order is created and sustained (Cox, 1981: 129). Thus, it is ultimately an analysis of social change, an attempt to re-embed the social in the political economy with the possibility of identifying alternate power-sharing arrangements (Payne, 2005). A critical approach calls for a more nuanced reading of power along with the possibilities of alternative power arrangements as opposed to traditional political economy discourses which conceptualized power in purely materialist terms. We will return to the question of power later in this chapter. In Cox's formulation, a 'method of historical structures' constitutes the political economy, where structures are essentially relationships between material capabilities, ideas and institutions. Configurations of these three forces shape prospects and impose constraints. Material capabilities involve inputs such as natural resources as well as the technology and industrial infrastructure required to transform natural resources into productive and surplus-generating outputs. Ideas refer to commonly held notions about social relations in a particular historical context as well as 'contested ideologies about alternative social orders' (Payne, 2005: 17). Institutions consolidate outcomes of particular configurations of ideas and material capabilities but are themselves the products of particular historical contexts and subject to the same forces of change. Although Cox used the notion of historical structures, his conceptualization was not necessarily structuralist in the strictest sense of the word, but more of a social constructivist approach that recognized that structures were social constructions, or 'persistent social practices, made by collective human activity and transformed by collective human activity' (Payne, 2005: 17). An important implication of Cox's formulation of political economy was its explicit recognition of agency embedded in the structures of political economy rather than privileging notions of structure that deny agency. Prioritizing both structure and agency also meant tapping into a richer methodological vein that allowed both questions of relationships between economic and political variables to be investigated as well as an analysis of the historical structures within which political and economic activity occurs. However, notions of agency that could be imagined in this political economy were bounded because the system provided opportunities as well as imposed constraints – agency was 'bound up' with structures.

According to Payne (2005), four theoretical strands constitute the basis for a critical political economy. First, an analysis of power and hegemony, in particular the Gramscian concept of hegemony as constitutive of both coercive and consensual power, shows how a dominant ideology is established and sustained in a political economy. Second, a critical political economy investigates how governments, global institutions, corporations and transnational managerial elites constitute what Gramsci (1971) called a 'transnational historic bloc' that in the present time has established a particular form of 'neoliberal globalization' (Scholte, 2000). Third, critical political economy analyses the role of the state in an era of neoliberal globalization. The state is a key player in the political economy and, while some theorists believe that the power of the state has greatly diminished in an era of global neoliberalism (Boggs, 1986; Regan, 1998; Rifkin, 1999), others argue that state power in recent years has been redistributed to be 'more tightly connected to the needs and interests of corporations and less so to the public interest [where] the diminishing role of the state in protecting citizens from corporations is accompanied by the expanding role of the state in protecting corporations from citizens' (Bakan, 2004: 154). Fourth, critical political economy in analysing the changing discourses of development goes beyond dependency theories of First and Third World relationships and argues instead that development is a problem for both the industrialized countries and the 'emerging economies'. Thus, analysing how different development strategies are formulated and played out at the international level, the power and politics underlying global development agendas, and how problems of development are articulated and solutions applied becomes a major task of critical political economy. Development strategies are analysed based on the recognition that they are contingent on the particularities of nations and regions as well as power relationships between regional and international actors and institutions. The concept of development in critical political economy has a different universality than that of traditional development theory of modernization or neoliberalism: whereas conventional views of development produced a universalism based on the commonality of the solution, critical political economy proposes a universalism based on the commonality of the problem (Payne, 2005). Thus, the key research agenda for critical political economy focuses on strategy, structure, agency and context. It examines the range of development strategies that are formulated and implemented by powerful global institutions whose structural power is balanced with the agential powers of states and societies historically situated in a world order, that encompasses different forms of hegemonies (Payne, 2005: 45).

In his analysis of macroeconomic country data and the functioning of global institutions like the United Nations, World Bank, International Monetary Fund and World Trade Organization, Payne (2005: 237) found a 'complex pattern of structured inequalities'. These institutions inevitably protected the interests of the wealthier nations of the world either by the way they were structured (the voting mechanisms of the World Bank and IMF for example) or by means of gentle and not so gentle coercion, threats of sanctions, and promises of sweeteners to dissenting countries in WTO negotiations. The G7 countries (Canada, France, Germany, Italy, Japan, the United Kingdom and the United States) by virtue of having a majority of votes determine World Bank policies and rules. However, they are not bound by the rules they create since they are creditor, not debtor, countries. Borrowing countries unable to influence the normative frameworks of the World Bank and the IMF invariably have to comply with stringent conditions that raise the cost of borrowing, which is ultimately borne by their already impoverished citizens (Randeria, 2007).

Inequality is not an antecedent or consequence of the global politics of development; rather it is 'fundamentally constitutive of contemporary global geopolitics' (Payne, 2005: 245). Inequalities in structural power also imply inequalities in agential power, which constrain a country's capacity to meet its preferred development goals. To borrow an analogy from strategic management, a resource-based view of global development shows that some countries have limited strategic capabilities not because they are classified as underdeveloped by UN indicators but because they have unequal access to development resources. This limits their ability to engage with global institutions and fight for a place at the dining table of global politics. What political economy lacks, as does the management discipline, is a comprehensive analysis of the 'hierarchies of power' (Mittelman, 2000: 5) that embed the global politics of unequal development. These hierarchies of power in contemporary political economy can be described as a 'new imperialism' (Harvey, 2003). Imperialism has been conceptualized in a variety of ways, primarily using a political framework. For instance, imperialism described theories and practices developed by a dominant metropolitan center to rule distant territories, by force, by political means or by economic, social and cultural dependence. Doyle (1986: 45) defines empire as 'a relationship, formal or informal, in which one state controls the effective political sovereignty of another political society. It can be achieved by force, by political collaboration, by economic, social or cultural dependence.' Colonialism, which is almost always a consequence of imperialism, involves the establishment of settlements on outlying territories. The traditional politics of power, i.e. military strength, diplomacy and weapons development, have evolved into an age of 'geo-economics' where winners and losers in the global economy are created by state-assisted private entities (Luttwak, 1999). Political and military imperialism shows itself clearly: the problem lies in articulating the different guises of imperialism in liberal 'free' market economies. Thus, if imperialism is to be viewed as a fundamental set of economic relations, then examining the range of relations (such as the relationship between nation states, international institutions and transnational corporations) becomes an important task in order to uncover the presence of imperialism in current institutional structures and processes. Placed in the context of imperialism, the operation of international finance capital becomes significant in its hegemonic institutionalization through the IMF, World Bank and WTO. Therefore, conflicts between North and South countries in various international trade fora as well as protests by peasants and workers in the poorer countries of the world over property and resource rights are often aptly framed as anti-imperialist struggles.

Thus, imperialism today is inextricably linked with culture, society, economy and polity. Its operation is often masked and, because imperialism has learned to 'manage' things better, it is difficulty to identify its disciplinary power in all its nuances: a power that normalizes and universalizes experiences, while constraining avenues for resistance and change (Patnaik, 1990). Imperialism is operationalized through different kinds of power: institutional power (agencies such as the IMF, WTO and World Bank), economic power (of corporations and nation states) and discursive power that constructs and describes uncontested notions of 'development', 'backwardness' and 'subsistence economies' while disallowing other narratives from emerging. Imperialistic practices such as creation of monopolies or oligopolies, restricted capital flows and rent extraction result from exploiting uneven geopolitical economies by taking advantage of existing structural inequalities in the political economy. Patterns of inequality, concentrations of wealth and zones of poverty are thus created which in turn sustain inequalities in power. Harvey (2003) argues that a key task of states is to create beneficial economic arrangements by leveraging their power, for example using their power to influence policies of the World Bank, IMF and WTO to serve the interests of wealthy member states. This exercise of power in the political economy is represented as being democratic and an example of free trade. Thus, the mission of the World Bank, which is 'to fight poverty by stimulating free market democracy', equates free trade with freedom while eliding inconsistencies between freedoms of self-determination on the one hand and the imposed discipline of free markets and unfair trade on the other. Imperialism in this domain amounts to 'foisting institutional arrangements and conditions upon others, usually in the name of universal wellbeing' (Harvey, 2003: 133).

So how does the 'social' fit into a critical political economy? The term 'social justice' appears frequently in discourses of development, sustainable development, corporate social responsibility and corporate citizenship, as well as in United Nations and World Bank policy documents. If social justice is about reducing inequalities to bring about a 'socially defensible distribution of income' (Galbraith, 2000: xii) and contemporary notions of CSR portray corporations as social change agents capable of solving global poverty (Prahalad and Hammond, 2002) then a critical interrogation of the 'social' as it is currently imagined will allow us to see the various actors, institutions and networks that constitute the social and the dynamics of power that frame these relationships. Prahalad and Lieberthal (1998) claim that the economic power of emerging economies like India and China signals the end of 'corporate imperialism' because to succeed in these markets requires not only cultural sensitivity but a rethinking and reconfiguring of existing business models. While it may be true that TNCs need different strategies to succeed in emerging markets it is rather naïve to think that this implies an end to corporate imperialism. Prahalad and Lieberthal's concept of the 'post-imperialist mindset' fails to recognize that Empire evolved from military conquest to a form of purely economic hegemony where imperialism became an 'economic system of external investment and the penetration and control of markets and sources of raw materials' (Williams, 1976: 159). Rather than signify the 'end of corporate imperialism', globalization and the rise of emerging economies do not merely represent a 'more dispersed base of power and influence' (Prahalad and Lieberthal, 1998) but are a new form of imperialism without colonies but with the collusion of postcolonial political elites in the former colonies where local states have emerged as sites of power for capitalist accumulation. Thus, rather than marking the death of the nation state, the globalization of markets is dependent on a system of multiple states which required a new doctrine of extra-economic coercion along with the manufacture of consent by the various global institutions that determine the parameters of global trade. The political economy of corporate social responsibility is part of this contested terrain.

The 'social' as it is imagined in the social sciences describes mainly how Western societies evolved during modernity. Every society has some sort of moral order regardless of what political formation it takes. Modern visions of moral order in most Western societies provided the normative basis for society on the assumption that society consisted of individuals consenting to a particular form of political governance where individuals had rights and obligations to each other. Society provided common benefits, security being the most important one. Taylor (2002) in developing his notion of the 'social imaginary' states:

> Central to Western modernity is a new conception of the moral order of society ... The mutation of this view of moral order into our social imaginary is the coming to be of certain social forms which are those essentially characterizing Western modernity: the market economy, the public sphere, the self-governing people, among others. The social imaginary is not a set of 'ideas'; rather it is what enables, through making sense of, the practices of a society. (Taylor, 2002: 92)

The modern corporation of course is a key player in the social imaginary. Taylor's concept of the social imaginary provides a way to analyse the macro-level political, economic, institutional and social structures that have shaped Western modernity and the rationality that informs them. Sociologists and social theorists have commented on the increasing penetration of the social by the economic in Western societies, a hallmark of what is commonly referred to as the 'neoliberal' agenda. Rejecting the key tenets of Keynesian economic theory, neoliberalism argued for reducing the role of government in managing the economy and giving greater freedom to business corporations. The main tenets of the neoliberal school of thought are: (1) protection of private capital interests and expansion of the process of capital accumulation by giving greater freedom of actions to corporations and curbing trade unionism; (2) primary reliance on market forces to achieve economic, political and social goals through the homogenization of state policies and reducing the role of states in economic management; and (3) development of a system of transnational institutional authority above and beyond the authority of the state (Boggs, 1986; Fine, 2001; Gills, 2000; Payne, 2005). Perhaps the most significant achievement of the neoliberal agenda was its ability to convert global institutions like the World Bank and IMF and influence their policies, leading to what is commonly referred to as the 'Washington Consensus' that dominated economic development policies in the 1980s and 1990s (Payne, 2005; Williamson, 1993). 'Washington' referred to not just the seat of the US government but also the head offices of the World Bank, IMF, think tanks, corporate lobbyists, investment bankers and the like along with their networks of power that constituted the 'world's de facto capital' (Krugman, 1995: 28). The Washington Consensus was no accident but was the culmination of years of efforts by business and their lobbyists in government to consolidate their power, especially in response to the counterculture movement of the 1960s and 1970s. Just prior to his elevation to the US Supreme Court by then President Richard Nixon, Lewis Powell wrote a memo to the US Chamber of Commerce in which he said:

> The time has come – indeed it is long overdue – for the wisdom, ingenuity and resources of American business to be marshaled against those that would destroy it ... The National Chamber of Commerce should lead an assault upon the major institutions – universities, schools, the media, publishing, the courts – in order to change how individuals think about the corporation, the law, the culture and the individual.

The 'assault' succeeded beyond Powell's wildest dreams – from 60 000 firms in 1972 membership to the Chamber of Commerce rose to 250 000 firms ten years later. The influential Business Roundtable, an organization of CEOs 'committed to the aggressive pursuit of political power for corporations', was founded in 1972 and continues to be a major force today engaged in vigorous lobbying against environmental and other forms of legislation at various regional, national and international levels. Neoliberalism became entrenched in the 1990s and, despite plenty of rhetoric from both sides of the Atlantic about a 'Third Way' that would allegedly keep some of the excesses of unbridled neoliberalism in check, the process of neoliberal globalization was wholeheartedly embraced.

However, there are deep divisions among academics, policy makers, institutional leaders and governments about the benefits of a neoliberal approach to economic development. A high-profile dissenter of neoliberalism came from its own ranks: Joseph Stiglitz, chief economist of the World Bank during 1996–99, criticized neoliberal policies of the World Bank for confusing 'privatization and trade liberalization as ends in themselves rather than as means to more sustainable, equitable and democratic growth'. Stiglitz (1998: 1) also pointed to the lack of attention paid to institutional infrastructure for markets to work better and too narrow a focus on budget deficits and money supply rather than attempts to strengthen local financial institutions. He called for a 'post-Washington Consensus' to overcome the inflexibilities of the neoliberal agenda, details of which were woolly apart from the need to include developing countries in policy development, a 'greater degree of humility', and an acknowledgment that the World Bank and IMF 'do not have all the answers'. Debates over the effectiveness of a neoliberal approach to economic development continue to this day – its proponents cite statistical evidence to claim that both world poverty and world inequality have fallen over the last 20 years (World Bank, 2002b). Others use different calculations to say the opposite – that world poverty and world inequality have increased (Wade, 2004). These scholars cite statistics that show that the distribution of wealth is grossly uneven and net poverty (measured by the change in number of people living on less than \$1 a day during 1987–98) has actually increased in sub-Saharan Africa, South Asia, Latin America, and parts of Europe and Central Asia (World Development Report, 2001). In 2004, about 3 billion people, making up half the world's population, lived on less than \$2 a day. This number will increase by another 2 billion by 2025, of which 1.95 billion will be born in the 'Third World' (World Development Report, 2001). Some claim that people who currently live on \$2 a day lived on much less before economic liberalization and hence they are better off. Profound ideological, theoretical and methodological differences underlie the debate whether economic growth is reducing or increasing poverty and inequality and this question is not going to be resolved easily. However, both sides accept that poverty exists in the world today and that the aim of governments, policy makers and global institutions is to remove poverty. Whether this should or can be a reasonable aim for corporations is open to debate. It is hard to believe that corporate social initiatives in an unregulated market system can reduce this polarity in income distribution. It is harder to believe that the neoliberal market system by itself will deliver social justice through the actions of private entities like business corporations; it cannot simply because it is not designed to do so.

Several environmental economists, social analysts and policy makers believe that ultimately the model of exponential growth will come up against at least three kinds of ecological limits: population limits, resource limits and pollution limits (Guha and Martinez-Alier, 1997; Hawken, 1995; Taylor, 1978). When these limits will be reached is a matter of speculation – the Club of Rome's prediction that these limits would be reached by the end of the twentieth century was premature, as technological advances increased efficiencies in energy production and use. However, most analysts seem to agree that the current pattern of growth is unsustainable. To move towards what Taylor (1978) calls a 'steady state society', economic systems will have to recognize and operate within these limits. While current discourses of sustainable development do recognize environmental and social consequences of economic growth, they still operate within the economic growth paradigm, only it is recast as 'sustainable' growth with little information as to how sustainable patterns will be achieved in the current system (Banerjee, 2003). There is also the problem of reaching agreement on global environmental or social principles: the breakdown of several international meetings in recent years and the problems in ratifying the Kyoto Protocol indicate that the so-called North–South divide is still quite deep despite more than 50 years of development.

According to Taylor (1978), the major challenge to a steady state society is 'intolerable inequality', which is made 'provisionally tolerable only by rapid growth'. The question is what can corporations and the private sector do to address this 'intolerable inequality' and how can they work toward the goal of a 'socially defensible distribution of income' (Galbraith, 2000: xii)? The answer is very little, given the structure and purpose of the modern corporation, as we have discussed in earlier chapters. This does raise serious problems because, if in a neoliberal economy governments are spending less on public and social welfare and the market system is not designed to address these issues, the onus seems to fall on corporations, which as we have seen earlier can only produce limited outcomes.

Privatization is a key tenet of the neoliberal agenda and is proceeding at a rapid pace in the developing economies of Asia, South America, Eastern Europe and Africa. In Latin America for example it is estimated that more than 2000 government industries were sold off between 1985 and 1992, many of them below their market value to private buyers 'with connections' to the military and US corporate and government interests (Grandin, 2006). The debates around privatization in these regions follow a similar pattern: the anti-privatization lobby bemoaning the sale of public assets to multinational companies and the pro-privatization lobby celebrating the end of large, inefficient, loss-making public sector undertakings and promising a leaner and more efficient sector. It is true that many of the large public sector undertakings in India, for example, were mismanaged and ran up huge losses. But it was also true that the public sector in India, as in several developing countries, had clear social goals: to provide employment and to contribute to education and training for disadvantaged populations, and to social welfare in general. Owing to a variety of factors, not least the pressures from the IMF's infamous structural adjustment programs, these industrial sectors were opened to privatization. Whether privatization does benefit the poor and deliver social justice in terms of reducing inequality and providing basic services like clean drinking water, health and education remains to be seen.

While the jury is still out on the decision about the overall benefits of the privatization process, current evidence indicates that a small minority enjoy the benefits (Fine, 1997; Harvey, 2005; Nash, 2001; World Development Report, 2001). There are a few case studies that have documented negative economic, environmental and social effects of development projects on indigenous communities (Banerjee, 2000; Nash, 2001). While privatization may have increased efficiencies in production, there is ample evidence to show that in Britain and South Africa, for example, the privatization of utilities 'according to an entrepreneurial logic meant a radical transformation in the dominant pattern of social relations and a redistribution of assets that increasingly favored the upper rather than the lower economic classes' (Harvey, 2005: 158). The privatization of water in Africa and South America is a case in point: in almost every case where water was privatized the poorer segments of society ended up not only paying higher

prices for water but paying with their lives as well. In South Africa during
2002–03 more than 100 000 people were infected with cholera leading to the
deaths of 200 people after the South African government (following World Bank
'recommendations') denied water and sanitation services to thousands of citizens in KwaZulu-Natal province who were too poor to pay their water bills
(Barlow and Clarke, 2002). World Bank water policies encourage 'cost recovery'; however, the problem is that corporate costs are recovered at the expense
of people who are denied access to clean water and sanitation. Race and class
also determine who suffers, who lives and who dies: in South Africa 600 000
white farmers consume 60 percent of the country's water supplies for irrigation
while 15 million black people have no access to clean water (Barlow and Clarke,
2002). Water tariffs rose 300 percent between 1994 and 1999 as a result of privatization and cost recovery stipulations laid down by the World Bank, with an
estimated 10 million people experiencing cut-offs in their water supply (Mc-
Donald and Pape, 2002; Mehta, 2006). The right to clean water, enshrined as a
human right, is violated by the state, the very institution that is supposed to
guarantee its citizens' rights, while South African and transnational corporations
reaped the benefits of the government's privatization strategies. A similar situation exists in the *maquiladoras* of Mexico where clean water is scarce because
it is mainly reserved for use by foreign-owned industries in the region. And
when Bolivia's economy was 'structurally adjusted' by the World Bank, one of
the conditions was to sell off the national water company, which the Bolivian
government did to Bechtel. Not long after the purchase water bills rose by 200
percent for an already impoverished citizenry, with the government even attempting to outlaw the collection of rainwater for personal use. Extended
protests by the people forced the Bolivian government to take over water supply
again, leading Bechtel to exit Bolivia, albeit with a $25 million payout (Grandin,
2006).

   There seems to be general agreement among social theorists that changes in
the economic environment over the last 20 years have produced significant social effects, effects that have been unevenly distributed across the globe. It also
appears that a neoliberal agenda is firmly in place (at least for now). The questions we want to ask are how and why did this come about? What are the
consequences for corporations? What are the consequences for different segments of society in different regions of the world? The work of Fine (1997,
1999, 2001) and Boggs (1986, 1997) provides some insights into the complex
dynamics that frame the interactions between the social and the economic. Both
Fine, a political economist, and Boggs, a sociologist, have written extensively
on the incursion of the economic into the social. Fine (2001) argues that the
emergence of what he calls the 'information-theoretic' approach to economics
marked a departure from conventional economics in the sense that its reach
extended to the non-economic as well. This 'colonization of the social sciences'

gave rise to a variety of sub-disciplines within the field including new political economics, new institutional economics, new development economics and new household economics (Fine, 2001: 10). For example, the editors of a volume profiling the work of Nobel Prize-winning economist Gary Becker state in their introduction:

> Many activities thought to be noneconomic in nature ... are actually economic problems. Economic theory can thus help explain phenomena traditionally located outside the scope of economics, in the areas of law, sociology, biology, political science, and anthropology ... The development of this economic imperialism ... is another significant contribution that Becker has made to modern economics. (Febrero and Schwartz, 1995: xx–xxi, cited in Fine, 2001)

Becker's work redefined the social as a form of the economic where the role of states was to govern the economic for the social, in contrast to the then West German model of a 'government of the social in the name of the economic' (Gordon, 1991: 43). Sociologists and social theorists have questioned the methodological reductionism that a primarily economic approach to social issues entails. Studying social relations requires different modes of inquiry because we are not dealing with markets but with people (Emerson, 1987; Fine, 2001). Traditional concepts of civil society and the public sphere were now interpellated by the neoclassical economic paradigm, which is ironic considering that these concepts first emerged because of the perceived shortcomings of economic models (Edwards and Foley, 1998; Fine, 2001). The dominance of the economic paradigm in the social sciences was also reflected in the consolidation of the market system in the global economy through the emergence and deployment of a particular kind of corporate rationality. Inevitably, corporate rationality overrules, co-opts or marginalizes interests that could threaten corporate advantage, and this polity–economy nexus penetrates civil society and the public sphere in more comprehensive ways resulting in technocratic imperatives dictating not only the functioning of the workplace but also 'education, housing, health care, cultural consumption, food production, and even neighborhood life' (Boggs, 1986: 28). Through the dynamics of discursive and institutional power, this market–state system positions itself 'above' society and its competing social forces while obscuring its key role in the accumulation process. As Fine (2001: 199) argues, despite the rhetoric of democracy and participation such a system is primarily about 'participation from below imposed from above'. The language of neoliberalism perpetuates this illusion by obscuring the role of wealth and capital – for instance Galbraith (1999) notes how the term 'capitalism' is no longer popular in the business press and policy documents of national governments and global organizations, having been replaced by the 'market system' or 'market forces'. The result is a diffusion of responsibility and accountability that minimizes the role of capital and wealth and focuses instead on the apparently impersonal nature of the market, giving the powerful interests that control capital a form of 'functional anonymity'.

One way to theorize the complex interactions between society, the economy and the polity and understand the rationality that produces particular institutions, mechanisms, knowledge and practices is to examine the interplay of different forms of power. In her analysis of the global environmental movement, McAfee (1999) describes three types of power that shaped meanings, practices and knowledge of concepts like 'nature', 'the environment' and 'biological diversity'. She describes how the *institutional power* of the World Bank and multilateral environmental institutions, the *economic power* of the 'advanced capitalist states and transnational corporations', and the *discursive power* of the 'environmental-economic paradigm' constructed particular notions of biological diversity that permitted its international trade as a commodity and the control of its accumulation and exchange (McAfee, 1999: 135). This process of 'green developmentalism' (McAfee, 1999) serves to further marginalize the poorer countries ('cash poor but natural resource rich') of the world by continuing the transfer of material and natural resources from developing regions to the industrialized countries thus reinforcing colonial modes of control (Adams, 1990; Banerjee, 2003; Escobar, 1995; Goldsmith, 1997; Jacobs, 1994; Shiva, 1993).

It is the concept of discursive power that is of interest to us in explaining how concepts of the social and economic are discursively produced at the political level and the practices and policies they shape at the meso- and micro-levels. While institutions and economic wealth are also sources of power, an analysis of the power of discourse allows us to see how social and economic domains are formed and transformed. Institutions are not immutable; they can be and have been transformed. And if we are to recover the social from the economic it is at the level of political economy that interventions need to be made because the political economy is informed by a particular kind of rationality that serves certain interests which are enacted through macro-social developmental issues and policies of global institutions like the World Bank, International Monetary Fund and World Trade Organization as well as micro-level strategies of corporations, non-governmental organizations and other agencies. My analysis of the power dynamics that underlie the politicization of the social and economic is based on Foucauldian notions of discourse, power/knowledge and governmentality.

Organization theorists have used Foucault's insights to problematize notions of subjectivity and power (Banerjee, 2003; Burrell, 1988; Knights, 1992; Knights and Willmott, 1989); human resource management practices (Townley, 1997); performance appraisal (Findlay and Newton, 1997); managerial competence (Du Gay *et al.*, 1996); and careers as labor process discipline (Grey, 1994; see also Newton, 1998, for a review of Foucauldian studies in organization and management theory). Foucault's analysis of discourse examined how the circulation of power produces a power/knowledge nexus where the effect of power relations on society is dependent on the production of discourses of truth through the production of knowledge (Clifford, 2001). Thus, 'we are subjected to the production of truth through power and we cannot exercise power except through the production of truth' (Foucault, 1980: 3). For Foucault, power was not something that resided in particular things but something that operated in a network of relationships (Burrell, 1988) that permeated all levels of social existence including private spheres of family and sexuality as well as the public spheres that constituted the legal, political and economic systems (Hall, 1997). The production of knowledge is intimately connected with questions of power through discourse, which he defined as a 'group of statements which provide a language for talking about – way of representing knowledge about – a particular topic at a particular historical moment' (Foucault, 1972: 143). Discourse, for Foucault, was not purely a mode of speech that presupposed a founding subject. It provided the very 'space of emergence and determined the possibilities for speech and speaking subjects' (Clifford, 2001: 182). Thus, notions of 'agency' and 'structure' are discursively constituted, allowing certain forms of agency to be created and denying the possibility of others within a discourse (Clegg, 1998). Rather than focus on notions of 'truth' or 'falsehood', the focus shifts to how certain forms of representation come to be constituted and accepted along with an analysis of the powers of representation and the ways in which that representation takes place (Clegg, 1998; Hall, 1997). This does not mean that truth does not exist but that truth is a function of power relations and is a place of struggle and contestation, what Foucault calls a 'truth effect'. Thus, 'knowledge linked to power, not only assumes the authority of "the truth" but has the power to make itself true' (Hall, 1997: 49).

Foucault's (1980) analysis of power reveals how disciplinary practices constitute the boundaries of discourse, determining 'what is and what is not, what can be done and what cannot, what should be and what should not' (Clegg, 1989: 142). These practices are discursive in the sense that they constitute and are constituted by knowledge appearing as specific institutional and organizational practices. They become discursive because they reproduce knowledge through practices that are made possible by the structural assumptions of that knowledge (Clegg, 1989). The rules generated by discourse thus become 'natural' rules or norms. The power of science and the scientific method in everyday discourse is an example of how science normalizes social and cultural realms, not because of the superior rationality of science but because of its procedures of normalization arising from its disciplinary power. This disciplinary power is not located at a 'legitimate' site of sovereign or state but transmits itself through a complex system of institutions, regulations, texts, policies and practices signifying not relations of sovereignty but relations of domination – what Foucault describes as 'subjugation through a constitution of subjects'. Thus,

> [Disciplinary power] is a mechanism of power that permits time and labor, rather than wealth and commodities, to be extracted from bodies. It is a type of power which is constantly exercised by means of surveillance rather than in a discontinuous manner through levies and obligations over time. It presupposes a tight knit grid of material coercions rather than the physical existence of a sovereign. This new type of power, which can no longer be formulated in terms of sovereignty is one of the great inventions of bourgeois society, a fundamental instrument in the constitution of industrial capitalism and the type of society that is its accompaniment. (Foucault, 1980: 105)

Not only are individual social and political identities and subjectivities produced under this power/knowledge discourse, but the knowledge produced also informs institutional and social practices. Truth does not reside outside power but results from the nexus of power and knowledge. Thus, every society is governed by a 'regime of truth', consisting simultaneously of 'the type of discourse which it accepts and makes function as true as well as political structures whose function it is to articulate such discourses in concrete forms into the social body resulting in practices that delimit space, determine possibilities, erect hierarchies and define individuals' (Foucault, 1980: 131). For example, definitions of 'progress', 'development', 'biodiversity' and 'natural resources' become truth effects that obscure the power relationships that govern the definitional process.

Foucault develops his notion of disciplinary power to explain the different mechanisms that have penetrated state apparatuses, resulting in a shift in the traditional authority of the state from sovereignty to what he calls governmentality emerging from a broader meaning of government. Foucault's use of the term 'government' is more complex than its common understanding of mechanisms of state apparatus or political parties. Governmentality is simultaneously about individualizing and totalizing, which is a process of defining what practices, mechanisms and institutions are needed for an individual and for societies to be governed or made governable, a 'conduct of conduct' aimed at shaping and guiding the conduct of populations (Foucault, 1979: 100). Governmentality produces a particular form of political rationality, a technology of power that

> isolates the economy as a specific sector of reality and political economy as the science and technique of intervention of the government in that field of reality. It is formed by the institutions, procedures, analyses and reflections, the calculations and tactics that allow the exercise of this very specific albeit complex form of power, which has as its target population, as its principal form of knowledge political economy and as its essential technical means apparatuses of security. (Foucault, 1979: 102)

Governmentality is not about the institutional power of states; rather it is a relational and discursive power that permeates society and directs social arrangements and informs juridical, legislative and democratic institutions. The problem was to develop a broader political framework, beyond legal, juridical or social contracts, that would incorporate individuals' economic agency within a governable order (Gordon, 1991). Classical political economy focused primarily on markets as autonomous systems without addressing the legal and institutional dimensions of the market. Governmentality was about the introduction of economy into political practice where the role of governments was to 'exercise power in the form of economy' (Foucault, 1979: 92). Civil society and the public spheres are also informed by this rationality whereby liberal tenets in Western societies assume an autonomous rationality to the processes of civil society. Gordon (1991: 42) describes this form of 'social government' as:

> an economy of the transeconomic, a methodology which straddles the formal bounds of the market. Thus, civil society becomes the concrete ensemble within which economic men [*sic*] need to be positioned in order to be made adequately manageable. It recasts the interface between state and society in the form of something like a second-order market of governmental goods and services. It becomes the ambition of neo-liberalism to implicate the individual citizen, as player and partner, into this market game. In liberal political economy discourse the social problem was not the anti-social effects of the economic market, but the anti-competitive effects of society.

Despite the rhetoric of stakeholder engagement and human rights, governmentality informs the political economy of CSR through a technology of power that governs the social in the name of the economic leading to an outcome where profits are privatized while losses become socialized. Recent debates about the role of public sector organizations seem to underscore Gordon's argument. The banking and financial sector in France, for example, was seen as being 'socially oriented'. Several multinational banks and financial institutions have argued against this orientation by claiming that the social role of the banking sector produces 'competitive distortions' (Rhodes and van Apeldoorn, 1998), citing the repeated bailing out of French public sector banks by the state. The future of public sector banks in France will depend on how discourses of 'social orientation' and 'competitive distortions' are played out based on their underlying power dynamics. A recent World Bank report on the state of the railways in India made a similar point, claiming that the poor productivity of that sector was due to its 'social' role, which the Bank described as 'bad economics'. The report called for the Indian government to 'resolve the conflict between railways' role as a commercial organization and one to serve social obligations' (*India Network News Digest*, 2005).

The 'exercise of power in the form of economy' is not the sole prerogative of governments but emanates from a loosely woven web of interconnected actors and institutions whose interests sustain existing material inequalities and forms of political power while allowing certain forms of resistance to emerge. The power, flexibility and global reach of capital have become even more pronounced over the last decade as a particular kind of corporate rationality further consolidated the market system in the global economy. This has resulted in a convergence of political, economic, military and institutional power where governments have either been complicit with transnational corporations in violating the human rights of their citizens in the name of development or been overthrown when they have attempted to resist the incursion of foreign capital. The involvement of US multinationals along with the CIA in fomenting military and political coups in Latin America, notably United Fruit Inc. in Guatemala and Colombia, and ITT in Chile and Brazil, is well documented (Dosal, 1993; Grandin, 2006). Millions of dollars were spent by the US government to destabilize Chile in the 1970s – on learning that Chile had elected a Marxist president in 1970, Nixon instructed the CIA to 'make their economy scream' in an effort to 'smash Allende' (Grandin, 2006). Corporate strategies to ensure 'safe havens' for their investment included obtaining US government support for dictatorial regimes, violent reprisals using state military and police to suppress dissent, and bribes and kickbacks to political elites. Transnational corporations were clearly complicit in the use of violence in these sites: Colombia in 1929, when the military gunned down striking United Fruit workers killing at least 400 (Kepner and Soothill, 1935), and the US-backed military coup in Guatemala in 1954 where more than 200 union leaders were killed are two of the more widely publicized cases involving violence and multinational capital (Chomsky and Herman, 1979). In a poem about the excesses of the United Fruit Company, the Chilean poet Pablo Neruda lamented:

> ... and Jehovah parceled out the earth
> to Coca-Cola, Inc., Anaconda,
> Ford Motors, and other entities:
> The Fruit Company Inc.
> reserved for itself the most succulent,
> the central coast of my own land,
> the delicate sweet of America.
> It re-christened its territories
> As the Banana Republics ...

In Foucault's sophisticated formulation of power and governmentality, notions of agency and resistance are not given sufficient attention. Agential power, however bounded it may be to structural inequalities, can still provide the space for resistance and perhaps a different configuration of power. Thus, it is important to realize that with power come new spaces of resistance and there are many ongoing battles waged by a variety of groups against powerful multinational corporations. The struggles of the Ogoni people against Shell; protests against World Bank-financed mega-dam projects in India and Latin America; peasant struggles against biopiracy; struggles against genetically modified foods and for recognition of indigenous production systems; conflicts between indigenous communities and logging companies over access to forest reserves; conflicts over land rights between indigenous communities, governments and corporations; political struggles against privatization; labor rights and women's rights movements in developing countries; campaigns to protect biodiversity; and protests against IMF-imposed austerity programs are just a few social movements that are well publicized in the media (Gills, 2000; Harvey, 2003). The power dynamics of these new social movements will determine whether corporate rationality can serve to create a kind of organizational closure around discourses of social and economic development or how these boundaries can be extended. And while it is easier to target abusive practices of multinational corporations, battling the 'regime of truth' that emanates from discursive power is more difficult. Based on the preceding analysis of the multiple sites of power and resistance and the discursive regimes that establish processes of domination and subordination, what are the new ways of theorizing the nature and role of corporations that can have more progressive outcomes for society? What implications arise for the theory of the firm? How do we make corporations more accountable? What are the effective forms of resistance against unbridled corporate power? What changes in the structures and processes in the political economy are required that can enable corporations to become agents for positive social change? I will attempt to explore these questions in the final chapter.

9. Alternate visions

It's not people who aren't credit-worthy. It's banks that aren't people-worthy.
(Muhammad Yunus, Founder, Grameen Bank)

Let us summarize what we have discussed thus far. We started our journey by taking a historical view of the emergence of the modern corporation in the nineteenth century. Early corporations chartered by the British monarchy were key agents that both drove global commerce and established colonies and colonial modes of governance across Asia, Latin America and Africa. In the United States royal charters were transferred to the independent states. Nineteenth-century America witnessed a legal and political revolution driven by powerful interests in the textile, railroad and energy industries that saw corporations free themselves from state control and established as artificial persons with constitutional rights, transforming their role from entities that were created to serve public interests to ones that served the interests of private shareholders. We then discussed the emergence of corporate social responsibility and the theoretical basis of alternate formulations of the corporation, in particular the stakeholder theory of the firm. We discussed the theoretical and practical shortcomings of stakeholder theory as well as the limitations of other discourses like corporate citizenship that attempted to describe the social responsibility of corporations. We described the dilemmas faced by corporations in practicing CSR and identified the limits of win–win situations. We examined the role of corporations in promoting sustainable development and described how environmental and social sustainability became reframed as growth opportunities for corporations, shifting the focus from planetary sustainability to corporate sustainability. We then examined the role of human rights and discussed the opportunities and challenges of employing a human rights approach to corporate social responsibility. We discussed how intellectual property rights regimes when applied to agricultural products through biotechnological patents produce destructive social and environmental effects on rural communities in developing countries. At this point of our analysis it became clear that it is difficult to promote and sustain any meaningful social initiatives at the level of the individual corporation, given the larger political and economic constraints faced by corporations. We then shifted our analysis to the level of political economy to understand how the social became increasingly framed by the economic in a neoliberal political economy and discussed the theoretical basis of a critical political economy where inequality became the

144

central concept in the global politics of development. We discussed how different forms of power – institutional, economic and discursive – produce particular forms of social arrangements of various actors, institutions and networks that constitute a particular image of the 'social' and the inclusions and exclusions that result. We showed how these power relations between the political, economic and social spheres produce a particular form of corporate rationality that determines the boundary conditions of corporate social initiatives. We also examined the structural inequalities between different countries and discussed the role of global institutions like the World Bank, IMF and WTO in the political economy. My basic argument highlights the fundamental weaknesses in theories and practices of corporate social responsibility that limit any attempts at social emancipation. These limits arise because of the structural and discursive effects of power that construct notions of a corporation as a shareholder maximizing entity, create a concept of the social using narrow economic criteria and construct an abstract notion of responsibility that is neither enforceable nor accountable.

Thus, the main conclusions that emerge from a critical analysis of CSR are:

- The corporation in its current form is an inappropriate agent for social change. If corporations are to make meaningful social contributions apart from making profits they will have to be transformed in order to serve society better and become more accountable. Any corporate governance reform within the existing structure and purpose of the corporation will have little impact on improving corporate accountability to society. Corporate governance reforms post-Enron were directed at protecting the interests of shareholders and other primary stakeholder groups like employees or creditors, not the interests of vulnerable communities impacted by socially and environmentally destructive corporate practices. Whether it is increasing accountability of directors, increasing the budget of the Securities and Exchange Commission, making boards independent, making CEOs accountable or even indicting them, all these reforms protect shareholder interests and simply serve to reinforce the shareholder view of the firm. Barring legislation there is no way that a profit-seeking corporation will not engage in environmentally destructive activity as long as that activity is profitable.
- There are no real 'leaders' or meaningful 'best practices' in CSR apart from a preoccupation with win–win situations. The same transnational corporations that are touted as CSR leaders in the business press have been accused of causing environmental destruction and human rights violations.
- The evidence linking CSR with better financial performance is dubious to say the least. All that can be concluded from the empirical evidence is

that companies that say they are socially responsible tend to perform better financially.

- The current neoliberal model represents an economic capture of the social. Economic assumptions of fundamentally competitive social relations can only produce a narrow and self-serving view of corporate social responsibility.
- The same rationality is reflected in the rhetoric of stakeholder theory – the current instrumental and pragmatic approach to stakeholders cannot address social ills in any meaningful way. Stakeholder 'dialogues', public–private 'partnerships' and 'citizenship' behaviors all take place under vastly unequal terms and conditions of power. Despite the important role they play in drawing attention to corporate abuses, NGOs and advocacy groups do not have the power to enforce corporate compliance with voluntary standards and codes of conduct. Stakeholder engagement can be a way for a corporation to deflect attention from its destructive social and environmental impact while gaining legitimacy through publicizing 'dialogue' with NGOs. There is also the danger of co-opting NGOs to the corporate agenda.
- The limits of corporate rationality determine the limits of corporate social responsibility – if a corporation can do good only to help itself do well, there is a profound limit on just how much good it can do. Win–win situations are not sustainable in the long run.
- A similar rationality informs discourses of sustainability. Any activity or transaction is sustainable only if it is profitable for corporations and if it can be transacted through the market. Sustainability of impoverished communities battling with transnational corporations for access to resources necessary for the communities' survival cannot be addressed meaningfully in any framework of corporate sustainability or CSR.
- Voluntary CSR practices such as codes of conduct cannot produce any meaningful social outcomes without regular monitoring and enforcement of labor and environmental standards.
- Socially responsible investment or ethical investment funds cannot address the social and environmental problems facing the world in any meaningful way. Consumer boycotts, despite their effectiveness in drawing public attention to corporate abuses, have little effect on long-term corporate profits. Transnational corporations under attack for their deplorable labor and environmental standards and the subject of several consumer boycotts (Nestlé, Shell and Nike to name a few) continue to be immensely profitable.
- CSR is more beneficial for corporations than for society. Corporations gain enhanced reputation because they are not legally required to document their CSR claims especially if they are made in general and vague

terms, as is normally the case. Avoiding or pre-empting legislation is another benefit that corporations can get from CSR strategies. When it suits them corporations also lobby *for* regulation: for example Shell and BP are lobbying governments for standards and regulations on climate change so that their competitors do not undercut them.

- Environmentally and socially responsible consumption as purely market-based solutions will not lead to sustainable economies. Green consumers represent a very small proportion of consumers, a majority of whom base their purchase decisions on cost, convenience and quality. Switching off the city lights of Paris, London, Berlin and New York for five minutes annually to help prevent global warming is about as effective as Prahalad and Hammond's (2002) prescription to solve global poverty by selling ice cream and cell phones to the poor.

- CSR does not challenge corporate power. Rather it can be seen as an ideological movement that consolidates the power of large transnational corporations. Corporations with high CSR profiles are also seen as being more legitimate partners for governments and businesses in the developing world, and CSR offers a way for transnational corporations to obtain access to emerging markets and the 'bottom of the pyramid' markets in developing countries.

Global organizations like the United Nations, World Bank and International Monetary Fund acknowledge that a majority of the world's people face severe social and economic hardships. These organizations jointly developed seven 'Millennium Development Goals' to address the world's social ills. These goals include: (1) reduce the proportion of people living in extreme poverty by half between 1990 and 2015; (2) enroll all children in primary school by 2015; (3) eliminate gender disparities in primary and secondary education by 2015; (4) reduce infant and child mortality rates by two-thirds between 1990 and 2015; (5) reduce maternal mortality ratios by three-quarters between 1990 and 2015; (6) provide access for all who need reproductive health services by 2015; and (7) implement national strategies for sustainable development by 2005 so as to reverse the loss of environmental resources by 2015 (World Development Report, 2001). The seven goals are 'mutually reinforcing' because they all address different aspects of poverty. The problem of course is a lack of any awareness that poverty is often a direct consequence of the economic policies of the very same organizations that are supposed to fight poverty. There is also a clear expectation that business corporations are 'partners' with global organizations in the fight against poverty. It is difficult to see how corporations in their current form can meaningfully address the Millennium Development Goals given how the social outcomes of contemporary discourses of CSR are limited by the constraints we have discussed earlier. Assuming it is somehow possible for a corporation to overcome financial and economic constraints in its effort to become socially responsible, what would a 'truly responsible' corporation look like? David Korten (1999: 149) offers one view:

> A truly responsible corporation would be one that produces and sells only safe and beneficial products, does not accept government subsidies or special tax breaks, provides secure jobs at a living wage, fully internalizes its environmental and social costs, and does not make any political contributions or otherwise seek to advance legislation or policies contrary to the broader public interest.

Whether such a corporation exists or can exist on this planet is very doubtful. Even if some sovereign power were to mysteriously appear and close down corporations that do not meet Korten's criteria of responsibility, tremendous social, economic and political upheaval would result. That is not a socially responsible outcome either. If we accept Korten's normative view of how a socially responsible corporation should behave the key question is how can such a dramatic and radical behavioral transformation take place? What are the structural conditions, dynamics of power relations, global and local governance mechanisms, institutional arrangements and realignment of actors required that can enable alternate forms of the corporation to emerge? In this chapter I will attempt to explore some alternate visions of the corporation and the political economy in which it must function. If the corporation is constrained in its ability to do social good because of the way it is currently constituted and the norms of the broader political economy in which it must function any alternate visions of a corporation must necessarily involve alternate visions of the economy and polity as well. Thus, we need to look at multiple units of analysis in our search for normative theories and practices that promote social well-being – both normative theories of the corporation and normative theories of the political economy.

Social theorists, management scholars, community groups, activist groups and NGOs have proposed a range of interventions at multiple levels that may redress some of the social ills caused by economic activity and corporate behavior as well as actively promote positive social outcomes. Both specific policy interventions and alternate theorizations of the nature of the firm and the nature of the political economy have been proposed. Social movements like the World Social Forum and other coalitions for social and environmental welfare have called for wide-ranging institutional reform in order to address global poverty, labor conditions, climate change, environmental destruction and biodiversity conservation. At the corporate level, these groups have called for more corporate accountability and democratic control over powerful transnational corporations. For instance, Friends of the Earth, an international environmental NGO, proposed a Framework Convention on Corporate Accountability at the Johannesburg Earth Summit (Bruno and Karliner, 2002). Governments and corporations, not surprisingly, largely ignored the proposal. Key elements of the proposal include:

- Mandatory corporate reporting requirements on environmental and social impacts, and a process for prior consultation with affected communities including environmental and social impact assessment and complete access to information.
- Extended liability to directors for corporate breaches of environmental and social laws and corporate liability for breaches of international laws and agreements.
- Rights of redress for citizens, including access for affected people anywhere in the world to pursue litigation, provisions for stakeholders to legally challenge corporate decisions and legal aid mechanisms to provide public funds to support such challenges.
- Community rights to resources, including indigenous peoples' rights over common property such as forests, fisheries and minerals.
- Veto rights over developmental projects and against displacement and rights to compensation for resources expropriated by corporations.
- Sanctions against corporations for breaching these duties including suspending stock exchange listing, fines and (in extreme cases) revoking the corporation's charter or withdrawal of limited liability status.

These and other alternatives and critiques have been popularized through books and articles in the popular press by a variety of writers and activists like Noreena Hertz, Martin Khor, Naomi Klein, David Korten, George Monbiot, Arundhati Roy and Vandana Shiva. Portrayed in the media (somewhat inaccurately) as being part of the 'anti-globalization movement' these writers offer radical alternatives to neoliberal market fundamentalism. I say somewhat inaccurately because I do not think any of these writers seriously considers rejecting globalization but rather they seek to harness the forces of globalization to promote social justice. And neither do these voices represent a single movement: the so-called anti-globalization movement consists of a diverse group of actors including 'statists' (who seek ways to defend and rebuild the role of the state that has been weakened as a result of neoliberal hegemony); 'alternatives' (who propose localization, smallness and decentralization and have a strong anti-corporate platform); and the 'reformists' (who advocate radical changes in current institutions and policies to address the worst excesses and injustices of globalization) (Green and Griffith, 2002: 55). One can add to this some voices from the established power blocs as well because movements for social change also contain voices from unexpected quarters – from Joseph Stiglitz, once the blue-eyed boy of the neoliberal establishment now considered a traitor to his cause as a result of his trenchant critique of the World Bank and IMF, to ultracapitalists like George Soros and Ross Perrot (both of whom opposed the North American Free Trade Agreement which saw them in the same camp as people like Jeremy Rifkin, the Zapatistas, George Monbiot, Naomi Klien, No-reena Hertz and a variety of green groups and community activists). The philosopher Slavoj Zizek points out that the claim of 'liberal communists' like George Soros, Bill Gates, Thomas Friedman and high-profile CEOs of several transnational corporations is that it is possible to have the 'global capitalist cake (thrive as entrepreneurs) and eat it (endorse the anti-capitalist causes of social responsibility, ecological concern etc)'. Zizek (2006) describes the liberal com-munist doctrine as 'a new, postmodernised version of Adam Smith's invisible hand' where the market and social responsibility are not opposites, but can be united for mutual benefit where the goal is not to earn money, but to change the world (and, as a by-product, make even more money). The enthusiastic endorse-ment by the neoliberal camp of the 'bottom of the pyramid' approach guru C.K. Prahalad exemplifies this win–win perspective of economic and social welfare.

This so-called new paradigm must be viewed with caution. As we have seen earlier there is not much difference between 'structural adjustment policies' and 'poverty reduction strategies' as regards sustaining the coercive and exploitative conditions in which the world's poor survive. The rhetoric of fighting poverty at the global level and engaging with the world's poor at the corporate level elides the key issue of complicity in and responsibility for much of the social and economic suffering in Third World regions. While the World Bank, IMF and WTO publicly proclaim their noble intentions of attacking global poverty, promoting literacy and education and eliminating child labor, their policies have the opposite effect. For instance, following its 'agreement' with the IMF in 1991 the Indian government slashed social spending dramatically in health and educa-tion. This had a direct effect on increasing the rate of child labor because poor families' dependence on child labor increased – child labor grew at an annual rate of 4 percent in the 1990s as the cost of living and unemployment soared (Tucker and Ganesan, 1997). The only options for poor families seeing their income shrink were to take their children out of school to reduce household expenses or to put them to work, or to take care of the family as mothers now had to enter the labor market (Arat, 2002). In patriarchal societies like India in more cases than not it was the girl who was 'structurally adjusted' and taken out of school as a result of the lending policies of the IMF, the same body which in a gesture of supreme irony identified 'eliminating gender disparities in pri-mary and secondary education by 2015' as one of its Millennium Development Goals. The same pattern was observed in 17 other IMF-adjusted countries where there was a steep decline in the ratio of girls to boys enrolled in secondary schools after structural adjustment programs were implemented (UNICEF, 1997).

Radical reformists acknowledge the complicity of global organizations and transnational corporations in creating the economic conditions that lead to social unrest. These voices propose a variety of alternatives to current unsustainable modes of development, including self-sufficiency, human activity in balance with nature, self-reliance instead of reliance on markets, local control, and democratic inclusion and participation (Thomas, 2000: 38). For example, in proposing a radical agenda to 'restore the rights of the living', Korten (1999: 188) calls for the creation of 'mindful markets' characterized by equity, diversity, ethics, stakeholder ownership, and accountability. Other proposals include restoring political democracy, ending the legal fiction of the corporation, establishing an international agreement regulating international corporations and finance, eliminating corporate welfare, restoring money's role as a medium of exchange and advancing economic democracy.

While the intent behind such critiques and alternatives is admirable because it stems from an ethical and political position that the current system is unjust and unfair to large segments of the world's population, the alternatives are not strong enough to counteract the ideology and hegemony of neoliberalism at this time. They do however provide multiple sites of resistance, and the challenge is to develop a global vision of the political economy that contains a coherent set of alternate views rather than an 'alternative package of ideas' (Payne, 2005). Theoretical development of these ideas has barely begun; rather a series of proposals have been put forward by a number of writers and activists and these are debated at various public or NGO meetings and on the internet. Some writers call for wide-ranging reforms of the UN, World Bank, WTO and IMF (Patomäki and Teivainen, 2004) while others call for the dissolution of these institutions because they are 'inherently unreformable' and the creation of more participatory forms of global governance in an effort to democratize globalization (Monbiot, 2004). George Monbiot in his book *The Age of Consent* advocates the creation of a 'world parliament', a genuinely representative global forum involving direct participation and representation of all citizens (not nation states) instead of including additional consultative groups like NGOs in various existing decision-making fora of global organizations. This rather ambitious and somewhat idealistic plan involves electing 600 representatives each with a constituency of 10 million people on a one person, one vote basis. Monbiot cites the World Social Forum as a starting point to identify potential constituencies; while there were no elected participants among the 100 000 people who participated at the Porto Alegre World Social Forum in 2003, they represented potential constituencies of a world parliament. The world parliament would not be a world government; instead its primary purpose would be to serve as an organization that holds other organizations accountable, especially non-democratic organizations like the World Bank and IMF as well as transnational corporations. Criticisms of a world parliament are wide and varied and come from the entire range of the political spectrum. Neoliberals dismiss the concept as being idealistic, foolish, utopian and unwieldy. Others more sympathetic to the global social justice agenda argue that a centralized body would suppress a plurality of forms and governance structures that are partially overlapping and mutually reinforcing (Patomäki and Teivainen, 2004). In fairness to Monbiot, however, he has consistently responded to criticisms about the unwieldiness and utopianism of his proposal by challenging his critics to come up with alternative proposals.

An analysis of the 'alternatives' discourse reveals two recurring themes – democracy and accountability. Reformists argue that there is a deficit of democracy in the present global economic system and decisions are made at the global level by non-democratic and unaccountable actors that have deleterious effects on large segments of the population, especially the poor. Critics point out that the very institutions that espouse democratic principles, albeit 'free market' ones, are not governed democratically themselves: the United Nations, World Bank and International Monetary Fund are all tightly controlled by a handful of rich and powerful countries. The World Bank and IMF operate on the principle of 'one dollar, one vote', where the largest contributor, the United States, controls 15 percent of the stock in both organizations, which enables it to block any resolution even if it is supported by every other member state. As if to underscore the centralization of interests in both organizations, the managing director of the IMF is always a European whose deputy is always North American. Since its inception in 1946 the IMF has had nine managing directors from one of five countries – Belgium, Sweden, France, the Netherlands and Germany – and, most recently, Spain (IMF, 2005). The World Bank president is always a US citizen nominated by the US Treasury Secretary. While the World Trade Organization is ostensibly more democratic because every member has one vote, in reality the trade agreements are negotiated in the backrooms, in so-called 'green room negotiations' which are controlled by the European Union, the United States, Canada and Japan and where the democratic process is controlled by a combination of bribes, threats, punishment and rewards (Monbiot, 2004; Woods and Narlikar, 2001). The ability of these organizations, given the way they are currently governed, to represent the interests of the world's poor, an overwhelming majority of whom live outside Europe and North America, is in serious doubt, and several critics argue that so-called poverty reduction policies developed by the World Bank and IMF tend to benefit the economies of the United States and Europe (Monbiot, 2004; Stiglitz, 2002). The basic aim of the reformist movement is to democratize global institutions and the governance of the world economy. While a variety of strategies at both global and local levels has been proposed, the problem lies in finding the political will in a democratic social justice framework to implement these strategies and ways to overcome the opposition of the various hegemonic blocs whose power is threatened by these reforms.

It is important to realize that, while all actors and institutions in the political economy hold the notion of democracy sacrosanct, there is a wide range of practices that constitute democracy and not all of them are automatically conducive to social justice. A democratic nation state does not guarantee that all segments of its population will be treated equally – in fact there are several resistance and separatist movements in the world that are currently fighting their own democratically elected governments over land and resource rights. Indigenous communities for instance all over the world probably have a dim view of parliamentary democracy because of the constant threat to their livelihoods as a result of national and global economic development policies. The challenge therefore is to find new forms of democracy that go beyond nation state modes of governance. Theoretical efforts to develop such transnational democratic modes of governance have focused on the notion of deliberative democracy first developed by Habermas (1996, 1998) in response to criticisms about the pragmatic difficulties presented by his theory of communicative action that involved an 'ideal speech situation' under the conditions of freedom of access, equal participation and absence of coercion. Deliberative democracy is posed as an alternative to conventional liberal democracies where there is a clear separation between the political and the economic (Bohman, 1998; Dryzek, 1999; Elster, 1998; Gutman and Thompson, 2004). In liberal democracies, individual rights are bestowed on citizens, and the role of the state is to protect individual freedom. The state obtains its legitimacy as a protector of rights, through violence if necessary, as part of a political process by obtaining a mandate from the electorate. Deliberative democracy is an attempt to disrupt the 'natural' political legitimacy of liberal democratic decisions by drawing attention to the power-laden discursive nature of the decision-making process. There are always overlapping and intersecting choices and preferences in any contested political decision-making process, and simple election-based outputs while being politically legitimate may not strictly be democratic if there are groups of people who are not represented or are unable to participate in the process. Deliberative democracy rejects the notion of fixed and stable preferences across the population and advocates political decision based on dialogue and consent – not in an ideal speech situation where every citizen participates and has equal access to information and there is comprehensive public deliberation over every political decision, but a more pragmatic approach that attempts to embed existing institutions and civil society into democratic forms of decision making (Fung, 2003; Scherer and Palazzo, 2007). Thus, civil society actors like NGOs and other non-state actors play a crucial role in deliberative democracy because of their ability to expand fixed choices and include less powerful voices in the decision-making process.

The Zapatista rebellion is an example of deliberative democracy attempting to broaden the scope of political decision making. The Zapatistas did not seek to overthrow the state but demanded to be included in political decision making. Their demands were articulated in different ways, through engagement with the state at certain times, disengagement with the state at other times, armed insurrection, mediations through civil society institutions, and direct action. They attempted to broaden the fixed political choices in a liberal democracy by highlighting the social and economic dislocations resulting from state economic policies and tried to ensure that the needs of their communities were taken into account in a more inclusive approach to political decision making. The needs of indigenous communities, until then a peripheral concern of state economic policies, were made central (Harvey, 2003; Nash, 2001). However, corporations did not play a direct role in any negotiation process (except Chase Manhattan Bank's recommendation to 'eliminate the Zapatistas' so that the Mexican government could demonstrate their 'effective control of the national territory and security policy', as we saw in Chapter 3). If deliberative democracy highlights the interface between the state and civil society, what is the role of the corporation as a key non-state actor in the political economy? While the majority of theories of the corporation have focused on its role as an economic and social actor, it is important to realize that a business corporation is also a political actor, enmeshed in relations of domination and subordination. According to Scherer and Palazzo (2007), in the context of deliberative democracy CSR can serve as the link between state, civil society and market actors through a system of participatory dialogue with civil society and state actors, an explicit political process that perhaps may permit a more 'democratic control on the public use of corporate power'. This theoretical perspective appears to be consistent with the more practical demands of the radical reformists. However it is not at all clear how corporate participation in deliberative democracy can give non-corporate actors 'democratic control' over corporate actions. There is little if any discussion on how 'control' will be achieved without any legally enforceable mechanism and despite claims that a 'deliberative concept of CSR' is more proactive than stakeholder strategies the argument that the former will lead to better social outcomes is not very convincing. The assumption is that active political engagement of civil society and state actors by corporations will ensure more transparency and accountability of corporate decision making. Whether this will actually occur or whether participation through initiatives like the Global Compact will make corporations less accountable remains to be seen. Although the notion of 'open dialogue' in the deliberative democracy concept is more pragmatic and less utopian than Habermas's earlier formulation of the 'ideal speech situation', there is still the problem of unequal power dynamics between state, corporate and civil society dynamics. Open dialogue between conflicting interests may manufacture an uneasy form of consent, perhaps offer better transparency, but it still does not address the notion of how accountability can be established and enforced in the context of deliberative democracy without the existence of a supranational body with the power to monitor and enforce standards of corporate behavior. Alternate visions of social justice have less to do with how corporations can penetrate civil society or enter into dialogue with it but more to do with how marginalized and impoverished communities who are non-corporate, non-market and non-state actors can ensure their rights are protected in a democracy, deliberative or otherwise. The deliberative concept of CSR also assumes that corporations will be motivated to enter into time-consuming, expensive, often hostile negotiations and dialogues with an expanded constituency base. As we have seen earlier, stated outcomes of enhanced legitimacy and a more democratic process of decision making leave most corporations singularly unimpressed and there is no reason to believe that corporations will voluntarily deploy significant resources in pursuing 'deliberative CSR'.

Establishing democratic control over economic policies developed by supranational institutions and business decisions of corporations in a transnational context implies some form of global governance. Governance involves understanding the rules, norms and institutions that define relationships between key actors, and processes of representation, decision making and accountability. Key questions underlying governance include who makes economic policy, who decides on particular courses of actions, who has influence, how is that influence exercised and how are decision makers held accountable? National legislation and international laws, treaties and agreements are examples of governance mechanisms. Private mechanisms such as voluntary codes of conduct, standards, processes and guidelines are also part of a governance system, sometimes referred to as 'soft governance' or soft laws. Increasing NGO and public pressure in a variety of arenas may not yet have been translated into legal mechanisms but corporations do change their strategies based on these external pressures. In the context of deliberative democracy, CSR could be positioned as a more democratically embedded form of governance as corporations engage in open dialogue with state and non-state actors (Scherer and Palazzo, 2007). However, while public–private partnerships, stakeholder dialogue and NGO involvement may have increased in recent years, these developments by no means challenge (in fact they deflect attention from) the fundamental assumptions of the neoliberal agenda, and serve instead to enhance the legitimacy of existing structures. Owing to the absence of any global monitoring and enforcement mechanism there is a danger that CSR could become a privatized system of governance lacking public accountability (Levy and Kaplan, 2007).

Thus, if corporate social responsibility is an inadequate mechanism to address social ills facing the world we need to explore if corporate social accountability can deliver more meaningful outcomes. Accountability is inextricably linked with resources and rights and is therefore a political process involving relations of domination and subordination. Struggles over resources are ultimately struggles to establish rights, such as the right to development, and thus the relationship between rights and accountability is contingent on the nature of resources, and levels of access and ownership, along with embedded relations of power and conflict (Newell and Wheeler, 2006). The key question is whether marginalized communities can forge transnational coalitions that enable them to claim rights over resources that are critical to their livelihood. If they are able to establish rights over resources only then can they demand accountability from states, transnational corporations and other non-state actors. But as we have seen in earlier chapters, establishing rights is a process imbued with relations of power and despite efforts to expand the notion of property rights to include community and common property rights the regime of property rights serves the interests of a narrow section of private property holders including corporations. Despite the rhetoric of human rights discourses, rights are not a given; they must be claimed for accountability to be established.

The notion of accountability is contested and often contradictory. The same institutions that are supposed to guarantee rights, such as the state, are often the ones that violate rights, as several indigenous communities have found out the hard way. Debates about accountability have revolved around developing a system of checks and balances to prevent the abuse of power. Accountability implies both answerability (accounts describing what actions have been taken) and enforceability (sanctions and penalties for not carrying out appropriate actions) (Newell, 2006; Schedler *et al.*, 1999). However, accountability is a moving target: as Newell (2006) points out, there is no global syntax that ensures accountability is deployed in the same way in different contexts. As we have seen in Chapter 6 on sustainability, different groups ascribe different meanings and value to nature, which in turn generates different systems of rights and responsibilities. Structural constraints like remoteness of locations, literacy and access to legal systems also ensure that accountability does not operate uniformly. Where there are established governance systems, accountability can operate passively in the sense that leaders and elected representatives of institutions have the authority to act on behalf of others along with a public responsibility to ensure they perform without harming others. This notion of 'delegative democracy' represents the self-governing mechanisms of political and managerial accountability (O'Donnell, 1994) and is different from 'deliberative democracy', which implies forms of active (but unenforceable) accountability that involves deliberation and continuous negotiations over public decisions in a community. There is an assumption that communities have both the right and the capacity to negotiate and voice their demands on issues affecting them while monitoring the performance of various actors responsible for community governance. While marginalized communities can work with NGOs and advocacy groups to demand rights, their capacity to obtain those rights is contingent on the institutional capabilities and political will of those that are responsible and accountable for delivering rights. One of the consequences of neoliberal globalization is that it has changed the dynamics of rights, resources and accountabilities between state, market and civil society actors by blurring boundaries between the three domains. The privatization of social welfare means that both the private and the NGO sector have taken over providing services that were once the purview of states; however new accountability mechanisms have not been developed to monitor performance in the social arena (Newell, 2006).

Ultimately the question of accountability is about the power to monitor, regulate and enforce social responsibility. Corporate actions have a wide range of destructive social impacts: exploitative labor conditions, environmental destruction, lack of access to resources, forced displacement of communities, erosion of land rights, and inequitable distribution of revenues from extractive industries to name a few. It is simply not possible to expect either corporations or governments to address all these issues fairly and justly especially when one or both actors are responsible for the problem. Social movements are constantly exploring new spaces of accountability involving the creation of new institutions and developing alternatives to the dominant development discourse, even disengaging with the state as the Zapatistas have done on numerous occasions (Newell and Wheeler, 2006). What is needed is some kind of supranational agency with enforcement powers working in partnership with a wide range of local advocacy groups and NGOs in order to ensure that vulnerable communities either have the right to say no to forms of development that further marginalize them or the right to demand accountability from their governments and from transnational corporations. While 'partnerships' seem to be the new mantra for the United Nations, World Bank, governments and NGOs, there is a need to identify the types of authority, governance structures and conflict resolution mechanisms that can allow for social outcomes that do not require economic rationalization. The problem with any partnership with corporations, whether by government or non-government agencies, is about authority, because a partnership implies some level of equality, which raises the question about who has sovereignty over corporations. As Bakan (2004: 108) points out, elected governments should have sovereignty over corporations that gives the former authority to decide on the appropriateness of corporate actions – the notion of partnerships implies a government has 'effectively abdicated its sovereignty over the corporation'.

Democracy, human rights, social justice and social welfare are not the current purpose of corporations or markets, and market-based measures can do little to meaningfully address these social issues. Unlike market-based solutions (like emissions trading to reduce greenhouse gas emissions), government and supranational regulations have the authority, capacity and democratic legitimacy to address the negative social impacts of corporations and to enforce CSR. An emphasis on responsibilities and voluntary mechanisms of control has resulted

in an imbalance between corporate rights and responsibilities and a corresponding imbalance in '*regulation for* business rather than *regulation of* business'
(Newell, 2006: 43, original emphasis). Market-based notions of accountability
dominate the plethora of World Bank reports that have appropriated the term
'accountability' after the Bank has faced decades of criticism for the destructive
effects of Bank-financed developmental projects. The 2004 World Development
Report stresses the importance of enabling the 'poor to monitor and discipline
service providers' (World Development Report, 2004). The assumption is that
private service providers are responsible for delivering services they have been
contracted for and are accountable to their 'customers' for non-delivery. Non-
performance means that the market will punish the firms for failure to provide
the service, as customers will find other providers. The astonishing naïveté of
this kind of reasoning obscures the fact that impoverished 'customers' often
cannot take their custom for basic services like water and sanitation elsewhere,
and such market-based accountability measures also overlook the historical
basis of exclusion and lack of access to key services and resources. As we have
seen in the previous chapter, the privatization of water in South Africa essentially
deprived poor people of water, supposedly their constitutional right, when they
were unable to pay their water bills on time. Accountability for the World Bank
is reduced to purchasing power, and World Bank policies despite their mission
of fighting poverty suffer from an anti-poor bias (Newell and Wheeler, 2006;
Whitfield, 2001). A complete refocusing of the mandate of supranational organizations like the United Nations, World Bank and World Trade Organization
is required in order to generate new understandings of both institutional and
corporate accountability instead of their current focus on forging partnerships
with the corporate sector.

   While globalization has resulted in a reconfiguration of the role of nation
states, the state continues to be a key agent in implementing neoliberal policies
dictated by the WTO, IMF and World Bank. Within the diversity of social movements and popular protests, recourse to national and international law is another
form of resistance. Globalization has also resulted in the creation of new spaces
and a plurality of legal and normative fora where NGOs and community organizations can plead their case. Randeria (2007) describes different 'pathways to
transnational legal plurality' such as the emergence of supranational norms (like
the Universal Declaration of Human Rights), which compete with other guidelines and codes of conduct that are not necessarily transposed to domestic law.
In addition, WTO resolutions imply changes in domestic laws of member countries or the creation of new laws, adding to legal plurality. Increased attention
to biodiversity protection and the common property rights of indigenous communities has resulted in the development of new norms and guidelines for
addressing the rights of dispossessed peoples. Whether NGOs and activist groups
can use these 'soft laws' (guidelines that cannot be enforced like the UN Global

Compact) to pressurize state and non-state actors to become more accountable is another matter. In her analysis of these alternative pathways, Randeria (2007) found that legal plurality also meant legal uncertainty, ambiguous outcomes regarding the enforceability of laws, and loss of transparency in decision making accompanied by a dilution of responsibility and accountability.

Neither governments nor corporations can be expected to solve the profound social problems facing the world when these institutions are at times the source of the problem. As we have seen in several cases, governments do not necessarily represent the interests of the poor and dispossessed. Successful resistance movements against repressive international and domestic trade policies have generally involved transnational coalitions that have used international law either to revoke prior legal rulings such as the successful revoking of Neem and Basmati rice patents or for compensation and reparation claims. While these coalitions have brought attention to the deleterious effects of economic and trade policies their influence in developing policies is negligible. Corporate social responsibility will not deliver true deliberative democracy: democratic interventions need to be made at the level of political economy, requiring a more inclusive approach to global economic development. While some believe NGOs and other community networks should be included as participants in meetings of supranational organizations like the WTO, World Bank and United Nations (Howse, 2002), others question the practicality of such arrangements given the diversity of interests represented by NGOs as well as the problematic nature of the politics of representation (Monbiot, 2004).

There are conflicts between market-based and rights-based frameworks to resource access, with each approach having different implications for accountability. In a scenario where there are clear property rights to resources, the resource consumer can hold the resource provider accountable in a market transaction. In a rights-based approach the onus of accountability falls on the state. As we have seen in the previous chapter, in relation to the provision of basic services like water (enshrined as a basic human right) a range of conflicts can arise between market- and state-based approaches where neither the state nor the market is accountable for service failures, resulting in poor communities becoming further impoverished owing to lack of access to water. While it is not clear whether a rights approach to development can deliver economic, social and cultural rights for poor and marginalized populations, conflicts over rights and resources can create possibilities to think about new ways of conceptualizing the relationship between rights and accountability instead of focusing on responsibility, which as we have seen produces limited results. The separation of the economic from the social, political and cultural is in many ways a 'Western' way of looking at the world and is at odds with other worldviews. Development struggles over resources may challenge the current preoccupation with property and economic rights and perhaps promote an understanding that delivering economic rights for those that are negatively impacted by development is contingent on securing social, cultural and political rights (Newell and Wheeler, 2006). As long as participatory democracy continues to elude marginalized communities they can resort to forming transnational coalitions that demand the right to participate in the production of hypernorms while challenging the sole right of the state to do so. Social movements and the intervention of non-state actors in the political economy have the potential to expand the domain of civil and human rights currently defined by the law and the state and instead develop a system of rights grounded in civil society. Just as states invoke concepts of human rights, 'the people' and national interest to legitimize exclusions and denial of rights to marginalized communities in the guise of state sovereignty, transnational civil coalitions can employ the same discourses to challenge state sovereignty and protect community rights (Chatterjee, 2004). For instance, NGOs and activists in India have mounted legal challenges that question unrestricted state ownership of land and resources through colonial legal principles of 'eminent domain'. Appropriation of land and natural resources using the principle of eminent domain can be challenged by invoking the tenet of 'public trust', which focuses on public rights to land and resources. The principle of public trust assumes that states hold land and natural resources in perpetual trust and thus have to accept the necessary obligations and constraints on the use or transfer of these resources (Randeria, 2007). This 'vernacularization of Western law' is an outcome of the political interactions between transnational civil coalitions, states and corporations where foreign norms are adapted, transformed and deployed as legal constructs in a different local context (Randeria, 2007: 20).

If, as Hardt and Negri (2000) claim, Empire is the new juridical–economic–political force that has replaced the sovereign nation state with powerful supranational institutions then resistance directed at states and institutions appears to be futile. However, evidence from social movements suggests that state-directed resistance can be effective because national and international laws and institutions function within the juridical practices and institutions of the state. Thus, while the 'multitude' can provide an extra-juridical and extra-state form of resistance, the importance of state- and international law-based resistance should not be overlooked (Randeria, 2007). The emancipatory possibilities of international and national legal systems could provide the basis of a normative shift in decision making when citizens and transnational civil coalitions engage with supranational institutions as well as national governments. However, as Randeria (2007) warns us, promoting participatory democracy and accountability through direct engagement with these institutions runs the risk of enhancing the authority and legitimacy of what are essentially undemocratic bodies while weakening the sovereignty of the very states that advocacy groups are trying to make accountable. Resistance movements deploy national and international laws, codes of conduct, human rights doctrines and international conventions and treaties as well as alternative notions of property rights such as common property and customary rights to challenge, modify or create new institutional norms for decision making. Depending on the context and the dynamics of power, interactions between states, transnational advocacy groups and international institutions can be hostile, cooperative, reactive, accommodating or violent; as Randeria (2007: 28) observes, NGOs and advocacy groups seek to form public–private partnerships with the state for pragmatic reasons 'even as they continue to challenge its legitimacy to represent the public interest and common good ... Civil society actors have neither permanent friends nor enemies but only permanent interests.'

The power dynamics of new social movements will determine whether corporate rationality can serve to create a kind of organizational closure around discourses of social and economic development or whether these boundaries can be extended. This then leads to the question: can an analysis of the multiple sites of power and resistance and the discursive regimes that establish processes of domination and subordination provide new ways of theorizing the nature and role of corporations that can have more progressive outcomes for society? What implications arise for the theory of the firm? How can our critique enhance our understanding of the role of corporations in society? What are the structures and processes that can enable corporations to become agents for positive social change? I will attempt to explore these questions in the next section by discussing a dual theory of the corporation.

TOWARDS A NEW (DE)ONTOLOGY OF THE CORPORATION: A DUAL THEORY OF THE FIRM

The prevailing orthodoxy in organization theory of the contractual view of the firm defines a corporation as a 'nexus of contracts' between wealth-maximizing rational actors. The focus is on identifying institutions, markets and governance structures that can align incentives of managers with interests of shareholders (Yingyi and Weingast, 1997). And as we have seen earlier, despite the contribution of stakeholder theorists, attempts to broaden the social role of corporations are limited because of the capture of the social by the economic. Stakeholder theory can tell us how to manage stakeholders but it does not provide managerial prescriptions on how to address social ills or a system for managing tradeoffs given the current form of the corporation. More than 70 years ago Berle recognized this dilemma when he stated: 'You cannot abandon emphasis on the view that business corporations exist for the sole purpose of making profits for their shareholders until such time as you are prepared to offer a clear and reasonably enforceable scheme of responsibilities to someone else' (Berle, 1932). And while stakeholder theory can provide the normative basis of recognizing corporate responsibilities to 'someone else' we are still far from developing a globally enforceable regime that can enforce corporate social responsibility. Perhaps fundamental changes in the identity and purpose of corporations are also needed if the social is to be recovered from the economic. Let us explore some theoretical avenues by which this could be achieved.

I argue that a different ontology is needed to imagine a radically different role for corporations to enable them to become agents for positive social change. Why a different ontology? Because our assumptions about the reality of objects and the nature and relations of being (ontology) influence how and what we know about it (epistemology). The way we imagine abstract entities like the corporation, the community or society influences the ways in which they become part of a particular language and knowledge system. If we want to change our assumptions about the reality of organizations as socially responsible entities then we need a deontological mode of ethics to imagine what new forms of corporations will look like. A deontological approach to ethics argues that how people achieve their goals is more important than what they achieve. If a corporation is an artificial profit-seeking person then understanding how those profits are made is equally important to, if not more important than, determining what profits are made. An analysis of dominant discourses of organizations can reveal the limits that may have been imposed on knowledge discourses and allow different discourses to emerge (Calás and Smircich, 1991: 569). Thus, we can reconstitute the corporation 'not as a bounded social entity, but as a generic organizing process involved in the creative structuring of social reality' (Chia and King, 1998: 463). As Clegg *et al.* (2005: 159) argue, 'being' a corporation is less about it being an ontologically stable object than about its existence as a result of a series of processes.

Rather than being a discrete legal entity or artificial person a corporation can be seen as being constituted by various processes, some independent, some path dependent, but mutually constitutive. Organization theory and neoclassical economics focus on the economic processes that constitute the firm. But as we have argued earlier the firm is also constituted by political, social and cultural processes. Its legal fiction of being an artificial person was produced by a particular set of political forces in eighteenth-century America that determined the conditions of economic and social exchange, resulting in the emergence of the modern corporation. It is this political space between a firm and its environment that needs to be transformed for a new image of the social to be created. If the firm is seen as a nexus of relationships (not all contractual) between shareholders, employees, suppliers and customers, then the ability of the firm to continue being an artificial person is dependent on its ability to reproduce processes and secure conditions that allow its continued existence. In its current form this means generating enough surplus value and distributing it to its key stakeholders. A crisis point is reached when a firm is unable to deliver value to key stakeholder groups, which remain to this day dominated by its shareholders. Delivering value to social groups other than employees, customers and suppliers implies that corporate social initiatives should not be evaluated only by their financial benefits to the firm. The problem is how can this be made a legitimate strategy to pursue for corporations? Transformations in the larger social and political economy along with a change in the fundamental identity and purpose of corporations are needed for this to occur.

Mantziaris (1999: 283), drawing on the work of the American philosopher John Dewey, argued that the corporation must be explained in two different ways – internally, as a legal category that serves to apply a set of legal rules, and externally, as a legal artifact called the corporation which ultimately 'facilitates the coordination of social action, whether this be in the economic system or the political system'. This dual nature of the corporation allows us to go beyond theorizing its existence as a legal person and see the corporation's being as the result of a series of political, economic, social, cultural and economic processes. If we extend Mantziaris's argument to CSR we can generate its normative assumptions based on an ontology of the corporation whose existence is not based on some fictional personhood or nexus of contracts but as a facilitator of social actions that can be assessed not just as market transactions but by the social outcomes they generate. A corporation's market activities can be assessed in terms of its contribution to enhancing shareholder value. Its legal status and fictional personality bestow it with property rights that can allow it to generate wealth for its shareholders. If a corporation is to be an agent that promotes social welfare then assessing its performance necessarily involves non-economic parameters along with a system of monitoring and enforcement.

In defining what a corporation is, Dewey (1929) distinguished between 'definition by essence' and 'definition by consequence'. Definition by essence focuses on identifying in the 'defined term an essential or inherent quality which exists independently of the process of definition' (Mantziaris, 1999: 293). Thus, the category corporation describes a set of corporate attributes that have a real existence outside the law. However, as we have seen in our earlier discussion of power and discourse, nothing escapes the 'process of definition' which is the basic poststructuralist critique against essentialism. Thus, when we ask what is a corporation we are looking for a definition that is generally based on its legal status as an artificial entity. The entity-based definition presupposes a particular reality of being that then determines how we can generate knowledge about it, what its role is in society and how it should be governed. Broadening the ontological basis of a corporation as an analytic device allows us to develop new forms of discourses about corporations and their role in society.

Definition by consequence on the other hand is an inherently pragmatic definition. It is less about what a corporation is and more about what it does

(Mantziaris, 1999). A corporation produces goods and services, engages in economic exchange, employs people and generates wealth. It also has negative impacts on the natural environment by generating waste, using non-renewable resources and creating pollution. And it has real social effects both positive and negative: it can create jobs for communities; it can destroy jobs for communities; it can alter local modes of social and economic exchange; its products and processes can enhance human welfare as well as diminish it. Thus, a corporation whether it is defined as essence or fiction operates in a larger society and therefore needs to be 'defined in terms of the functions it fulfills not only within the law but within the social system as a whole' (Mantziaris, 1999: 293). Whether entity-based or transaction-based, legal definitions of the corporation do not allow it to address any 'social' issue outside its economic realm because the 'economic' continues to be outside and at times closed to the 'social' or constructs the social in its image. This limits the range of social initiatives a corporation can develop even in a social contract situation because recognizing and honoring a social contract assume all segments of society, however dispossessed and marginalized, can enter, monitor and enforce social contracts with powerful economic actors. We have seen earlier some examples where 'good social policy' becomes 'bad economics' because it creates 'competitive distortions' and cases where 'good economics' can have 'bad social consequences'. Any process of selecting one or the other option or devising a process of managing tradeoffs has to be normative. There was a time when trading in slaves was a legitimate corporate activity, and no doubt created many efficiencies for the corporation (Cooke, 2003). Some banks regularly used slaves as collateral for loans and, when borrowers defaulted on their loans, the banks took ownership of the slaves and sold them to recover their debts (*New York Times*, 2005). Changing social norms resulted in the outlawing of slavery, which in an economic sense meant that human beings were taken out of the market as tradeable commodities. Financial accounting models used by corporations and government agencies are inherently biased toward the economic – as Kelly (2001) points out, when CEOs and mission statements of corporations say 'Our employees are our greatest assets', the opposite is true because in financial terms they appear on income statements as an expense.

A dual theory of the firm involves recognizing two simultaneous processes, what Dewey called *normative closure*, where the defined term 'corporation' could never be independent of the process of definition, and *cognitive openness*, an 'ongoing process of redefinition where the law responded to phenomena within the social system which it experienced as new'. A corporation 'becomes' a corporation as a result of both these processes. Focusing primarily on the entity view of a corporation as a nexus of contracts is an example of normative closure that does not permit any meaningful articulation of a corporation's social role. For this to occur there needs to be (hence the normative assumptions of a dual theory) an understanding that the corporation's 'being', form, role and purpose are also influenced by social systems. This should be accompanied by a politico-legal system of enforcement of rules and regulations that govern corporate behavior. What is lost by not articulating the social processes that constitute a corporation is a more meaningful notion of social accountability (as opposed to responsibility) where the focus is less on the amounts of profits or surplus value generated by corporations and more on how these profits were generated, at what social and environmental cost, which segments had to bear these costs and which segments reaped the rewards. The focus shifts from responsibility to accountability because focusing primarily on the responsibilities of the corporation as a legal entity, even in its progressive stakeholder form, will still produce limited social outcomes where a corporation is responsible for everything but accountable to no one (but its shareholders).

Extending Dewey's concepts of normative closure and cognitive openness to corporate social responsibility may enable us to imagine a different form of the corporation and its role in society. There is a corporate closure around most social issues when social outcomes are evaluated by the self-interested, utility-maximizing corporate actor. If we take the view that corporations are the bearers of civic virtue, the cognitive openness of corporate social responsibility would be reflected in their ability to respond to new challenges and tensions, to embrace non-financial stakeholder interests and to honor social contracts. Parallel developments in the political, economic and legal environments would be needed to ensure monitoring, compliance and enforcement. While social responsibility and stakeholder theory are often described as normative theories, there seems to be an underlying assumption that the shareholder value model is somehow a 'natural law' instead of also being an economic and legal norm (Kelly, 2001). Social movements can play a role in changing norms governing economic activity at the level of political economy by engaging with corporate actors, states and non-state actors. A process of cognitive openness can enable new forms of governance based on net social welfare produced by corporate activity as opposed to narrow financial and economic criteria.

The task of a dual theory is to expand the range of 'social action coordination' practices that are recognized as legitimate corporate actions to enable a re-imagining of corporate legal forms and relationships with civil society. As Mantziaris (1999: 303–4) argues:

> The dual view provides the theoretical framework for a renewed emphasis on the coadaptation between the legal and other social systems. It offers the promise of a richer and less dogmatic explanation of the social, political and economic processes which the law interprets and serves through the category 'corporation'. By focusing on the legal artefact of the corporation as a device for the coordination of action, much can be learnt about the way in which legal categories produce effects in the

external world, perhaps provide a powerful force in the shaping of the social action by legislation, perhaps a realignment of powers between actors.

Thus, a dual theory of the firm is a normative theory in the sense that it redefines the meaning and existence of a corporation based on social norms. Operationalizing this view of the corporation involves expanding the fiduciary duties of a corporation, supported by legal mechanisms that can enforce these duties and a more democratic mode of governing the corporation that combines public and private interests. Kelly (2001: 168) proposes such a view of the corporation, where a corporation cannot claim the rights of individual persons but is a 'semi-public body composed of both property and persons, and these persons include employees. The public corporation is to be chartered by states to serve public and private interests and is to be governed internally by democratic processes.' This view of the firm eliminates shareholder primacy and while not explicitly promoting a stakeholder view assumes that stakeholder interests can be subsumed in the 'public interest'.

Current theories of corporate social responsibility cannot provide a system for managing social and economic tradeoffs except in a limited way because they attempt to reconcile social issues with the economic entity of the firm. Unless we change the way current political economies are organized it is very difficult to see how an ontological shift in the nature of a corporation will occur. Only then can we see corporations address social issues in a more meaningful manner where corporate decision making is organized around delivering key social outcomes even at the expense of diminishing shareholder value. A new ontology of the corporation would see this as a legitimate activity. What will it take for such a fundamental shift to occur? A cynic would argue that only a major global ecological or social crisis could ensure this transformation. A more optimistic approach would be to look at the burgeoning social movements across the globe and examine their potential for transforming the political economy and the role of corporations. Perhaps social movements can bring about a 'realignment of powers between actors' for corporations to address social ills in a meaningful way. Thus, there is no escaping the inherently normative basis of any theory of corporate social responsibility. Ironically, some theorists propose that a redefined concept of property rights may provide the normative basis of CSR (Donaldson and Preston, 1995). They argue that property rights are 'embedded in human rights' and there are restrictions against the harmful and unrestrained use of property. However, while the concept of property rights may be expanded to include responsibility and restrictions of the use of these rights there is no normative or instrumental framework that specifies what these restrictions are and which groups of non-property owners have the right to restrict the rights of property holders. A dual theory of the firm may provide the normative basis for legal theorists to address how 'stakes' of non-property holders can constitute legally enforceable rights in the political economy.

A new ontology of the corporation would imply that corporate decision making is organized around delivering key social outcomes. This ontology would overcome the economic hegemony of organizations and open the way to 'polyphonic' forms of organization (Hazen, 1993), which implies the active presence of a plurality of voices and actors from economic, social, cultural, political, juridical and pedagogical spheres. If social action is to be shaped by legislation then studying the extended social impact of corporate activity becomes important. The real challenge, as Boggs (1986: 16) points out, is to imagine possibilities that can 'transform the state apparatus, revitalize the public sphere, and create new forms of authority so that fundamental change can be initiated consistent with the radical potential of new social movements'. Countering current economic hegemony implies questioning the hierarchy of issues and priorities in social, cultural, political and economic arenas. Asking these questions will allow new parameters of organizational performance as well as new forms of accountability and institutions to emerge.

PARTING THOUGHTS

So where do we go from here? What are the new directions for research and practice given my critique of contemporary discourses of CSR? I believe a critical research agenda for CSR requires a theoretical and policy framework that encompasses all three aspects of CSR – the good, the bad and the ugly. A critical research agenda that explores the 'good' in CSR will focus on corporations and their partners that follow a more proactive approach to CSR – corporations that have signed up to the Global Compact, for instance, and others that have engaged with civil society actors to work on various social initiatives. Key questions to explore in this area are: what are the specific outcomes of CSR practices? To what extent have the espoused outcomes of particular social initiatives been realized? What are the limits of win–win situations in a particular CSR context, whether it is environmental protection, poverty reduction, community development, labor standards or economic development? What are the areas of conflicts and points of tension and disagreement between corporations and civil society organizations and how have the conflicts been resolved? The focus shifts from trying to find a positive relationship between CSR and financial performance to exploring the effects of corporate social initiatives on a different 'dependent variable' – outcomes for society not corporations. Perhaps this approach may allow us to recover the 'social' in CSR rather than corporatize the social, which is the basis of current research. A critical research agenda that focuses on the 'good' of CSR will thus allow us to test the assumption that corporations can indeed be effective agents of positive social change (Margolis and Walsh, 2003).

Apart from critically analysing the good that corporations can do there is also a need to explore the effects of the bad. We have discussed numerous cases of corporate abuses: environmental destruction, exploitative labor conditions, complicity with repressive regimes, inadequate product and process safety standards, relocation of polluting industries to regions with weak environmental protection regimes, destruction of local livelihoods and violence against indigenous communities. There is a need for more research on modes of corporate accumulation through dispossession. The focus shifts from identifying the antecedents and analysing the conditions of win–win situations to understanding the conditions that create win–lose situations as well as developing monitoring and enforcement regimes. Going beyond win–win situations involves acknowledging that there are profound tensions between efficiencies and shareholder value maximization and the detrimental effects that shareholder value-maximizing strategies have on certain segments of society. Rather than focusing on identifying whose claims and which stakeholders are legitimate or assuming that conflicting interests can be resolved, research is needed to understand how corporations resolve conflicting objectives. As Margolis and Walsh (2003: 282) point out, most research on CSR has 'theorized away the collision of objectives and interests' and there is a need for research that describes how corporations analyse and manage tradeoffs and dilemmas. How do corporations deal with their negative social and environmental impacts? How can these be documented? What monitoring and enforcement mechanisms are needed to prevent negative social and environmental outcomes? What institutional arrangement and modes of governance are needed to minimize the bad that corporations do? What mandatory reporting requirements and other accountability measures are required? What roles do civil society organizations and supranational organizations play in the global governance of corporate activity?

The ugly face of CSR is the covert and sometimes not so covert abuse of corporate power while attempting to portray a caring and responsible citizen image through relentless public relations campaigns. More research is needed to uncover the extent of greenwashing that takes place in the public relations arena and to design monitoring mechanisms that can hold corporations to the claims they make in their PR campaigns. What are the political strategies adopted by corporations? What is the range of corporate lobbying efforts and to which actors are these efforts directed? How do corporations respond to pressures from civil society actors or accusations of misconduct by activist groups? How is corporate influence exerted in the political economy? What is the extent of corporate contribution to political campaign financing? What kind of tax relief, concessions and other forms of corporate welfare do corporations obtain? What kinds of legal actions have corporations taken, against which actors, and what were the outcomes? What legal actions do corporations face and how do they respond?

Based on the above questions it is clear that a critical research agenda requires multiple levels of analysis as well as multiple methods of investigation. While there are many accounts of corporations abusing their power and their complicity with fascist and military regimes in the popular press, these 'corporate strategies' remain under-theorized in the management literature where they are dismissed as examples of organizational deviance – good corporations doing bad things. This is far too simplistic an analysis and more research is needed to understand the conditions that sustain this 'deviance' which may allow us to shift the focus on the institutional forces that constitute the corporation and recognize that corporate social (ir)responsibility is symptomatic of a flawed institution (Bakan, 2004). Mainstream research on international business focuses on directions and flows of foreign direct investment, joint ventures, offshore production and outsourcing, exports, or cross-cultural issues, with very little attention paid to the social and cultural transformations produced by international business activity. The bland and impersonal econometric models that describe much of this research need to be illuminated by rich ethnographic accounts of social dislocations, cultural transformations and political and economic marginalization wrought by foreign investment and transnational corporate activity along with accounts of local and global resistance movements that inevitably accompany any exercise of power in the political economy (Harvey, 2003). Investigation needs to be done at multiple levels of analysis: the organizational level, the institutional level and the societal level. A critical research agenda for CSR involves exploring relationships between corporations and other actors using partnerships, industries and coalitions as units of analysis through critical discourse analysis of the power dynamics that underlie interactions between corporations and their stakeholders.

At the societal level, more research is needed to investigate, using a variety of theoretical and methodological perspectives, the rise of social movements and organized collective efforts to address social problems all over the world. The environmental movement is a case in point: from a fringe movement in the 1960s it has now become a mainstream issue. Public concern and media pressure have changed policies and practices at governmental, institutional and corporate levels (Banerjee *et al.*, 2003; Bansal, 2005). If using an economic lens creates an image of society that marginalizes the world's poor then perhaps studying social movements might allow us to construct a new image of society. As we have seen earlier, any social theory of the firm is based on normative assumptions. Only by changing the normative framework of political decision making can meaningful corporate social initiatives be sustained. Social movements can provide a basis for changing the normative framework. The World Social Forum (WSF) represents one such movement. The WSF is an annual meeting organized as a challenge to the World Economic Forum meetings. The WSF is

> not an organization, not a united front platform, but an open meeting place for reflec-
> tive thinking, democratic debate of ideas, formulation of proposals, free exchange of
> experiences and inter-linking for effective action, by groups and movements of civil
> society that are opposed to neo-liberalism and to domination of the world by capital
> and any form of imperialism, and are committed to building a society centered on
> the human person. (Sen *et al.*, 2004)

Obviously, any alternative vision of the world will contain an economic dimension. The challenge is to integrate political, social and cultural dimensions into
this vision. The history of social movements shows that they play an important
role in this process. By challenging beliefs, norms and values of existing institutions these movements effectively de-institutionalize established norms and
institutionalize new beliefs, norms and values through collective action (Rao *et
al.*, 2000). These new social movements also represent alternate forms of social
organization of resistance to corporate power to the traditional forms of resistance such as unions, political parties and governments, which are 'hopelessly
compromised' according to Harvey (2003: 189). A critical research agenda on
social movements does not assume that NGOs automatically hold the moral
high ground when it comes to social and environmental issues. NGOs and civil
society actors might not be profit driven, but their power and legitimacy to represent marginalized groups must also be scrutinized along with their motives
and intentions. The burgeoning movement of non-governmental organizations
(sometimes sponsored by governments and corporations) means that a large
number of NGOs are battling for market share as they seek ways to achieve
sustainable competitive advantage and identify long-term funding sources in
the NGO market. All NGOs do not necessarily have a revolutionary agenda and
neither are all outcomes of NGO strategies beneficial to the communities they
represent. Corporations and governments also seek to influence the direction of
social movements to suit their own agendas and through 'partnerships' and
'dialogue' try to accommodate conflicting objectives to neoliberal regimes of
power (Harvey, 2003). A critical perspective in analysing social movements
would examine the policies, practices, modes of governance and power dynamics underlying their interactions with other stakeholders and the conflicting
discursive rationalities they produce. This might yield valuable insights on how
social problems are articulated, along with the contradictions, modes of resistance, struggles and tensions between social movements and neoliberal agendas
(Grewal, 2005; Zald, 2002).

   Another direction is to explore alternate organizational forms that allow
corporations to pursue social initiatives. For instance, what kind of organizations would we need to achieve the Millennium Development Goals? It seems

obvious corporations as they are currently constituted can do little. The new mantra of 'public–private partnerships' needs to be scrutinized critically to identify the types of authority, governance structures and conflict resolution mechanisms that can allow for social outcomes without requiring economic rationalization. There are useful insights to be gained by investigating alternate forms of organizations, perhaps hybrid forms of organization similar to the quasi-autonomous non-governmental organizations (or quangos as they are called in the UK) that are funded out of corporate profits, whose purpose is to implement projects promoting social welfare. New organizational and institutional forms emerge when market structures and incentives do not produce social good (Rao *et al.*, 2000). This is primarily a political process where new organizations attempt to gain legitimacy in order to be able to mobilize resources to ensure their survival so that they can serve specific needs of different social groups. These accounts may allow us to say that in some instances the corporation is a useful vehicle for social change but in other circumstances there will be a need for more regulation and community involvement. Emerging research on social entrepreneurship may offer some insights. A social enterprise is defined as a 'market based venture for a social purpose' (Dees and Anderson, 2002: 16). Social enterprises produce goods and services on an ongoing basis, have explicit social aims to serve the community, involve the direct participation of community members, and can be either for-profit or non-profit (Borzaga and Defourny, 2004). Such enterprises are usually locality or community based and part of a stakeholder economy; they are structured and governed by and for stakeholder interests to ensure that surpluses are principally reinvested to achieve agreed community aims. Perhaps social enterprises with a separate governing body can be created from the profits accrued by corporations in a particular industry to address the social and environmental problems caused by that industry.

There are profound contradictions between societal expectations of corporations and what corporations can actually deliver. Corporations cannot replace governments and, despite the neoliberal push for diminished regulation, a stronger regulatory environment may be required to address social ills in a more meaningful manner. Broader social goals such as democracy, social justice, citizens' health and welfare, environmental integrity and cultural identity are sometimes incompatible with the narrower corporate goals of self-interest and shareholder value and require a regulatory system with authority and democratic legitimacy that go beyond those provided by a market-based system (Bakan, 2004). What kind of future awaits us depends on how we negotiate these profound contradictions and challenges. Albert Einstein once said, 'imagination is more important than knowledge'. If this is true then we need to demand that our theories act with an 'organizational imagination' in order to address questions of social inequality, cultural marginalization and ecological crisis which will enable researchers 'to make linkages between history, structures and individual lives in the service of an intellectual and political purpose' (Mir and Mir, 2002: 115). If our theories of globalization and economic development were developed without people in mind then it is time to retheorize these processes by putting people back in. The ideology of neoliberal market fundamentalism is so prevalent that it has almost become immune to empirical disconfirmation. New perspectives may allow us to envision a future where sustainable development does not mean sustainable corporations, where the poor are not structurally adjusted by tightening their belts while the belts of the rich are loosened, where biotechnology does not reduce the diversity of life into a replication of uniformity, where food exports do not lead to an increase in a nation's GNP while their children starve, and where billions of dollars are not spent developing drugs to cure balding or impotence while millions die elsewhere of malaria and tuberculosis. Perhaps a more fertile organizational imagination will allow us to recover the social from the economic and rephrase the former World Bank president's words to say instead, 'At the level of people, the system is working.' But that is another story.

Statistical appendix

Table A.1   World's ten biggest corporations

Company	2005 Revenues	2005 Profits
ExxonMobil	$340 billion	$36 billion
Wal-Mart Stores	$316 billion	$11 billion
Royal Dutch Shell	$307 billion	$25 billion
BP	$268 billion	$22 billion
General Motors	$192 billion	($11 billion)
Chevron	$190 billion	$14 billion
DaimlerChrysler	$186 billion	$3.5 billion
Toyota Motors	$186 billion	$12 billion
Ford Motors	$177 billion	$2 billion
ConocoPhillips	$167 billion	$14 billion

Notes:

To put these figures in some perspective: there are 190 countries listed in the 2004 World Development Report. The revenues of the ten biggest companies listed above are greater than the Gross National Income of 168 countries in the world. Only Australia, Austria, Belgium, Brazil, Canada, China, France, Germany, India, Italy, Japan, South Korea, Mexico, the Netherlands, Norway, Russia, Spain, Sweden, Switzerland, Turkey, the United Kingdom and the United States have higher Gross National Income than the Big Ten corporations. In 2006 ExxonMobil's profits rose to $39.5 billion.

Six of the Big Ten are US-based corporations, three are European and one is Japanese.

Five of the Big Ten corporations are from the oil industry. This industry is also the most profitable industry in the world (see Tables A.4 and A.5) as well as one of the fastest-growing industries in the world (see Table A.6). Four of the Big Ten corporations are from the automobile industry and one from retail. The individual corporations listed above as well as the industries to which they belong pose serious social and environmental problems.

A similar industry pattern can be observed when we look at Europe's ten biggest corporations (Table A.2), with the main difference being the presence of the financial services and insurance sectors.

The pattern in Asia is different, with electronics, utilities and telecommunications sectors also represented in Asia's biggest ten corporations.

Source: All figures compiled from *Fortune* magazine's list of Global 500 companies, http://money. cnn.com/magazines/fortune/global500/2006/.

Table A.2   Europe's ten biggest corporations

Company	2005 Revenues	Country
Royal Dutch Shell	$307 billion	Netherlands
BP	$268 billion	Britain
DaimlerChrysler	$186 billion	Germany
Total	$152 billion	France
ING Group	$138 billion	Netherlands
AXA	$130 billion	France
Allianz	$121 billion	Germany
Volkswagen	$119 billion	Germany
Fortis	$112 billion	Belgium/Netherlands
Crédit Agricole	$111 billion	France

Source: All figures compiled from *Fortune* magazine's list of Global 500 companies, http://money.cnn.com/magazines/fortune/global500/2006/.

Table A.3   Asia's ten biggest corporations

Company	2005 Revenues	Country
Toyota Motor	$187 billion	Japan
Sinopec	$99 billion	China
Nippon Telegraph	$95 billion	Japan
Honda Motor	$87 billion	Japan
State Grid	$87 billion	China
Hitachi	$84 billion	Japan
China National Petroleum	$84 billion	China
Nissan Motor	$83 billion	Japan
Samsung Electronics	$79 billion	Japan
Matsushita Electric	$79 billion	Japan

Source: All figures compiled from *Fortune* magazine's list of Global 500 companies, http://money.cnn.com/magazines/fortune/global500/2006/.

Table A.4 *World's most profitable industries (profits as percentage of revenue)*

Industry	2005 Profits as percentage of revenue
Mining, crude oil production	29.9
Internet services and retailing	23.8
Commercial banks	18.3
Network/communications equipment	15.8
Pharmaceuticals	15.7
Medical products and equipment	13.2
Securities	12.7
Railroads	12.5

Source: All figures compiled from *Fortune* magazine's list of Global 500 companies, http://money.cnn.com/magazines/fortune/global500/2006/.

Table A.5 *World's most profitable industries (return on assets)*

Industry	2005 Return on assets
Mining, crude oil production	14.9
Network/communications equipment	12.8
Homebuilders	11.1
Pharmaceuticals	10.5
Petroleum refining	10.1
Household and personal products	9.2
Food consumer products	8.7
Specialty retailers	8.7
Tobacco	8.3
Computer services and software	7.7

Source: All figures compiled from *Fortune* magazine's list of Global 500 companies, http://money.cnn.com/magazines/fortune/global500/2006/.

Table A.6 World's fastest-growing industries

Industry	% Increase 2004–05
Pipelines	46.0
Internet services and retailing	39.2
Securities	37.2
Petroleum refining	35.7
Mining, crude oil production	34.3
Homebuilders	27.4
Engineering, construction	23.2
Oil and gas equipment	22.0

Source: All figures compiled from *Fortune* magazine's list of Global 500 companies, http://money.cnn.com/magazines/fortune/global500/2006/.

References

Abrahamsen, R. and Williams, M.C. (2005). *The Globalization of Private Security*, http://users.aber.ac.uk/rbh/privatesecurity. Accessed 15 March 2007.

Abrams, F. (1951). Management's responsibilities in a complex world. *Harvard Business Review*, **29** (3): 29–34.

Adams, W.M. (1990). *Green Development: Environment and Sustainability in the Third World.* New York: Routledge.

American Bar Association (1990). Other constituencies statutes: potential for confusion. *Business Lawyer*, **45**: 2261.

Amis, L., Brew, O. and Ersmarker, C. (2005). Human rights: is it your business? International Business Leaders Forum, www.iblf.org/humanrights. Accessed 15 March 2007.

Annan, K. (2000). A compact for the new century, www.un.org/partners/business/davos.htm. Accessed 15 March 2007.

Annan, K. (2001). Unparalleled nightmare of AIDS. Address to the United States Chamber of Commerce, Washington, DC, http://www.un.org/News/Press/docs/2001/sgsm7827.doc.htm. Accessed 15 March 2007.

Arat, Z.F. (2002). Human rights issue: its causes, aggravating policies, and alternative proposals. *Human Rights Quarterly*, **24**: 177–204.

Asad, T. (2000). What do human rights do? An anthropological enquiry. *Theory and Event*, **4** (4): 1–17.

Australian Institute of Aboriginal Studies (1984). *Aborigines and Uranium: Consolidated Report to the Minister for Aboriginal Affairs on the Social Impact of Uranium Mining on the Aborigines of the Northern Territory (1979–84).* Canberra: AGPS.

Bakan, J. (2004). *The Corporation: The Pathological Pursuit of Profit and Power.* Toronto: Viking Canada.

Balibar E. (1997). *La crainte des masses: politique et philosophie avant et après Marx.* Collection La Philosophie en effet. Paris: Galilée. Cited in Zizek (2006).

Banerjee, S.B. (1998). Corporate environmentalism: perspectives from organizational learning. *Management Learning*, **29** (2): 147–64.

Banerjee, S.B. (1999). Corporate environmentalism and the greening of strategic marketing. In M. Charter and M.J. Polonsky (eds) *Greener Marketing: A Global Perspective to Greening Marketing Practice*, 2nd edn. Sheffield: Greenleaf Publishing, pp. 16–40.

Banerjee, S.B. (2000). Whose land is it anyway? National interest, indigenous stakeholders and colonial discourses: the case of the Jabiluka uranium mine. *Organization and Environment*, **13** (1): 3–38.

Banerjee, S.B. (2001a). Managerial perceptions of corporate environmentalism: interpretations from industry and strategic implications for organizations. *Journal of Management Studies*, **38** (4): 467–91.

Banerjee, S.B. (2001b). Corporate citizenship and indigenous stakeholders: exploring a new dynamic of organizational stakeholder relationships. *Journal of Corporate Citizenship*, **1**: 39–55.

Banerjee, S.B. (2003). Who sustains whose development? Sustainable development and the reinvention of nature. *Organization Studies*, **24**: 143–80.

Banerjee, S.B., Iyer, E. and Kashyap, R. (2003). Corporate environmentalism and its antecedents: influence of industry type. *Journal of Marketing*, **67** (2): 106–22.

Bansal, P. (2005). Evolving sustainability: a longitudinal study of corporate sustainable development. *Strategic Management Journal*, **26**: 197–218.

Barlow, M. and Clarke, T. (2002). *Blue Gold: The Battle against Corporate Theft of the World's Water*. Toronto: McClelland and Stewart.

Baron, D.P. (2001). Private politics, corporate social responsibility and integrated strategy. *Journal of Economics and Management Strategy*, **10** (1): 7–45.

Beck, U. (2000). *The Brave New World of Work*. Cambridge: Polity Press.

Beder, S. (1994). Revoltin' developments: the politics of sustainable development. *Arena Magazine*, June–July: 37–9.

Berle, A.A. (1932). For whom are corporate managers trustees? *Harvard Law Review*, **45**: 1365–7.

Birch, D. (2001). Corporate citizenship: rethinking business beyond corporate social responsibility. In J. Andriof and M. McIntosh (eds) *Perspectives on Corporate Citizenship*. Sheffield: Greenleaf Publishing, pp. 53–65.

Blakeney, M. (1997). Bioprospecting and the protection of traditional medical knowledge of indigenous peoples: an Australian perspective. *EIPR*, **6**: 298–303.

Boggs, C. (1986). *Social Movements and Political Power*. Philadelphia, PA: Temple University Press.

Boggs, C. (1997). The great retreat: decline of the public sphere in the late twentieth century America. *Theory and Society*, **26**: 741–80.

Bohman, J. (1998). The coming of age of deliberative democracy. *Journal of Political Philosophy*, **6** (4): 400–425.

Borzaga, C. and Defourny, J. (2004). *The Emergence of Social Enterprise*. London: Routledge.

Bowen, H. (1953). *The Social Responsibilities of the Businessman*. New York: Harper.

Brenner-Beck, D. (1992). Do as I say, not as I did. *UCLA-Pacific Basin Law Review Journal*, **11**: 84–118.

Bruno, K. and Karliner, J. (2002). Marching to Johannesburg. *Corpwatch*, 21 August, www.corpwatch.org/campaigns/PCD.jspa?articleid=3588. Accessed 15 March 2007.

Buchholz, R.A. (1993). *Principles of Environmental Management: The Greening of Business*. Englewood Cliffs, NJ: Prentice Hall.

Bugge, H.C. and Tvedt, M.W. (2000). A legal look at Article 15 in the Convention on Biological Diversity: access to genetic resources. In H. Svarstad and S.S. Dhillion (eds) *Responding to Bioprospecting: From Biodiversity in the South to Medicines in the North*. Oslo: Spartacus Forlag As, pp. 169–92.

Bunting, A. (1996). Theorizing women's cultural diversity in feminist international human rights strategies. *Journal of Law and Society*, **20** (1): 6–22.

Burrell, G. (1988). The contribution of Foucault. *Organization Studies*, **9**: 221–35.

Business Week (2000). Too much corporate power? 11 September.

Calás, M.B. and Smircich, L. (1991). Voicing seduction to silence leadership. *Organization Studies*, **12**: 567–602.

Carroll, A. (1979). A three-dimensional conceptual model of corporate social performance. *Academy of Management Review*, **4**: 497–505.

Carroll, A. (1998). The four faces of corporate citizenship. *Business and Society Review*, **100**: 1–7.

Carson, R. (1962). *Silent Spring*. Boston, MA: Houghton Mifflin.

Center for Corporate Public Affairs (2000). *Corporate Community Involvement: Establishing a Business Case*. Melbourne: Center for Corporate Affairs.

Cernea, M. and McDowell, C. (eds) (2000). *Risks and Reconstruction: Experiences of Resettlers and Refugees*. Washington, DC: World Bank.

Chadha, M. (2005). Patent laws shake up India's drug sector, http://news.bbc.co.uk/2/hi/business/4148903.stm. Accessed 15 June 2007.

Chatterjee, P. (2004). Empire after globalization. *Economic and Political Weekly*, **39** (37): 4155–64.

Chea, T. (2006). Chevron fights rights abuse allegations. ABC News, 1 January, http://abcnews.go.com/Business/wireStory?id=1461727&CMP=OTC-RSS-Feeds0312. Accessed 15 March 2007.

Chevron (2006). Nigeria fact sheet, http://www.chevron.com/news/current_issues/nigeria.asp. Accessed 15 March 2007.

Chia, R. and King, I.W. (1998). The organizational structuring of novelty. *Organization*, **5**: 461–78.

Chomsky, N. and Herman, E.S. (1979). *The Washington Connection and Third World Fascism: The Political Economy of Human Rights*. Boston, MA: South End Press.

Christianson, A.C. (2002). Beyond Petroleum: Can BP deliver. Fridjotf Nansen

Institute Report, http://www.fni.no/pdf/FNI-R0602.pdf. Accessed 15 March 2007.

Chua, A. (2004). *World on Fire: How Exporting Free Market Democracy Breeds Ethnic Hatred and Global Instability.* London: Arrow Books.

Clapman, A. and Jerbi, S. (2001). Categories of corporate complicity in human rights abuses. *Hastings International and Comparative Law Review*, **24** (3): 339–49.

Clarkson, M.B.E. (1995). A stakeholder framework for analyzing and evaluating corporate social performance. *Academy of Management Review*, **20** (1): 92–117.

Clegg, S. (1989). *Frameworks of Power.* London: Sage.

Clegg, S. (1998). Foucault, power and organizations. In A. McKinley and K. Starkey (eds), *Foucault, Management and Organization Theory.* London: Sage, pp. 29–48.

Clegg, S., Kornberger, M. and Rhodes, C. (2005). Learning/becoming/organizing. *Organization*, **12**: 147–67.

Clifford, M. (2001). *Political Genealogy after Foucault.* New York: Routledge.

Coase, R.H. (1937). The nature of the firm. In O.E. Williamson and S.G. Winter (eds) *The Nature of the Firm: Origins, Evolution and Development.* New York: Oxford University Press, pp. 18–33.

Cooke, B. (2003). The denial of slavery in management studies. *Journal of Management Studies*, **40**: 1895–1918.

Cole, L. and Foster, S. (2001). *From the Ground Up: Environmental Racism and the Rise of the Environmental Justice Movement.* New York: New York University Press.

Collier, P. (2000). *Economic Causes of Civil Conflict and their Implications for Policy.* Washington, DC: World Bank.

Corporate Watch (2006). Corporate Watch CSR report 2006, http://www.corpwatch.org. Accessed 15 March 2007.

Cox, R.W. (1981). Social forces, states and world orders: beyond international relations theory. *Millennium: Journal of International Relations*, **10** (2): 126–55.

Crane, A. (2000). Corporate greening as amoralization. *Organization Studies*, **21** (4): 673–96.

Cunningham, L. (1999). Corporate governance roundtable. *Cornell Law Review*, **84** (5): 1289–95.

Cyert, R.M. and March, J.G. (1963). *A Behavioral Theory of the Firm.* Englewood Cliffs, NJ: Prentice Hall.

Dahl, R.A. (1973). Governing the giant corporation. In R. Nader and M.J. Green (eds) *Corporate Power in America.* New York: Grossman Publishers.

Dasmann, R. (1988). National parks, nature conservation, and future primitive.

In J.H. Bodley (ed.) *Tribal Peoples and Development Issues*. Pao Alto, CA: Mayfield, pp. 303–10.

Davenport, K.S. (2000). Corporate citizenship: a stakeholder approach for defining corporate social performance and identifying measures for assessing it. *Business and Society*, **3** (2): 210–19.

Davis, K. (1973). The case for and against business assumption of social responsibilities. *Academy of Management Journal*, **16**: 312–22.

Davis, M. (1990). *City of Quartz: Excavating the Future in Los Angeles*. London: Verso.

Dawkins, K. (1997). *Gene Wars: The Politics of Biotechnology*. New York: Seven Stories Press.

Dean, T.J. and Brown, R.L. (1995). Pollution regulation as a barrier to new firm entry: initial evidence and implications for future research. *Academy of Management Journal*, **38**: 288–303.

deButts, J.D. (1978). And profits shall lie down with responsibility. *Business and Society Review*, 7–8.

Dees, J.G. and Anderson, B.B. (2002). For-profit social ventures. *International Journal of Entrepreneurship Education*, **2** (1): 8–21.

de George, R.T. (2005). Intellectual property and pharmaceutical drugs: an ethical analysis. *Business Ethics Quarterly*, **15** (4): 549–75.

De Muth, S. (2003). Power driven. *Guardian*, 20 November.

Denoon, D. (2000). *Getting under the Skin: The Bougainville Copper Agreement and the Creation of the Panguna Copper Mine*. Carlton South: Melbourne University Press.

Derber, C. (1998). *Corporation Nation*. New York: St Martin's Griffin.

DeSimone, L.D. and Popoff, F. (1997). *Eco-efficiency: The Business Link to Sustainable Development*. Cambridge, MA: MIT Press.

Dewey, J. (1929). *The Quest for Certainty*. New York: Putnam Publishing.

Dobson, A. (1998). *Social Justice and the Environment*, Oxford: Oxford University Press.

Doe v. Unocal Corporation (1997). 963 F Sup. 880 (C.D. California).

Donaldson, T. and Preston, L.E. (1995). The stakeholder theory of the corporation: concepts, evidence and implications. *Academy of Management Review*, **20** (1): 65–91.

Dosal, P. (1993). *Doing Business with Dictators: A Political History of United Fruit in Guatemala 1899–1944*. Wilmington, DE: Scholarly Resources Books.

Dow Jones Sustainability Group Index (2000), http://www.dowjones.com/djsgi/index/concept.html. Accessed 15 March 2007.

Downes, D.R. (1996). Global trade, local economies, and the Biodiversity Convention. In W.J. Snape and O.A. Houcj (eds) *Biodiversity and the Law*. Washington, DC: Island Press.

Downing, T. (1996). Mitigating social impoverishment when people are involuntarily displaced. In C. McDowell (ed.) *Understanding Impoverishment: The Consequences of Development-Induced Displacement.* Oxford: Berghahn Books.

Doyle, M. (1986). *Empires.* Ithaca, NY: Cornell University Press.

Driessen, P. (2003). *Eco-imperialism.* Bellevue, WA: Free Enterprise Press.

Dryzek, J.S. (1999). Transnational democracy. *Journal of Political Philosophy*, **7** (1): 30–51.

Du Gay, P., Salaman, G. and Rees, B. (1996). The conduct of management and the management of conduct: contemporary managerial discourse and the constitution of the 'competent' manager. *Journal of Management Studies*, **33**: 263–82.

Duncan, N. (1996). *Body Space: Destabilizing Geographies of Gender and Sexuality.* London: Routledge.

Dutt, R. (1970). *India Today.* New Delhi: Navjivan Press.

Edwards, B. and Foley, M. (1998). Civil society and social capital beyond Putnam. *American Behavioral Scientist*, **42** (1): 124–39.

Egri, C.P. and Pinfield, L.T. (1996). Organizations and the biosphere: ecologies and environments. In S.R. Clegg, C. Hardy and W.R. Nord (eds), *Handbook of Organization Studies.* London: Sage.

Elkington, J. (1997). *Cannibals with Forks: The Triple Bottom Line of 21st Century Business.* Oxford: Capstone.

Elster, J. (1998). *Deliberative Democracy.* Cambridge: Cambridge University Press.

Emerson, R. (1987). Toward a theory of value in social exchange. In K. Cook (ed.), *Social Exchange Theory.* London: Sage.

Enriquez, J. and Goldberg, R.A. (2000). Transforming life, transforming business: the life-science revolution. *Harvard Business Review*, (March–April): 96–104.

Enron (2002). Corporate responsibility annual report, http://www.enron.com/corp/pressroom/responsibility/CRANNUAL.pdf. Accessed 1 December 2006.

Entine, J. (1995). Rain-forest chic. *Toronto Globe & Mail Report on Business*, October: 41–52.

Escobar, A. (1992). Imagining a post-development era: critical thought, development and social movements. *Social Text*, **31/32**: 20–56.

Escobar, A. (1995). *Encountering Development: The Making and Unmaking of the Third World, 1945–1992.* Princeton, NJ: Princeton University Press.

Esteva, G. (1992). Development. In W. Sachs (ed.) *The Development Dictionary.* London: Zed Books, pp. 6–25.

European Commission (2005). Promoting a European framework for corporate social responsibility, http://www.europa.eu.int/comm/employment_social/ soc-dial/csr. Accessed 15 March 2007.

Farmer, P. (2005). *Pathologies of Power: Health, Human Rights and the New War on the Poor.* Berkeley: University of California Press.

Febrero, R. and Schwartz, P. (1995). The essence of Becker: an introduction. In R. Febrero and P. Schwartz (eds), *The Essence of Becker.* Stanford, CA: Hoover Institution Press.

Fernandes, W. (2000). From marginalization to sharing the project benefits. In M. Cernea and C. McDowell (eds) *Risks and Reconstruction: Experiences of Resettlers and Refugees.* Washington, DC: World Bank.

Ferraro, F., Pfeffer, J. and Sutton, R.I. (2005). Economics language and assumptions: how theories can become self-fulfilling. *Academy of Management Review*, **30**: 8–24.

Findlay, P. and Newton, T. (1997). Reframing Foucault: the case of performance appraisal. In A. McKinlay and K. Starkey (eds) *Foucault, Management and Organization Theory.* London: Sage, pp. 211–19.

Fine, B. (1997). Privatization: theory and lessons from the UK and South Africa. *Seoul Journal of Economics*, **10** (4): 373–414.

Fine, B. (1999). A question of economics: is it colonizing the social sciences? *Economy and Society*, **28** (3): 403–25.

Fine, B. (2001). *Social Capital versus Social Theory: Political Economy and Social Science at the Turn of the Millennium.* London: Routledge.

Food and Agriculture Organization (2000). Food and population: FAO looks ahead, http://www.fao.org/news/2000/000704-e.htm. Accessed 15 March 2007.

Ford, H. (1978). No magic from the corporate genie. *Business and Society Review*, **5**.

Ford, W.C. (2000), http://www.princeton.edu/main/news/archive/A94/88/20Q00/index.xml. Accessed 15 March 2007.

Foucault, M. (1972). *The Archeology of Knowledge and the Discourse on Language.* New York: Pantheon Books.

Foucault, M. (1979). Governmentality. In G. Burchell, C. Gordon and P. Miller (eds) *The Foucault Effect: Studies in Governmentality.* Chicago, IL: University of Chicago Press, pp. 87–104.

Foucault, M. (1980). *Power/Knowledge: Selected Interviews and Other Writings, 1972–1977.* New York: Pantheon Books.

Frankel, C. (1998). *In Earth's Company: Business, Environment and the Challenge of Sustainability.* Gabrieola Island, BC: New Society Publishers.

Frederick, W.C. (2006). *Corporation Be Good: The Story of Corporate Social Responsibility.* Indianapolis, IN: Dog Ear Publishing.

Freeman, R.E. (1984). *Strategic Management: A Stakeholder Approach.* Boston, MA: Pitman.

Freeman, R.E. and Evan, W.M. (1990). Corporate governance: a stakeholder perspective. *Journal of Behavioral Economics*, **19** (4): 337–59.

Friedman, A.L. and Miles, S. (2002). Developing stakeholder theory. *Journal of Management Studies*, **39** (1): 1–21.

Friedman, M. (1962). *Capitalism and Freedom.* Chicago, IL: University of Chicago Press.

Frynas, J.G. (2001). Corporate and state responses to anti-oil protests in the Niger Delta. *African Affairs*, **100**: 27–54.

Fung, A. (2003). Deliberative democracy and international labor standards. *Governance*, **16**: 51–71.

Galbraith, J.K. (1999). Free market fraud. *Progressive*, **63** (1): 17–31.

Galbraith, J.K. (2000). The social left and the market system. In B.K. Gills (ed.), *Globalization and the Politics of Resistance*. New York: Palgrave.

Galeano, E. (1998). *Upside Down: A Primer for the Looking Glass World*. New York: Picador.

Gathii, J.T. (2001). Construing intellectual property rights and competition policy: consistency with facilitating access to affordable AIDS drugs to low-end consumers. *Florida Law Review*, **53**: 727–34.

GEMI (1992). *Total Quality Environmental Management: The Primer*. Washington, DC: Global Environmental Management Initiative.

Ghoshal, S. and Moran, P. (1996). Bad for practice: a critique of the transaction cost theory. *Academy of Management Review*, **21**: 13–47.

Gibbons, B. (2007). H.L. Mencken's quotations, http://www.io.com/gibbonsb/mencken/megaquotes.html. Accessed 15 June 2007.

Gibson, R. (1998). *Political economy for the earnest*, http://www.pipeline.com/~rgibson/POLIECO.html. Accessed 15 March 2007.

Gills, B.K. (2000). *Globalization and the Politics of Resistance*. New York: Palgrave.

Gladwin, T.N., Kennelly, J.J. and Krause, T.S. (1995). Shifting paradigms for sustainable development: implications for management theory and research. *Academy of Management Review*, **20** (4): 874–907.

Goldsmith, E. (1997). Development as colonialism. *Ecologist*, **27** (2): 60–79.

Gordon, C. (1991). Government rationality: an introduction. In G. Burchell, C. Gordon and P. Miller (eds), *The Foucault Effect: Studies in Governmentality*. Chicago, IL: University of Chicago Press, pp. 87–104.

Gramlich, J.D. and Wheeler, J.E. (2003). How Chevron, Texaco, and the Indonesian government structured transactions to avoid billions in U.S. income taxes. *Accounting Horizons*, **17** (3): 107–22.

Gramsci, A. (1971). *Selections from the Prison Notebooks*. New York: International Publishers.

Grandin, G. (2006). *Empire's Workshop: Latin America, the United States and the Rise of the New Imperialism*. New York: Metropolitan Books.

Granovetter, M. and Swedberg, R. (2001). *The Sociology of Economic Life.* Boulder, CO: Westview Press.

Grassé, P.P. (1977). *Evolution of Living Organisms: Evidence for a New Theory of Transformation.* New York: Academic Press.

Green, D. and Griffith, M. (2002). Globalization and its discontents. *International Affairs*, **78** (1): 49–68.

Greider, W. (1996). Citizen G.E. In J. Mander and E. Goldsmith (eds) *The Case against the Global Economy.* San Francisco, CA: Sierra Club Books, pp. 323–34.

Grewal, I. (2005). *Transnational America: Feminisms, Diasporas, Neoliberalisms.* Durham, NC: Duke University Press.

Grey, C. (1994). Career as a project of the self and labor process discipline. *Sociology*, **28** (2): 479–98.

Grice, S. and Humphries, M. (1997). Critical management studies in postmodernity: oxymorons in outer space? *Journal of Organization Change Management*, **10** (5): 412–25.

Guha, R. and Martinez-Alier, J. (1997). *Varieties of Environmentalism.* London: Earthscan.

Gunningham, N., Kagan, R. and Thornton, D. (2003). *Shades of Green: Business, Regulation and Environment.* Stanford, CA: Stanford University Press.

Gutman, A. and Thompson, F. (2004). *Why Deliberative Democracy.* Princeton, NJ: Princeton University Press.

Habermas, J. (1996). *Between Facts and Norms: Contributions to a Discourse Theory of Law and Democracy.* Cambridge, MA: MIT Press.

Habermas, J. (1998). Three normative models of democracy. In J. Habermas (ed.) *The Inclusion of the Other: Studies in Political Theory.* Cambridge, MA: MIT Press, pp. 239–52.

Hall, S. (1997). *Representation: Cultural Representations and Signifying Practices.* London: Sage.

Hallman, D.G. (1995). Ethics and sustainable development. In D.G. Hallman (ed.) *Ecotheology: Voices from South and North.* New York: Orbis Books.

Hardt, M. and Negri, A. (2000). *Empire.* Cambridge, MA: Harvard University Press.

Harness, E.G. (1978). No charity for charity's sake. *Business and Society Review*, **10**.

Harrison, J.S. and St John, C.H. (1994). *Strategic Management of Organizations and Stakeholders.* Eagan, MN: West.

Hart, S.L. (1995). A natural-resource-based view of the firm. *Academy of Management Review*, **20** (4): 986–1014.

Hart, S.L. (1997). Beyond greening: strategies for a sustainable world. *Harvard Business Review*, January/February: 6–76.

Hart, S.L. and Ahuja, G. (1996). Does it pay to be green? An empirical examination of the relationship between emission reduction and firm performance. *Business Strategy and the Environment*, **5**: 30–37.

Harvard Law Review (1989). Incorporating the Republic: the corporation in antebellum political culture, 1883–1903.

Harvey, D. (1996). *Justice, Nature and the Geography of Difference*. Oxford: Blackwell.

Harvey, D. (2003). *The New Imperialism*. Oxford: Oxford University Press.

Harvey, D. (2005). *A Brief History of Neoliberalism*. Oxford: Oxford University Press.

Hawken, P. (1995). *The Ecology of Commerce: A Declaration of Sustainability*. London: Phoenix.

Hayes, P. (1987). *Industry and Ideology: IG Farben in the Nazi Era*. Cambridge: Cambridge University Press.

Hazen, M.A. (1993). Towards polyphonic organization. *Journal of Organizational Change Management*, **6**: 15–26.

Hemphill, T. (2004). Corporate citizenship: the case for a new corporate governance model. *Business and Society Review*, **109** (3): 339–61.

Hertz, N. (2001). *The Silent Takeover: Global Capitalism and the Death of Democracy*. London: Arrow.

Hessen, R. (1979). *In Defense of the Corporation*. Stanford, CA: Hoover Institution Press.

Hill, C.W.L. and Jones, T.M. (1992). Stakeholder-agency theory. *Journal of Management Studies*, **29**: 131–54.

Hillman, A. and Keim, G. (2001). Shareholder value, stakeholder management, and social issues. What's the bottom line? *Strategic Management Journal*, **22** (2): 125–39.

Holmberg, J. and Sandbrook, R. (1992). Sustainable development: what is to be done? In J. Holmberg (ed.) *Policies for a Small Planet*. London: Earthscan.

Howitt, R. and Douglas, J. (1983). *Aborigines and Mining Companies in Northern Australia*. Chippendale: Alternative Publishing Cooperative.

Howse, R. (2002). From politics to technocracy – and back again: the fate of the multilateral trading regime. *American Journal of International Law*, **96** (94): 94–117.

Human Rights Watch (1999). The price of oil: corporate responsibility and human rights violations in Nigeria's oil producing communities, http://www. hrw.org/reports/1999/nigeria. Accessed 15 March 2007.

ICCPR (1976). International Covenant on Civil and Political Rights, http://www. ohcr.org/english/law/ccpr.htm. Accessed 15 March 2007.

ICESCR (1976). International Covenant on Economic, Social and Cultural

Rights, http://www.unhchr.ch/html/menu3/b/a_cescr.htm. Accessed 15 March 2007.

ICME (1999). *Mining and Indigenous Peoples: Case Studies*. Ottawa: International Council on Metals and the Environment.

IIFC (International Indigenous Forum on Climate Change) (2000). Declaration of Indigenous Peoples on climate change. Second International Indigenous Forum on Climate Change, The Hague, 11–12 November.

IMF (2005). IMF managing directors, http://www.imf.org/external/np/exr/chron/mds.asp. Accessed 15 March 2007.

India Network News Digest (2005). Dragon runs, India barely walks. *India Network News Digest*, **20**: 11.

International Herald Tribune (2005), http://www.iht.com/articles/2005/12/20/business/toyota.php. Accessed 15 March 2007.

Iwanowa v. Ford Motor Company. 67 F Suppl. 2d 424 (DNJ 1999).

Jacobs, M. (1994). The limits to neoclassicism: towards an institutional environmental economics. In M. Redclift and T. Benton (eds), *Social Theory and the Global Environment*. New York: Routledge, pp. 67–91.

Jensen, M. (1988). Takeovers: their causes and consequences. *Journal of Economic Perspectives*, **2** (1): 21–44.

Johnson, G. and Scholes, K. (2002). *Exploring Corporate Strategy*, 6th edn. Harlow, Essex: Pearson Education.

Johnson, H.L. (1958). Can the businessman apply Christianity? *Harvard Business Review*, **36** (4): 68–76.

Jones, T.M. (1995). Instrumental stakeholder theory: a synthesis of ethics and economics. *Academy of Management Review*, **20**: 404–38.

Joseph, S. (2003). Pharmaceutical corporations and access to drugs: the 'fourth wave' of corporate human rights scrutiny. *Human Rights Quarterly*, **25**: 425–52.

Judge, W.Q. and Douglas, T.J. (1998). Performance implications of incorporating natural environment issues into the strategic planning process: an empirical assessment. *Journal of Management Studies*, **35**: 241–62.

Kahn, J. and Yardley, J. (2004). Amid China's boom, no helping hand for young Qingming. *New York Times*, 1 August: 1.

Katona, J. (1998). If Native Title is us, it's inside us: Jabiluka and the politics of intercultural negotiation. Interview with S. Perera and J. Pugliese. *Australian Feminist Law Journal*, **10** (March): 1–34.

Kauffman, P. (1998). *Wik, Mining and Aborigines*. St Leonards: Allen & Unwin.

Kell, G. (2003). The Global Compact: origins, operations, progress, challenges. *Journal of Corporate Citizenship*, **11**: 35–49.

Kelly, M. (2001). *The Divine Right of Capital: Dethroning the Corporate Aristocracy*. San Francisco, CA: Berrett-Koehler.

Kennedy, D. (2002). The international human rights movement: part of the problem. *Harvard Human Rights Journal*, **15**: 101–25.

Kepner, C.D. and Soothill, J.H. (1935). *The Banana Empire: A Case Study of Economic Imperialism.* New York: Vanguard Press.

Kilbourne, W., McDonagh, P. and Prothero, A. (1997). Sustainable consumption and the quality of life: a macromarketing challenge to the dominant social paradigm. *Journal of Macromarketing*, **14**: 42–63.

Kinley, D. and McBeth, A. (2003). Human rights, trade and multinational corporations. In R. Sullivan (ed.) *Business and Human Rights*. Sheffield: Greenleaf Publishing, pp. 52–81.

Kirkby, J., O'Keefe, P. and Timberlake, L. (1995). *Sustainable Development.* London: Earthscan.

Klassen, R.D. and McLaughlin, C.P. (1996). The impact of environmental management on firm performance. *Management Science*, **42**: 1199–214.

Knights, D. (1992). Changing spaces: the disruptive impact of a new epistemological location for the study of management. *Academy of Management Review*, **17** (3): 514–36.

Knights, D. and Willmott, H. (1989). Power and subjectivity: from degradation to subjugation in social relations. *Sociology*, **23** (4): 535–58.

Knights, D. and Morgan, G. (1993). Organization theory and consumption in a post-modern era. *Organization Studies*, **14** (2): 211–18.

Kochan, T.A. and Rubinstein, S. (2000). Toward a stakeholder theory of the firm: the Saturn partnership. *Organization Science*, **11** (4): 367–86.

Koku, O., Akhigbe, A. and Spronger, T. (1997). The financial impact of boycotts and threat of boycotts. *Journal of Business Research*, **40** (1): 15–20.

Korten, D.C. (1995). *When Corporations Rule the World.* West Hartford, CT: Kumarian Press.

Korten, D.C. (1999). *The Post-Corporate World: Life after Capitalism.* West Hartford, CT: Kumarian Press.

Kothari, S. (1997). Whose independence? The social impact of economic reform in India. *Journal of International Affairs*, Summer: 44–61.

Kotler, P. and Lee, N. (2005). *Corporate Social Responsibility: Doing the Most Good for Your Company and Cause.* Hoboken, NJ: John Wiley & Sons.

Krastev, I. (2002). The Balkans: democracy without choices. *Journal of Democracy*, **13** (3): 39–53.

Kristof, K.M. (2003). Study ties biggest CEO raises to largest layoffs. *Los Angeles Times*, 26 August: B4.

Krugman, P. (1995). Dutch tulips and emerging markets. *Foreign Affairs*, **74** (4): 28–44.

Lawrence, A.T. (2002). The drivers of stakeholder engagement: reflections on the case of Royal Dutch/Shell. *Journal of Corporate Citizenship*, **6**: 71–85.

Leflaive, X. (1996). Organizations as structures of domination. *Organization Studies*, **17** (1): 23–37.

Leisinger, K.M. (2003). Opportunities and risks of the United Nations Global Compact. *Journal of Corporate Citizenship*, **11**: 113–31.

Leisinger, K.M. (2005). The corporate social responsibility of the pharmaceutical industry: idealism without illusion and realism without resignation. *Business Ethics Quarterly*, **15** (4): 577–94.

Levitt, T. (1958). The dangers of corporate social responsibility. *Harvard Business Review*, **36** (3): 41–50.

Levy, D.L. (1997). Environmental management as political sustainability. *Organization and Environment*, **10** (2): 126–47.

Levy, D.L. and Egan, D. (2003). A neo-Gramscian approach to corporate political strategy: conflict and accommodation in the climate change negotiations. *Journal of Management Studies*, **40**: 803–30.

Levy, D.L. and Kaplan, R. (2007). CSR and theories of global governance: strategic contestation in global issue arenas. In A. Crane, A. McWilliams, D. Matten, J. Moon and D. Siegel (eds) *The Oxford Handbook of CSR*. Oxford: Oxford University Press.

Lifsher, M. (2005). Unocal settles human rights lawsuit over alleged abuses at Myanmar pipeline. *Los Angeles Times*, 22 March.

Lippman, M. (1995). War crime trials of German industrialists: the 'other' soldiers. *Temple International and Comparative Law Journal*, **173**: 229–49.

Lohman, L. (2005). Marketing and making carbon dumps: commodification, calculations and counterfactuals in climate change mitigation. *Science as Culture*, **14** (3): 203–35.

Luke, T.W. (1993). Green consumerism: ecology and the ruse of recycling. In J. Bennett and W. Chaloupka (eds) *In the Nature of Things*. Minneapolis, MN: University of Minneapolis Press, pp. 154–72.

Luttwak, E. (1999). *Turbo-Capitalism: Winners and Losers in the Global Economy*. London: Orion Books.

Lyon, T. and Maxwell, J. (2004). *Corporate Environmentalism and Public Policy*. Cambridge: Cambridge University Press.

Maas, P. (2005). Road to hell: Niger Delta dispatch. *New Republic*, 25 February: 2–4.

McAfee, K. (1999). Selling nature to save it? Biodiversity and green developmentalism. *Environment and Planning D*, **17** (2): 133–54.

McCalman, P. (2001). Reaping what you sow: an empirical analysis of international patent harmonization. *Journal of International Economics*, **55** (1): 161–86.

McDonald, D. and Pape, J. (2002). *Cost Recovery and the Crisis of Service Delivery in South Africa*. London: Zed Books.

McDowell, C. (2003). Privatizing infrastructure development: 'development refugees' and the resettlement challenge. In R. Sullivan (ed.) *Business and Human Rights*. Sheffield: Greenleaf Publishing, pp. 155–68.

Macnaghten, P. and Urry, J. (1998). *Contested Natures*. London: Sage Publications.

McWilliams, A. and Siegel, D. (2000). Corporate social responsibility and financial performance: Correlation or misspecification? *Strategic Management Journal*, **21**: 603–9.

McWilliams, A. and Siegel, D. (2001). Corporate social responsibility: A theory of the firm perspective. *Academy of Management Review*, **26** (1): 117–27.

Madrick, J. (2004). Economic sense. *New York Times*, 28 October: C2.

Magretta, J. (1997). Growth through global sustainability: an interview with Monsanto's CEO, Robert B. Shapiro. *Harvard Business Review*, January/February: 79–88.

Mantziaris, C. (1999). The dual view of the corporation and the Aboriginal corporation. *Federal Law Review*, **27** (2): 283–321.

Marcos, S. and the Zapatista Army of National Liberation (1995). *Shadows of Tender Fury: The Letters and Communiqués of Subcomandante Marcos and the Zapatista Army of National Liberation*. New York: Monthly Review Press.

Margolis, J.D. and Walsh, J.P. (2003). Misery loves companies: rethinking social initiatives by business. *Administrative Science Quarterly*, **48**: 268–305.

Marshall, T.H. (1965). *Class, Citizenship and Social Development*. New York: Anchor Books.

Martin, A. (2007). Tobacco's stigma aside, Wall Street finds a lot to like. *New York Times*, 31 January.

Martin, R.L. (2002). The virtue matrix: calculating the return on corporate responsibility. *Harvard Business Review*, **80** (3): 69–75.

Martin, W.F. (1978). The wish to be welcomed. *Business and Society Review*, **16**.

Martinez-Alier, J. (1987). *Ecological Economics: Energy, Environment and Society*. Oxford: Blackwell.

Mateo, N. (2000). Bioprospecting and conservation in Costa Rica. In H. Svarstad and S.S. Dhillion (eds) *Responding to Bioprospecting: From Biodiversity in the South to Medicines in the North*. Oslo: Spartacus Forlag As, pp. 45–56.

Matten, D. and Crane, A. (2005). Corporate citizenship: toward an extended theoretical conceptualization. *Academy of Management Review*, **30**: 166–79.

May, C. and Sell, S.K. (2006). *Intellectual Property Rights: A Critical History*. London: Lynne Rienner Publications.

Mehta, L. (2006). Do human rights make a difference to poor and vulnerable people? Accountability for the right to water in South Africa. In P. Newell and J. Wheeler (eds) *Rights, Resources and the Politics of Accountability*. London: Zed Books, pp. 63–79.

Milmo, C. (2005). India's suicide epidemic is blamed on the British, http://news. independent.co.uk/world/asia. Accessed 15 March 2007.

Mir, R. and Mir, A. (2002). The organizational imagination: from paradigm wars to praxis. *Organizational Research Methods*, **5** (1): 105–25.

Mitchell, H. (2005). *A Call to Action: Taking Back Healthcare for Future Generations*. New York: McGraw-Hill.

Mitchell, N.J. (1989). *The Generous Corporation: A Political Analysis of Economic Power*. New Haven, CT: Yale University Press.

Mitchell, R., Agle, B. and Wood, D. (1997). Toward a theory of stakeholder identification and salience: defining the principle of who and what really counts. *Academy of Management Review*, **22** (4): 853–86.

Mitra, S. and Singh, V.B. (1999). *Democracy and Social Change in India: A Cross-sectional Analysis of the National Electorate*. New Delhi: Sage Publications.

Mittelman, J.H. (2000). *The Globalization Syndrome: Transformation and Resistance*. Princeton, NJ: Princeton University Press.

Monastersky, R. (2007). International scientific panel on climate change is 90% sure that human actions have warmed the planet. *Chronicle of Higher Education*, 3 February.

Monbiot, G. (1997). Seeds of destruction in Monsanto conspiracy. *Sydney Morning Herald*, 20 September.

Monbiot, G. (2004). *The Age of Consent: A Manifesto for a New Global Order*. New Delhi: Harper Collins.

Moon, J., Crane, A. and Matten, D. (2005). Can corporations be citizens: corporate citizenship as a metaphor for business participation in society. *Business Ethics Quarterly*, **15** (3): 429–53.

Mooney, P.R. (2000). Why we call it biopiracy. In H. Svarstad and S.S. Dhillion (eds) *Responding to Bioprospecting: From Biodiversity in the South to Medicines in the North*. Oslo: Spartacus Forlag As, pp. 37–44.

Muchlinski, P. (2003). The development of human rights responsibilities for multinational enterprises. In R. Sullivan (ed.) *Business and Human Rights*. Sheffield: Greenleaf Publishing, pp. 32–51.

Muecke, S. (1992). *Textual Spaces: Aboriginality and Cultural Studies*. Sydney: University of New South Wales Press.

Munshi, N.V. (2004). Conversations on business citizenship. *Business and Society Review*, **109** (1): 89–93.

Munson, A. (1995). The United Nations Convention on Biological Diversity. In J. Kirkby (ed.), *The Earthscan Reader in Sustainable Development*. London: Earthscan.

Murphy, C. (2002). Is BP beyond petroleum? Hardly. *Fortune*, 20 September: 44.

Nader, R., Green, M. and Seligman, J. (1976). *Taming the Giant Corporation.* New York: W.W. Norton.

Nash, J.C. (2001). *Mayan Visions: The Quest for Autonomy in an Age of Globalization.* New York: Routledge.

New York Times (2005). Editorial: an update on corporate slavery, 31 January.

Newell, P. (2005). Citizenship, accountability and community: the limits of the CSR agenda. *International Affairs*, **81** (3): 541–57.

Newell, P. (2006). Taking accountability into account: the debate so far. In P. Newell and J. Wheeler (eds) *Rights, Resources and the Politics of Accountability.* London: Zed Books, pp. 37–58.

Newell, P. and Wheeler, J. (2006). Introduction. In P. Newell and J. Wheeler (eds) *Rights, Resources and the Politics of Accountability.* London: Zed Books, pp. 1–36.

Newton, T. (1998). Theorizing subjectivity in organizations: the failure of Foucauldian studies? *Organization Studies*, **19**: 415–47.

Newton, T. and Harte, G. (1997). Green business: technicist kitsch? *Journal of Management Studies*, **34** (1): 75–98.

Norman, W. and Macdonald, C. (2004). Getting to the bottom of 'triple bottom line'. *Business Ethics Quarterly*, **14** (2): 243–62.

O'Connor, J. (1994). Is sustainable capitalism possible? In M. O'Conner (ed.) *Is Capitalism Sustainable? Political Economy and the Politics of Ecology.* New York: Guildford Press, pp. 152–75.

O'Donnell, G. (1994). Delegative democracy. *Journal of Democracy*, **5** (1): 29–43.

Ong, A. (2005). Graduated sovereignty in South East Asia. In J.X. Inda (ed.) *Anthropologies of Modernity: Foucault, Governmentality and Life Politics.* Oxford: Blackwell.

Orlitzky, M., Schmidt, F.L. and Rynes, S.L. (2003). Corporate social and financial performance: a meta-analysis. *Organization Studies*, **24**: 403–41.

Osland, J.S., Dhanda, K.K. and Uthas, K. (2002). Globalization and environmental sustainability: an analysis of the impact of globalization using the Natural Step framework. In S. Sharma and M. Starik (eds) *Research on Corporate Sustainability: The Evolving Theory and Practice of Organizations in the Natural Environment.* Cheltenham, UK and Northampton, MA, USA: Edward Elgar, pp. 31–60.

Parry, G. (1991). Paths to citizenship. In U. Vogel and M. Noran (eds), *The Frontiers of Citizenship.* New York: St Martin's Press, pp. 166–201.

Patnaik, P. (1990). *Whatever Happened to Imperialism and Other Essays.* New Delhi: Tulika.

Patomäki, H. and Teivainen, T. (2004). *A Possible World: Democratic Transformation of Global Institutions*. London: Zed Books.

Payne, A. (2005). *The Global Politics of Unequal Development*. New York: Palgrave Macmillan.

Pearce, D.W., Markandya, A. and Barbier, E.B. (1989). *Blueprint for a Green Economy*. London: Earthscan.

Perera, S. and Pugliese, J. (1998). Parks, mines and tidy towns: enviro-panopticism, 'post'colonialism, and the politics of heritage in Australia. *Postcolonial Studies*, **1** (1): 69–100.

Perriere, T. and Seuret, G. (2000). *Brave New Seeds*. Sydney: Pluto Press.

Perrow, C. (2002). *Organizing America: Wealth, Power and the Origins of Corporate Capitalism*. Princeton, NJ: Princeton University Press.

Peterson, S. (1990). Whose rights? A critique of the 'givens' in human rights discourse. *Alternatives*, **15** (3): 303–44.

Pettersson, B. (2002). Development-induced displacement: internal affair or international human rights issue? *Forced Migration Review*, **12**: 16–19.

Philip Morris (2002). Listening, learning and changing: the path to corporate responsibility at Philip Morris Companies, http://www.philipmorris.com/pressroom/executive_speeches/speech_nicoli_fresno.asp. Accessed 15 March 2007.

Piasecki, B.W., Fletcher, K.A. and Mendelson, F.J. (1999). *Environmental Management and Business Strategy: Leadership Skills for the 21st Century*. New York: John Wiley.

Pitelis, C. (1993). Transnationals, international organization and deindustrialization. *Organization Studies*, **14** (4): 527–43.

Polanyi, K. (1944). *The Great Transformation: The Political and Economic Origins of Our Time*. Boston, MA: Beacon Press.

Porter, M.E. (1995). Green and competitive: ending the stalemate. *Harvard Business Review*, **73** (5): 120–34.

Post, J.E. and Berman, S.L. (2001). Global corporate citizenship in a dot com world. In J. Andriof and M. McIntosh (eds) *Perspectives on Corporate Citizenship*. Sheffield: Greenleaf Publishing, pp. 53–65.

Post, J.E., Preston, L.E. and Sachs, S. (2002). *Redefining the Corporation: Stakeholder Management and Organizational Wealth*. Stanford, CA: Stanford University Press.

Prahalad, C.K. and Hamel, G. (1990). The core competence of the corporation. *Harvard Business Review*, **68** (3): 79–91.

Prahalad, C.K. and Lieberthal, K. (1998). The end of corporate imperialism. *Harvard Business Review*, **76** (1): 69–79.

Prahalad, C.K. and Hammond, A. (2002). Serving the world's poor, profitably. *Harvard Business Review*, **80** (9): 48–57.

Preston, L.E. and Post, J.E. (1975). *Private Management and Public Policy:*

The Principle of Public Responsibility. Englewood Cliffs, NJ: Prentice Hall.

Puckett, J. and Smith, T. (eds) (2002). *Exporting Harm: The High-Tech Trashing of Asia.* Seattle, WA: Basel Action Network.

Quarter, J. (2000). *Beyond the Bottom Line: Socially Innovative Business Owners.* Westport, CT: Quorum.

Rahman, S.S. (2002). Stakeholder discourse and critical-frame analysis: the case of child labor in Bangladesh. *Journal of Corporate Citizenship*, **6**: 111–29.

Rajagopal, B. (2001). The violence of development. *Washington Post*, 8 August.

Ramasastry, A. (1998). Secrets and lies: Swiss banks and international human rights. *Vanderbilt Journal of Transnational Law*, **31** (2): 325–523.

Ramasastry, A. (2002). Corporate complicity: from Nuremberg to Rangoon – an examination of forced labor cases and their impact on the liability of multinational corporations. *Berkeley Journal of International Law*, **20** (9): 91–159.

Randeria, S. (2007). The state of globalization: legal pluralities, overlapping sovereignties and ambiguous alliances between civil society and the cunning state in India. *Theory, Culture and Society*, **24** (1): 1–33.

Rao, H., Morrill, C. and Zald, M.N. (2000). Power plays: how social movements and collective action create new organizational forms. In B.M. Staw and R.I. Sutton (eds) *Research in Organizational Behavior*, Vol. 22. New York: JAI.

Redclift, M. (1987). *Sustainable Development: Exploring the Contradictions.* London: Methuen.

Regan, M.C. (1998). *Debating Democracy's Discontent: Essays on American Politics, Law and Public Philosophy.* Oxford: Oxford University Press.

Reich, S. (2002). The Ford Motor Company and the Third Reich. *Dimensions: A Journal of Holocaust Studies*, **13** (2), http://www.adl.org/braun/dim_13_2_ford.asp. Accessed 15 March 2007.

Renner, M. (1997). *Fighting for Survival: Environmental Decline, Social Conflict and the New Age of Insecurity.* London: Earthscan.

Rhodes, M. and Apeldoorn, B. van (1998). Capital unbound: the transformation of European corporate governance. *Journal of European Public Policy*, **5**: 406–27.

Rifkin, J. (1999). *The Biotech Century: How Genetic Commerce Will Change the World.* London: Phoenix.

Rio Tinto (2007). Global citizen, local partner, http://www.riotinto.com/community. Accessed 15 March 2007.

Roberts, J. (1981). *Massacres to Mining: The Colonization of Aboriginal Australia.* Victoria: Globe Press.

Roberts, J. (2003). The manufacture of corporate social responsibility. *Organization*, **10**: 249–65.

Rossi, M.S., Brown, H.S. and Baas, L.W. (2000). Leaders in sustainable development: how agents of change define the agenda. *Business Strategy and the Environment*, **9**: 273–86.

Roy, A. (2001). *Power Politics*. Cambridge, MA: South End Press.

Russo, M.V. and Fouts, P.A (1997). A resource-based perspective on corporate environmental performance and profitability. *Academy of Management Journal*, **40**: 534–59.

Sample, I. (2007). Scientists offered cash to dispute climate study. *Guardian*, 3 February.

Schedler, A., Diamond, L. and Plattner, M. (1999). *The Self-Restraining State: Power and Accountability in New Democracies*. London: Lynne Rienner Publishers.

Scherer, A.G. and Palazzo, G. (2007). Toward a political conception of corporate responsibility: business and society seen from a Habermasian perspective. *Academy of Management Review*, **32** (4).

Schoenberger, K. (2000). *Levi's Children*. New York: Grove Press.

Scholte, J.A. (2000). *Globalization: A Critical Introduction*. Basingstoke: Palgrave Macmillan.

Schot, J., Brand, E. and Fischer, K. (1997). The greening of industry or a sustainable future: building an international research agenda. *Business Strategy and the Environment*, **6**: 153–62.

Scudder, T. (1993). Development-induced relocation and refugee studies: 37 years of change and continuity among Zambia's Gwembe Tonga. *Journal of Refugee Studies*, **6** (3): 123–52.

Sen, A. (1999). *Development as Freedom*. New York: Anchor Books.

Sen, J., Anand, A., Escobar, A. and Waterman, P. (2004). *World Social Forum: Challenging Empires*. New Delhi: Viveka Foundation.

Sengupta, A. (2002). On the theory and practice of the right to development. *Human Rights Quarterly*, **24**: 837–89.

Sethi, P. (1979). A conceptual framework for evaluative analysis of social issues and evaluation of business response patterns. *Academy of Management Review*, **4**: 63–74.

Sharma, S. and Vredenburg, H. (1998). Proactive corporate environmental strategy and the development of competitively valuable organizational capabilities. *Strategic Management Journal*, **19**: 729–53.

Shiva, V. (1991). *The Violence of the Green Revolution: Third World Agriculture, Ecology and Politics*. London: Zed Books.

Shiva, V. (1993). *Monocultures of the Mind: Perspectives on Biodiversity and Biotechnology*. London: Zed Books.

Shiva, V. (2001). *Protect or Plunder: Understanding Intellectual Property Rights*. London: Zed Books.

Shrivastava, P. (1994). Castrated environment: greening organizational studies. *Organization Studies*, **15** (5): 705–21.

Smith, C. (1994). The new corporate philanthropy. *Harvard Business Review*, **72** (3): 105–16.

Speed, S. and Collier, J. (2000). Limiting Indigenous autonomy in Chiapas, Mexico: the state government's use of human rights. *Human Rights Quarterly*, **22** (4): 877–905.

Stiglitz, J.E. (1996). Some lessons from the East Asian Miracle. *The World Bank Economic Observer*, **11** (2): 151–77.

Stiglitz, J.E. (1998). More instruments and broader goals: moving toward the post-Washington Consensus. The 1998 World Institute for Development Economic Research Annual Lecture, 7 January, Helsinki, http://www.world-bank.org.html/extdr/extme/jssp101998.htm. Accessed 15 March 2007.

Stiglitz, J.E. (2000). The insider. *The New Republic Online*, 17 April.

Stiglitz, J.E. (2002). *Globalization and its Discontents*. New York: W.W. Norton.

Stokes, G. (2002). Democracy and citizenship. In A. Carter and G. Stokes (eds) *Democratic Theory Today*. Cambridge: Polity Press.

Strauss, G. (2003). CEOs still sitting on piles of pay. *USA Today*, 25 August: C3.

Swanson, D. and Niehoff, B.P. (2001). Business citizenship outside and inside organizations: an emergent synthesis of corporate responsibility and employee citizenship. In J. Andriof and M. McIntosh (eds) *Perspectives on Corporate Citizenship*. Sheffield: Greenleaf Publishing, pp. 104–16.

Swanson, T. M. (1995). The appropriation of evolution's values: an institutional analysis of intellectual property regimes and biodiversity conservation. In T.M. Swanson (ed.) *Intellectual Property Rights and Biodiversity Conservation: An Interdisciplinary Analysis of the Values of Medicinal Plants*. Cambridge: Cambridge University Press.

Tatz, C. (1982). *Aborigines and Uranium and Other Essays*. Victoria: Heinemann Educational Australia.

Taylor, C. (1978). The politics of the steady state. *NUQ*, Spring: 157–84.

Taylor, C. (2002). Modern social imaginaries. *Public Culture*, **14** (1): 91–124.

Thérien, J.P. (1999). Beyond the North–South divide: two tales of world poverty. *Third World Quarterly*, **20** (4): 723–42.

Thomas, C. (2000). *Global Governance, Development and Human Security: The Challenge of Poverty and Inequality*. London: Pluto Press.

Thomas, P. (1999). Stakeholders and strategic management: the misappropriation of discourse. Paper presented at the Critical Management Studies Conference, Manchester, UK, July.

Townley, B. (1997). Beyond good and evil: Foucault and HRM. In A. McKinlay and K. Starkey (eds) *Foucault, Management and Organization Theory.* London: Sage, pp. 191–210.

Toyota (2005). Toyota in the World Data Book, http://www.toyota.com.jp/en/about_toyota/pdf2005/index.html. Accessed 15 March 2007.

Truby, M. (2003). Sierra Club ads may dim Ford party: environmentalists press automaker to boost fuel economy. *The Detroit News*, 4 June.

Tucker, L. and Ganesan, A. (1997). The small hands of slavery: India's bonded child laborers and the World Bank. *Multinational Monitor*, http://www.third-worldtraveler.com/IMF_WB/SmallHands_MNM.html. Accessed 15 March 2007.

Turton, D. (1996). Migrants and refugees. In T. Allen (ed.) *In Search of Cool Ground: War, Flight and Homecoming in Northeast Africa.* London: James Currey.

UNICEF (1997). The state of the world's children, http://www.unicef.org/sowc97. Accessed 15 March 2007.

United Nations (1994). *International Convention on the Rights of Indigenous Nations.* New York: UN Publications.

United Nations (2002). Draft norms on responsibilities of transnational corporations and other business enterprises with regard to human rights. UN Doc. E/CN.4/Sub.2/2002/13, www.umn.edu/humanrts/links/tncreport-2002.html. Accessed 15 March 2007.

United Nations (2006). The Global Compact: corporate citizenship in the world economy, www.unglobalcompact.org. Accessed 15 March 2007.

United States v. Krauch *et al.* (1952). *The I.G. Farben Case: Trials of War Criminals before the Nuremberg Military Tribunals*, iii–iv.

United States v. Krupp (1952). *Trials of War Criminals before the Nuremberg Military Tribunals*, IX.

United States v. Von Weiszaecker (1952). *Trials of War Criminals before the Nuremberg Military Tribunals*, XIV: 621–2.

Victor, D.G. (2001). *The Collapse of the Kyoto Protocol and the Struggle to Slow Global Warming.* Princeton: Princeton University Press.

Visvanathan, S. (1991). Mrs Brundtland's disenchanted cosmos. *Alternatives*, **16** (3): 377–84.

Vogel, D. (2005). *The Market for Virtue: The Potential and Limits of Corporate Social Responsibility.* Washington, DC: Brookings Institution Press.

Waddington, C.H. (1977). Whitehead and modern science. In J.B. Cobb and D.R. Griffin (eds) *Mind in Nature: Essays on the Interface of Science and Philosophy.* Washington, DC: University Press of America.

Waddock, S. (2001). Integrity and mindfulness: foundations of corporate citizenship. In J. Andriof and M. McIntosh (eds) *Perspectives on Corporate Citizenship.* Sheffield: Greenleaf Publishing, pp. 26–38.

Wade, R. (2003). What strategies are available for developing countries today? The World Trade Organization and the shrinking of development space. *Review of International Political Economy*, **10** (4): 621–44.

Wade, R. (2004). On the causes of increasing world poverty and inequality, or why the Matthew effect prevails. *New Political Economy*, **9** (2): 163–88.

Walley, N. and Whitehead, B. (1994). It's not easy being green. *Harvard Business Review*, **72** (3): 46–52.

Wartick, S.L. and Cochran, P.L. (1985). The evolution of the corporate social performance model. *Academy of Management Review*, **10**: 758–69.

Waters, M. (1995). *Globalization*. London: Routledge.

Watts, M.J. (1999). Petro-violence: some thoughts on community, extraction and political ecology, http://repositories.cdlib.org/iis/bwep/WP99-1-Watts.

WCED (World Commission for Economic Development) (1987). *Our Common Future*. New York: Oxford University Press.

Welford, R. (1997). *Hijacking Environmentalism: Corporate Responses to Sustainable Development*. London: Earthscan.

Welsh, H.J. (1988). Shareholder activism. *Multinational Monitor*, **9**: 12–14.

Whetten, D.A., Rands, G. and Godfrey, P. (2002). What are the responsibilities of business to society? In A. Pettigrew, H. Thomas and R. Whittington (eds) *Handbook of Strategy and Management*. London: Sage, pp. 373–408.

Whitfield, D. (2001). *Public Services or Corporate Welfare: Rethinking the Nation State in the Global Economy*. London: Pluto Press.

Wiesen, S.J. (2002). German industry and the Third Reich: fifty years of forgetting and remembering. *Dimensions: A Journal of Holocaust Studies*, **13** (2), http://www.adl.org/braun/dim_13_2_forgetting.asp. Accessed 15 March 2007.

Williams, O.F. (2004). The UN Global Compact: the challenge and the promise. *Business Ethics Quarterly*, **14** (4): 755–74.

Williams, R. (1976). *Keywords: A Vocabulary of Culture and Society*. London: Fontana Press.

Williamson, J. (1993). Democracy and the 'Washington Consensus'. *World Development*, **21** (8): 1329–36.

Williamson. O.E. and Winter, S.G. (eds) (1991). *The Nature of the Firm: Origins, Evolution and Development*. New York: Oxford University Press.

Willmott, H. (1995). What has been happening in organization theory and does it matter? *Personnel Review*, **24** (8): 33–53.

Wilson, E.O. (1992). *The Diversity of Life*. London: Penguin Books.

Windsor, D. (2001). Corporate citizenship: evolution and interpretation. In J. Andriof and M. McIntosh (eds) *Perspectives on Corporate Citizenship*. Sheffield: Greenleaf Publishing, pp. 39–52.

Wolf, M. (2001). What the world needs from the multilateral trading system. In

G. Sampson (ed.) *The Role of the World Trade Organization in Global Governance.* Tokyo: United Nations University Press, pp. 183–208.

Wolfensohn, J. (2002). Interviewed by S. Bernhut. *Ivey Journal of Business*, March/April: 28–34.

Wood, D. (1991). Corporate social performance revisited. *Academy of Management Review*, **16** (4): 691–718.

Wood, D.J. and Logsdon, J.M. (2001). Theorizing business citizenship. In J. Andriof and M. McIntosh (eds) *Perspectives on Corporate Citizenship.* Sheffield: Greenleaf Publishing, pp. 83–103.

Wood, E.M. (2003). A manifesto for global capital? In G. Balakrishnan (ed.) *Debating Empire.* London: Verso Books.

Woods, N. and Narlikar, A. (2001). Governance and accountability: the WTO, the IMF and the World Bank. *International Social Science Journal*, **53** (170): 569–83.

World Bank (1995). *Global Economic Prospects and the Developing Countries.* Washington, DC: World Bank.

World Bank (2002a). *Global Economic Prospects and the Developing Countries.* Washington, DC: World Bank.

World Bank (2002b). *Globalization, Growth and Poverty: Building an Inclusive World Economy.* Oxford: Oxford University Press for the World Bank.

World Business Council (2005). Corporate social responsibility, http://www.partnerships.gov.au/csr/corporate.shtml. Accessed 15 March 2007.

World Development Report (2001). *Attacking Poverty.* New York: Oxford University Press.

World Development Report (2003). *Sustainable Developing in a Dynamic World: Transforming Institutions, Growth and Quality of Life.* New York: Oxford University Press.

World Development Report (2004). *Making Services Work for Poor People.* New York: Oxford University Press.

World Trade Organization (2000). Trade related intellectual property rights, http://www.wto.org/english/tratop_e/trips_e/t_agm3_e.htm#1. Accessed 15 March 2007.

Yingyi, Q. and Weingast, B.R. (1997). Federalism as a commitment to preserving market incentives. *Journal of Economic Perspectives*, **11**: 83–92.

Yunus, M. (with Alan Jolis) (1998). *Banker to the Poor: The Story of the Grameen Bank.* London: Aurum Press.

Zadek, S. (2001). *The Civil Corporation: The New Economy of Corporate Citizenship.* London: Earthscan.

Zadek, S. (2004). The path to corporate responsibility. *Harvard Business Review*, **82**: 125–32.

Zald, M.N. (2002). Spinning disciplines: critical management studies in the context of the transformation of management education. *Organization*, **9** (3): 365–85.

Zapatista (1998). Documentary film produced by Big Noise Films, Cambridge, MA.

Zizek, S. (2006). Nobody has to be vile. *London Review of Books*, **28** (7), http://www.lrb.co.uk/contribhome.php?get=zize01. Accessed 15 March 2007.

Index

Abrams, Frank 5
accountability 60, 98, 99, 122–3,
     155–61
activists 36, 37, 123, 126, 158–9, 168
     see also environmental activists
Africa *see* Nigeria; South Africa
African National Congress (ANC) 31–2
agency, and critical political economy
     128, 129–30, 139, 142–3
agency theory of the firm 23–4
     see also stakeholder-agency theory of
     the firm
Agreement on Trade-Related Aspects of
     Intellectual Property Rights (TRIPS)
     56, 103–5, 106, 108, 109, 110, 112,
     117
Alien Tort Claims Act (ATCA) 62, 63–4,
     96
Annan, Kofi 1, 97
anthrax scare 104
anti-globalization movement 149–50
Asea Brown Boveri (ABB) 86–7
Asia 75, 119, 174
     see also China; India; Iraq; Japan;
     Malaysia; Myanmar; Philippines
Auschwitz 60–61
Australia 34–6, 37–8, 43–4
automobile industry 87–8

Bakan, Joel 2, 9–10, 29, 50, 55, 56, 58,
     129, 157, 169, 171
Banerjee, Subhabrata Bobby 20–21, 28,
     33, 36, 37, 43, 48, 53, 78, 83, 84,
     90, 91, 134, 135, 138, 169
banking industry 141, 164, 175
Bayer 104
Becker, Gary 137
behavioral theory of the firm 23
beneficiary complicity 63
Berle, A.A. 161
Berman, S.L. 44–5

Big Pharma 56–7
biodiversity 73, 105, 106–9, 110,
     111–12, 114, 115, 138
biopiracy 111, 116–17
bioprospecting 110–11
biosphere people 115
biotechnology 80, 105, 108, 111–12,
     115–16
Birch, D. 42–3
Body Shop, The 17
Boggs, C. 132, 136, 137, 166
Bolivia 136
Bowen, Howard 7
BP 55–6, 147, 173, 174
bribery 75, 100, 101
Britain 7, 15, 135
Brundtland Commission 67, 92
Business Council for Sustainable
     Development 75, 90

campaigning coalitions 37, 159, 160
Canada 104, 152
capabilities 77, 82, 83, 122, 128, 130
capital 72–3, 114–15, 118, 137–8
carbon 114
Carroll, A. 16, 18, 19, 20, 35, 44
Carsons, Rachel 66
chartered corporations 7–8, 15
Chevron 45, 54–5, 173
child labor 49–50, 150
China 102
citizenship 45–7
civic virtue 12, 13, 14, 165
'civil corporation' 89–90
civil rights 95, 96, 103
Clarkson, M.B.E. 21–2, 24–5, 30
climate change 29, 75, 113–14, 134
coalitions, campaigning 37, 159, 160
codes of conduct, voluntary *see* voluntary
     codes of conduct
colonialism 7, 15, 130

deontology of the corporation 162–7
design for environment (DFE) 79, 89
developed countries 67, 68, 69, 74, 75, 132
developing countries
and biodiversity 73, 106–7
and codes of conduct 59
crises 68–9
and development concept 67
drug supply 56–8, 103–4
economic development 74, 104–5
and green developmentalism 138
hazardous waste disposal 59
and human rights 100–105, 117–18, 142
and intellectual property rights 56–8, 103–5
sustainable development 79–80
and TNC malpractices 52–5
see also indigenous communities; North-South divide; 'Third World'
development 67–8, 92
see also economic development; economic growth; sustainable development
development projects 120, 122, 123, 126, 135
development strategies 36–7, 68–70, 119–20, 129, 151, 159–60
Dewey, John 163, 164–5
disciplinary power 139–40
discourse 138–43
discretionary business practices 16, 18
discursive power 138
displaced and dispossessed people 120, 122, 123, 158, 159
Donaldson, T. 24, 25, 26, 27, 166
Douglas, T.J. 82–3
Dow Jones Sustainability Group Index 89, 90
Doyle, M. 130
Draft Norms on Responsibilities of Transnational Corporations and Other Businesses Regarding Human Rights (UN) 95–6
drugs 56–8, 103–4
dual theory of the firm 163–7

'economic', and 'social' 136–8

economic development 72, 74, 104–5, 133–4
economic growth 70–71, 72, 74, 118, 126, 134
economic power 138
economic responsibility 18
economic rights 95, 96, 103, 117, 118, 121, 159–60
economic theories, corporate social responsibility 12–13
ecosystem people 115
Ecuador 54–5
education 35, 147, 150
efficiency 12–13, 23–4, 26
Elkington, J. 85
empire 130, 160
enforcement 45, 96, 98, 99, 154
enlightened self-interest 7, 19–20, 87–8
Enron 43
environmental activists 30–31, 36, 37, 66, 75, 126
environmental auditing and reporting 17
environmental destruction 70–71, 74, 126, 145, 168
environmental international standards 81
environmental performance 82, 83
environmental protection 17–18, 66, 71, 72, 74, 76–89, 90, 118
see also Global Compact (UN)
Environmental Protection Agency 29, 113
environmental responsibility 37, 78, 82, 87–8, 118
Escobar, A. 68, 69–70, 71
Esteva, G. 67–8
ethical investment funds 90, 146
ethics 18, 41
Europe 152, 174
see also Britain; Germany
European Union 59, 102, 117
ExxonMobil 41–2, 75, 173

Farben 60–61
Farmer, P. 38, 39
farmers 80, 117, 121–2, 136
farmers' organizations 108
financial performance 2, 25–6, 28, 76, 78, 82, 101–2, 145–6, 167
Fine, B. 126, 132, 135, 136–7

self-interest, of corporations 7, 12–14,
  19–20, 87–8, 145, 162
Sen, Amartya 115–16, 122
Sen, J. 170
Shapiro, Robert 112
shareholder value maximization 2, 6,
  13–14, 90, 161, 165
shareholder value maximization theory
  of the firm 23–4, 25, 26
Sharma, S. 82
Shell 40, 53–4, 62, 147
Shiva, V. 105, 106, 107, 111, 116, 117
Siegel, D. 16, 26, 27
slave labor *see* forced labor
social auditing and reporting 16–17, 42,
  86
social capital 72–3
social change 145
social citizenship reporting 42, 43
social development goals 126
social enterprises 171
social imagery 132
social initiatives 58–9, 170–71
social interests, versus corporate interests
  13–14, 145
social issues
  classification 19–20
  and corporate social responsibility
    versus corporate social respon-
    siveness 20
  and corporations 13–14, 145, 164
  and deontology of the corporation
    162–3
  and 'economic' interactions 136–8
  and neoliberal agenda 132–6, 146,
    157
  and political economy 131–3, 141
  versus stakeholder issues 21–2
  and stakeholder theory of the firm
    27–8, 161–2
  and triple bottom line 85–6
social justice 73–4, 131, 135
social movements 169–70
  see also activists; anti-globalization
    movement; campaigning coali-
    tions; community groups;
    consumer groups; environmental
    activists; farmers' organizations;
    resistance movements
social obligations 6, 141

social performance 16–17, 25–6, 28,
  145–6
social rights 95, 96, 103
social role, corporations 51–2, 165–7
social welfare 23, 47, 52, 135, 157
society 7, 132, 134–5
South Africa 57, 75, 102, 104, 135, 136,
  148–9, 158
stakeholder-agency theory of the firm 26
stakeholder colonialism 33–40
stakeholder engagement, and corporate
  citizenship 42, 43
stakeholder issues, versus social issues
  21–2
stakeholder surveys 17
stakeholder theory of the firm
  and contracts 26–7, 28, 32
  and corporate social responsibility
    27–8, 161–2
  as descriptive 25
  as instrumental 25–6, 27–8, 29–30, 40
  and knowledge 30, 32, 39
  legitimacy, and stakeholder salience
    30–32
  and marginalized groups 31–3
  multilateral contracts 26–7
  as normative 26, 27, 28, 29, 30, 40,
    162
  and organizational stakeholders 28
  and poststructuralism 39–40
  and power 30–32, 146
  and social issues 27–8, 161–2
  and stakeholder colonialism 33–40
  stakeholders defined 24–5, 28
  urgency, and stakeholder salience 30,
    31, 32
  see also stakeholder-agency theory of
    the firm
stakeholders
  in corporate social responsibility
    definitions 16, 18
  defined 24–5, 28
  and human rights compliance 101
  legal rulings 14
  legitimacy 30–32, 36, 37, 38
  power 30–32, 36, 146
  urgency 30, 31, 32
standards 81, 82, 97, 98–9
state 9, 128–9, 140, 158, 160–61
  see also governments